THE GREAT REVOLT AND ITS LEADERS

THE GREAT REVOLT AND ITS LEADERS

The History of Popular American Uprisings in the 1890's

by carleton beals

ABELARD - SCHUMAN

LONDON/NEW YORK/TORONTO

Second Printing 1970

LONDON	NEW YORK	TORONTO
Abelard-Schuman	*Abelard-Schuman*	*Abelard-Schuman*
Limited	*Limited*	*Canada Limited*
8 King St. WC2	*257 Park Ave. S.*	*200 Yorkland Blvd.*
	10010	*425*

An Intext Publisher

Printed in the United States of America

Latin America: World in Revolution
Cyclone Carry: The Story of Carry Nation
John Eliot: The Man Who Loved the Indians
Dawn Over the Amazon
The Story of Huey P. Long
Porfirio Díaz: Dictator of Mexico
Mexican Maze

TO MY FATHER
LEON ELI BEALS
A GREAT KANSAS POPULIST

CONTENTS

THE GREAT REVOLT AND ITS LEADERS

I
THE GRIM
GAY NINETIES

January 24, 1890, Comet G reached its maximum brilliancy and twelve new asteroids were discovered — celestial events that provided frontier astrologers with more prophetic power, brought numerous prognostications of trouble, and lengthened the columns of seersucker ads in the New Orleans and San Francisco papers, where uprooted people needed the solace of crystal balls and cardsharpers.

The decade that followed was mauve, it was gay, it was grim. It was stormy. The adjective selected will likely depend upon your liver, your income, or the authority you prefer; or whether your taste is for the cancan girls or for Sockless Jerry Simpson, the Socrates of the prairie farmers. As in every era there were the "boom" or "razoop" writers, who saw everything in bright Wizard of Oz colors; but "calamity" writers held a large part of the stage.

For Thomas Beer, writing in retrospect, the period was mauve; though so delicate a tint — despite much pressed-violet literature and children in Lord Fauntleroy suits — scarcely jibes with Beer's own descriptions of the rip-snorting Titanesses, reformers, and good-willers; it scarcely backgrounds the bitter partisanship, verbal violence, Bible-quoting, red-light blare and patriotic braggadocio of the end-century years. "What a bubbling, steaming, complaining period it was!" exclaimed Hamlin Garland, the first realistic chronicler of the Middle Border, in his *Roadside Meetings*. He himself had done much of the bubbling and complaining. It was painter James Abbott McNeil Whistler who defined mauve as merely pink trying to be purple. It was the favorite color of the day. Prudery had not caught up with reality, or maybe a new middle-class gentility was floating to the top.

An old frontier way of life was dying; a new urban life was rising; a new era of money, factories, commercialism, and an uprooted proletariat; a new age of steel was taking over the ramparts of power. A whole people had swept across a virgin continent, clearing the forests, killing the buffalo and Indians, building roads, digging mines. Hordes had rushed in from Europe; they had clambered over the Appalachians; they had reached the Rockies and the California gold fields. They could go no farther, and a population, keyed up to rapid settlement and expansion, was largely stopped in its tracks.

Europe's westward movement was also halted. The population backlash created stresses far into the European hinterland that badly wrenched the Old World political structure and helped cause social upheavals and future wars that would also engulf the United States.

The great westward putsch carried over into an industrial revolution and the incipient imperialism of the Spanish-American War. The American farming population — so far as family farms were concerned — was never fully to recover. Large-scale farming became more efficient. More and more farm machinery was being introduced. In 1855, it had required 4½ hours of labor to produce a bushel of corn. By 1895, it required 10 minutes. In 1820, it had taken from 50 to 60 man-hours to produce 20 bushels of wheat per acre; by 1890, this had been cut from 8 to 10 hours. By 1930, it

[2]

would be down to 3 to 4 hours. More wheat with less labor. Bigger farms. Everybody seemed to profit except the small farmer, and in the early nineties farm prices were lower than they had been for 7 generations. There were new costs for him; machinery, fertilizer, mounting taxes, which in themselves make self-sufficient family farming an impossibility today.

Government reports reiterated the warning by Henry George twenty years earlier that the free lands of America were almost gone. By 1893, Frederick Jackson Turner discovered the momentous change; that earlier motivations of American life were disappearing. It was, in fact, a revolution. From Plymouth Rock to 1890 the high-ticking adventure of rapid expansion across the land continued. After the Civil War, the shoe began to pinch. After 1890, finis was put on old-style land settlement, and before long family farming began to decline. There stood "Turner's Peak," blocking the old way of life.

The new frontier was the machine, science, technology. The Bible ceded ground to the engineer's manual and the test tube. The free will of the steel piston, at least its power and smoothness of operation, became more important than that of many human beings. These, among other things, shaped the political battle of the nineties. The farmers made a last ditch fight against the new order. Out of the collision of those two epochs — before and after 1890 — many fine traditions of colonial America, and evil ones too, were swept away; new ones emerged, some fine, some lamentable. Though here again, judgment depends upon the yardstick: taste, aesthetics, efficiency, productive output, comfort versus culture. Acquisitive but not always creative talents were sharpened. Isolationism, for centuries a proud boast, became provincial, almost a disgusting crime, as overseas expansion pushed into Latin America, on to Europe, to Africa and China. It was, in any event, a strenuous time of readjustment.

Ironically, those who fought for the old freedoms, the old moralities, the old-style individual rights, were branded as fanatics and

[3]

often were, whereas the true revolutionists of the day, the builders of factories, the so-called "plutocrats," the builders of the empires of oil, steel, coal and copper, those smashing up the old scheme by bringing into being the new industrialism and the new ball-bearing society of efficiency and conformity, were the ones who posed as the true guardians of tradition and order — so rapidly had their hold been cemented on the economic and political life of the country. The centers of new power — though most of the nation now lived west of the Appalachians — more than ever were on the Eastern seaboard, not in the ruined South or the debt-ridden West.

The shattering of many rural hopes and the general dislocation of the nation's former economy made the people of the West and the South, hard-hit by the change-over, ready to listen to any panacea, however visionary. Out of this confusion, and adding to it, sprang every sort of crusade, some righteous and sound, others wrong-headed, many just plain crack-pot.

Unfortunately for the farmers, they had to make their quixotic stand at a time when agriculture was declining in importance in the overall scheme of American life, when foreign markets for farm products were growing more competitive, or being choked off, when new and more fertile lands in Argentina, Australia, and Russia were being opened up. Soon vast crop surpluses and human hunger were piled up all over the earth. The farmers had to fight at a time when the railroads had seized the bottlenecks of profit, when the labor market was being flooded with European immigrants.

The clash of these two systems — the old frontier America with its free lands, its individualistic egalitarian democracy, versus the growing power of industry and finance — was epic while it lasted. It was the anarchism of untrammeled endeavor and opportunity pitted in a losing game against those building industrial empires. It was the battle of a dying agricultural system — often wasteful, mostly unscientific — versus the new industrialized large-scale plantation agriculture to meet mass production and urban needs. The old-time farmers' fight was lost before it started, but it set up some land-marks that have endured, guide-posts that have helped salvage a modicum of individual human freedom in the mechanized superstate system no farmer of the nineties envisaged. Even the new owners of the loaves and fishes failed to foresee the colossal political outcome of their larger efforts.

For the small farmers being flattened out by the new jugger-naut of industrial might, the nation, those years of the eighties and nineties, was certainly going to the dogs, but to the successful in the great cities, it was to be *the* American century. The golden towers of the new imperial metropolises continued to rise, hit or miss, at the buffalo crossroads and alongside the old moccasin trails. And among those promoting the new order, it was not meet to question the wisdom of unholy haste, waste and wealth-grabbing, or to concern oneself with the wreckage also piling up. Few took pause, that bustling year of 1890, to listen to the growing com-plaints coming like a young cyclone out of the West — or to read Jacob J. Riis' book, *How The Other Half Lives.*

But by kerosene lamps and by the cracker barrels at the rural crossroads, the inlanders were talking and reading about far worse things having to do with "the hated trusts," "monopoly," "blood-sucking Wall Street," and the dire fate of the farmer. They now read the discouraging realism with which Hamlin Garland punc-tured prairie romance; they read the propaganda of the Farmers' Alliance and the sensational novels by Ignatius Donnelly and Edward Bellamy. Life on the frontier was depicted not as glorious adventure but as grim hardship and repeated defeat — dust and sweat and disaster for the tillers of the soil, who enjoyed little of the good life or spiritual communion with nature. The contrast with city glamor was sharp.

Donnelly, in his *Golden Bottle,* put the matter in bathetic terms in describing the fate of a Kansas farmer's daughter, Sophie:

"One bright morning a pitiful cortege of grim visaged men and weeping women went forth from that little paradise of fields and

woods and prolific greenery, and took their sad way to the great
city of Omaha, to struggle with thousands of hungry ones for daily
bread. And Sophie — became a store girl at starvation wages; and
stories began to come back to us — but enough!"

During the 1892 campaign, he stated: "A farmer in a good suit
of clothes is so rare a sight in much of the western United States
that the presumption is he was a member of the last legislature."

Donnelly's Kansas farmer-boy character says, "I am Ephraim
Benegert. . . . It is the old story. Grasshoppers, poor crops, pools,
trusts, burning the candle at both ends; increasing taxation to support a lot of office-holding non-producers; an increasing family with
another lot of non-producers to support . . . debt, pinching economy
and, at last that conditional sale of a homestead which is disguised
under the name of a 'mortgage' . . . the end, foreclosure — wiping
out — starting adrift . . . " The Song of Emigration was the "Hymn
of Fugitives."

"The gay 'nineties of the cities of the North," wrote Roscoe Cole-
man Martin in his story of Texas Populism, "were the starvation
'nineties of the Texas farmers." In Georgia, according to Alex
Matthew Arnett, chronicler of Populism in Tom Watson's hot-
blooded state, they were the "heartbreaking 'nineties." But the
North also had its rural woes. The drab story of New York State
farm life, its blight and failures, its mean cheaters and ugly country
louts, was set forth in Harold Trideck's powerful *Seth's Brother's
Wife*.

But the men of industry, city-dwellers, felt the pulse of power
and new opportunity. Romance found a pattern in stone and steel
and factory smoke. There, under the glowing brilliance of the lights
of Edison, the bigger and better era was duly celebrated.

And so, as Hollywood romanticists later pictured it, the decade
of the nineties was really quite gay. The booming cities of the time
were flush with easy virtue eager to be plucked by the easy money
from the raping of the new West. Quickly garnered wealth and
the adventurous spirit had returned from the open spaces arm in

[6]

arm, sex-starved and tired of religious orgies, to squander themselves where the lights were bright around the fleshpots. Romance was returning from the gold rushes, the land stampedes, the Cherokee Strip rush, the panhandlers, the cattle-sheep feuds, the vigilante hangings, the Indian wars, to the corrupt gangster cities and the jangling dives, the hogwallows of the New Orleans tan-and-white tenderloin, the cowbarns and cribs and melodeons of the Frisco Barbary Coast, the Chicago Slide, and the overrated Manhattan Bowery. The "Barlow Knife" was giving way to the sawed-off shotgun. So was Jim Bowie's fame diminished, soon to be blotted out by the Capones and Costellos, all the daring exploits of the bootleggers and one-arm bandits.

Romance now raised its proud head among the jumbled architecture of the garish mansions of the "Robber Barons" on Central Park East, along Chicago's Lake Shore, atop San Francisco's Nob Hill. Newport's Casino of Belmont fame was already catering to the super-rich; and, though monitors saw to it that women went bathing "fully dressed," clear to the soles of their feet, at balls, "shameless décolleté" — a difficult word to pronounce — was already in vogue and all the more "dazzling and disgusting" because of the extreme upper and nether bulges. Whatever might be happening out on the Middle Border, frontier "coarseness" now entrenched itself in cosmopolitan luxury, draped its ungainly form in velvets and fluff and grossly shot the works. *The Mauve Decade!* Before long the "Mink Decade" would arrive, along with hipflasks and semen-spotted auto seats. The great middle class, with its queer shoddy snobbishness and social climbing, soon to erupt in Suburbia, was also in the making.

Good taste was not one of the strong points of the changing order. Much fine colonial craftsmanship died after the Civil War. Already in the Gilded Age, the eighties, there was a monstrous piling up of ponderous classic imitations and grotesque carpenters' gothic which soon degenerated into jigsaw gingerbread. Out in Carson City, Nevada, government buildings looked like a misplaced Roman city, but surrounded by wooden shacks, and main street stores stood with high fake foreheads branded, like that of Cain, with hopeful legends of harness and hardware, drugs and meat. Of American art there was little (save that imported from Europe) to annoy either the money-grabbers, the revelers, or the good folk.

Even so, there was much yearning for art out on the plains. The Kansas pavilion at the 1893 Chicago World's Fair had a larger showing of local painting than did any other state, but most of it was remote from reality — moonlight over continental castles, episodes from Greek, Roman, and biblical mythology, from old English romances — and none depicted sunflowers and tumbleweeds, lonely houses on flat acres or cottonwood bottoms. It would be many decades before Thomas Hart Benton would paint his powerful scenes of actual western harvests. But by then, the general yen for art had largely subsided, and he painted mostly for urban eastern sophisticates — except for his *History of Indiana* at the Chicago Exposition.

Lack of taste was also displayed by the clumsy forces of puritanical morality — "hot black silks screaming at naked boys in the old swimming hole." The blue-law battalions were a busy nuisance everywhere, trying to chastise both enjoyment and art. They are found in every age, and perhaps they were no more unpleasant and obnoxious in the nineties than in colonial and post-revolutionary days, but they seemed more incongruous and pathetic, their psychological aberrations and self-revealing displays of sex privation or perversion a bit more ridiculous. This fascism of morals, exported from Boston, had been originally an ignorant part of early English revolt against wealth and aristocracy; it was the least intelligent and least pleasant aspect of the farmers' revolt.

Doctors and family had to defend Ulysses S. Grant, when he lay dying in 1883, against "Committees of ladies and ancillary clergymen demanding he sign warnings against tobacco and alcohol." Carry Nation began smashing saloons, and Frances Willard, whose high forehead looked down from the heart of a sunflower, with petals labeled Truth, Purity, Temperance, at the

[8]

Chicago World's Fair, was most annoying about liquor and vice. Queasy Anthony Comstock, of the ginger-colored whiskers — "the smut-hound of heaven," Heywood Broun called him — was carrying on his perverted "purity" forays and with his big feet and obese body clumsily tried to imitate in court and elsewhere the contortions of the dancers and drunks he sought to convict.

In due time, Prohibition arrived and departed in a scandal of crime and intemperance. But already in the nineties, the guardians of pure living were overwhelmed by the urban hosts of Bohemianism, material ostentation, wasteful spending, and *nouveau riche* exhibitions. Today, when boardwalk beauty contests are hailed in song and picture, the 1893 Chicago Midway hootchie-kootchie contortions of Little Egypt, a much-swathed non-stripper, scarcely seem sinful, merely absurd. Even to the most righteous small-town preacher, the bikini has since become commonplace, and it now requires a topless female swimsuit to start the geese cackling.

Nevertheless, such clumsy sideshow goings-on accentuated the feud of West and South against the East. A further barrier was raised between farm and city. The westerner not only took his stand on the battlements of economic survival and better prices against the hated railroads and middlemen, but also raised the flag of temperance and purity, of righteousness versus sin. The new city, with its wealth and dazzle, became the symbol of all evil. The westerners chanted constantly about the pure honest virtues of farm life and closed their eyes to fornication and incest in the haystacks.

Nothing aroused such indignation beyond the Alleghenies as President Cleveland's praise of missionary efforts to check drunkenness, vice, and violence on the frontier. Governors of the hinterland (especially those who believed in a silver rather than a gold standard) railed back at him for maligning the wholesome West. The governor of Colorado (though Denver was a hell-hole of brothels, gambling, political viciousness, and thuggery) poured out horrendous descriptions of the painted infernos to be found within range of the President's hoarse, cancer-thickened voice.

But the documents of frontier sin and crime were there to be examined. The attorney general of Kansas complained in 1890 that though the age of consent had been raised to eighteen, this gave no protection to young men of immature years who were snared, blackmailed, and even sent to prison by under-age girls plying a life of shame, on occasion even by "a prostitute in a house of ill-fame."

Most frontier towns had their "West Ends" or "Chicagos." The *Cheyenne Daily Leader* (July 12, 1892) reported that Flureé Turenne of Company D of the Seventeenth Infantry "sent a ball through the breast of Genie Poiquette, a girl of easy virtue in the house of Margaret Hume." But the local bootleg joints, the blowsy run-down whores who had migrated for their last stand to the cross-roads, the gambling, gunfights, bank robberies, and general desper-adoism of the latest settled areas could not compete in yokel imagination with the evils of the large cities. The farmers saw life in black-and-white terms of Everyman simplicity, of innocent bucolic virture versus city-slicker and handlebar-moustache villains. Real sin existed only under the lurid gas jets of the nations greatest metropolis. New York became Babylon, Sodom and Gomorrah, and all other biblical hot spots combined, "an eating house and a gilded lupanar irresistible to the peasant mind."

Out on the Kansas plains, Populist orator, Mary E. Lease, in Cassandra accents, told her broken-shoe, sun-bonneted audiences that annually 100,000 poor shop girls of New York, unable to make body and soul meet, were forced "to sell their virtue for the bread their niggardly wages deny them." She probably slightly exagger-ated the market for shop-girl virgins, quite likely also the supply, but people believed and wept.

The cities heard not. The ta-ra-ra boom-dee-ay rose in growing crescendo until it blended into the cannon fire of the Spanish-American War and the romance of Teddy's Rough Riders.

Everybody, of course, believed in sacred womanhood. Farmers' wives had held rifles that shot redskins from cabin windows, and they had stood by the plow. The farmers backed the brewing revolution for women's rights, and women joined the farmers' great crusade in droves, vocally and otherwise. It was the female revolution, both rural and urban, which went on to success, while that of the farmers was to fail. Thus the nineties could well be called also the sentimental decade, overstuffed with eloquent passages about the purity of womanhood and ringing apostrophes to the nobility of the weaker sex.

Farm leader "Cyclone" Davis of Texas dedicated his *Memoir* to his wife with the following hyperbole: "As the sharon and the rose have shed their fragrance upon the dew drops of earth, so has the bright star of motherhood, in the galaxy of heaven, held sway, alike in the bosom of heroes and heretics." His cow-lipped palaver was most effective in those end-century years.

August 18, 1891, Evan Jones, head of the Texas Farmers' Alliance, told convention delegates that woman was "the crowning work of God." She had been "the inspiration of man's endeavors, through all the ages of the world. Without her influence, home would be a blasted shrine; the foundations upon which civil and religious liberties stand would be a wreck and chaos inevitable. Anarchy would remain supreme and darkness like a pall would devour this fair land of ours."

Such fulsomeness was not confined to western prophets. Roscoe C. Conkling, New York Republican boss and corporation lawyer, never missed an opportunity to drip honeyed discourses about sacred womanhood and the sacrifices of "pure, enlightened and progressive mothers" into the gluttonous minds of his auditors. Over six hundred babies, most of them legitimate, were named after him.

Many people were shocked by the daring bloomer-clad suffragettes who scoured the land with their pleas for women's rights, except that it was a great bicycle decade, and the immoral bloomer was the only practical answer. It kept naked thighs concealed a bit longer.

Some aspects of the female revolt were more subtle. In its January 1, 1890 issue, the *Barber County Index*, Farmers' Alliance

[11]

organ of Medicine Lodge, Kansas, insisted that the fair sex also had great inventive capacities; to it "we are indebted for corsets and moustache cups."

Though tight corsets, with bone or steel stays, suddenly became a symbol of importance and of female inventiveness for the editor of the *Index*, they were an ancient binding institution, but being used by Caucasian Christian females instead of Chinese foot-binders, were never considered heathenish, even when accompanied by padlocks. In the nineties, however, corsets were being loosened more and more. One woman's magazine told a touching story of a young man who led his hour-glass fiancée into the garden and tied a tight string about the stem of a lily. In a few days the lily withered, and he tactfully explained that it would produce no seed. After that, realizing that her tight corsets would choke off healthy offspring, the girl appeared in loose flowing garments, "which had all the beauty of the apparel of the ancient Greeks."

It would have been wholly gross in those days to have told a girl she had a womb — or even legs. The boy's fiancée would have fainted in tears, and he would have gotten his engagement ring back. Female legs, hidden by ankle-length skirts, were stammeringly referred to as "limbs." Girls knew absolutely nothing of the facts of life, although it seemed they could, by subtle indirection, understand them. For females, "gonorrhea" and "syphilis" did not exist. No decent woman was supposed to know about such things, at most would mention "social diseases" with self-conscious stammering. In 1899, the publishers, faced by a storm of public fury, hastened to call back the first copies of Frank Norris' *McTeague, the Brute* — not because it portrayed savage crime and pathological degeneracy but because on page 106 little Aggie soiled his clothes.

The new women were so intrepid, yet had their feelings hurt so easily, were so readily shocked by honest words, especially those relating to sex, that they confused immorality with plain-speaking, not with the deed. Yet in ordinary etiquette their consciences could not rest without the most rigid technical truth. The magazines featured long tortured essays on whether "white lies" were justified. It was the old Puritan black-white standard, the literal mind, humorless unbending adherence to biblical mandates. Henry Demarest Lloyd, of the *Chicago Tribune,* used to tell of an uncle employed by the New York Gas Company, who was so honest he always carried two pencils, his own and that of his employer, and never wrote a line of personal matter with the latter. He worked twelve hours a day, receiving no overtime pay or fringe benefits.

Even the Titanesses and bloomer-girls, who so disturbed the mauve dreams of Beer and alarmed contemporaries, demanded, even more than their shyer sisters, all the old trappings of obeisance and chivalry, and felt, according to foreign observers, that they had a right to treat their husbands "as rudely as though they were servants." They were having their cake and eating it too.

For such a touchy age, all the bold new bloomer business was phenomenal. Women everywhere were becoming very vocal. Increasingly, frontier housewives, hardened and seared by barren toil, made frigid by puritanic doctrines, were aroused to shrillness over both economic injustice and "sin." Some became great crusaders. F.A. McNeal, Republican, of Kansas, who lived in holy terror of Populist Mary E. Lease, characterized her as the greatest orator he had ever heard. The Board of Lady Managers, under Mrs. R. Palmer, took over the Chicago World's Fair — except for its scandalous midway adjuncts, which Comstock tried to get them to suppress — and used the great commercial emporium as a sounding board for suffrage, prohibition, and a whole congeries of righteous causes. The aroused women of that day, even if they wielded no Carry Nation hatchets and found bowel movements so disgusting in print, went forth into the heat and dust and smoke of battle. They followed Frances Willard for prohibition. They followed Elizabeth Cady Stanton in a demand for suffrage. Clara C. Hoffman of Kansas City, known as the "Missouri Cyclone," stormed the male cellars in behalf of suffrage, and revered Anna G. Shaw of Boston, called by the *Medicine Lodge Cresset* "probably as good a lady orator as there is in the world," toured the nation time and again, to the remotest country towns, in the cause of women's votes. "The man opposed to equal suffrage will be out of luck in this country." The women soon swelled the ranks of the third party of the day, the new "People's Party," which, at least theoretically, recognized no difference of race, color, or sex. Tom Watson of Georgia was campaigning, whip and gun in hand, to protect Negroes speaking on his platform. But in some places the presence of women was more startling. As Josh Billings put it, "Wimmen is everywhere." They still are.

In 1873, Anthony Comstock wrote in his diary, "For Christmas I received a pair of slippers, a moustache cup and saucer and a gold tooth pick." Moustache cups, whatever the year of their initial appearance, and whether due to female inventiveness and re-belliousness against male coffee-sieving, had considerable vogue in the nineties. My childish birthday gift to my father in 1900 or so was such a cup. Willy-nilly the revolters of the Middle Border were being impregnated with the new middle-class gentility.

This drinking contrivance was a sign that the Civil War and the Gilded Age — the Gelded Age, Gerard Carson calls it — were well behind. Men were taming down; the frontier was really gone. The Titanesses of reform helped tame them — harbingers of the semi-matriarchate henceforth to feature American life.

The Civil War had sanctified the beard, just as the later Cuban Revolution does — and beatniks do. Shaving could not be allowed to intrude upon the noble business of mass murder, and the heroic virtues were emphasized for several decades afterwards — the long dreary bloody-shirt era of politics. Every member of Grant's first cabinet wore a facial mattress. Since most of the so-called Robber Barons and corporation heads also used big beards William Allen White, of Kansas, considered them a mask for duplicity and con-niving. But in most regions a politician without a beard, which usually meant a war record, had small chance of success. The Mid-dle Border revolt was not a youth movement; it was in good part

[14]

an overage Civil War veterans' movement, and the passing of the beard was in itself a symbol of its eventual defeat.

Even before the nineties, the moustache cup heralded the subtle change. The beard, gruffness, and a military record were growing less potent in successful pursuits. Brains and good manners were dampening down rampant victorious War-Republicanism and were beginning to have influence in social life and political affairs. Undoubtedly, the refinement typified by a mere moustache revealed the growing flabbiness of the national fiber, so typified later by Emily Post becoming a best seller and the middle-class search for shortcuts to aristocratic snobbery and discovery of quickie culture and knowledge in radio quiz programs — the "victory of the neat," poet Vachel Lindsay called it. Emerson had written about "creative manners," a disturbing concept; and his books, mostly self-published, sold only a few hundred copies, even in his own day. But in the late nineties and thereafter, he would have sold big, had he only written about "table manners." Even clean-shaven politicians, chiefly members of corporation law firms, were beginning to appear.

If the passing of the beard and the arrival of the Titanesses were symptoms that the Civil War was growing dimmer and that the long plundering rule of the veterans was now also on its way out, it was also an index of the growth of industrialism. It is not wise to have whiskers in the vicinity of whirring belts and gears.

Solemnity, like the female form and the male face, was taking on new style. To Cassandra Mary of Wichita and Sockless Jerry of Medicine Lodge, both close to the wreckage wrought by drouth, the collapse of boom times, and the foreclosure of farms, the nineties were wholly grim. But the grim apostles were not all political puff-guts, often they displayed humor and sometimes wit.

Henry Demarest Lloyd of Chicago wrote that Standard Oil had done "everything to the Pennsylvania legislature except refine it." To a colleague in the House of Representatives, who taunted him that Kansas farmers were burning corn needed by poor folk elsewhere, Jerry Simpson retorted: "Yes, and by the light of that burning they read the record of the Republican Party." When Jerry attended the Farmers' Alliance convention in Ocala, Florida (December, 1890), and big wigs entertained him at dinner at the flamboyant Ponce de Leon Hotel in Saint Augustine, he wise-cracked: "I'm going back to Kansas and sell my year's crop of corn so I can put up here for a single day." "Raise less corn and more hell," cried Mary Lease, but the wit was mostly dimmed by the horrifying word "hell" issuing from a woman's lips.

Jerry and Mary were part of a farming class caught in the end-squeeze of a closed frontier and a "heartless transportation monopoly!" The farmer's standards of life and security and hope had been lowered by the juggernaut of industrialism, by the declining importance of agriculture in the national economy and in politics, and by the competition of new lands in other countries. But before the inevitable debacle, the group fought valiantly for itself and for western-style democracy. It went down—almost—with flying colors, and Lease and Simpson and a score of similar prairie Jeremiahs must be included by the synod of time in the true American political bible.

II
KINGDOM
OF EARTH

"I felt that the talent intrusted to me had been accounted for — felt more fully satisfied, more deeply grateful than if all the kingdoms of the earth had been laid at my feet."

So wrote Henry George in March, 1879, on completing *Progress and Poverty*, eventually to have as wide a circulation of any book on economics except Karl Marx's *Das Kapital*.

For the time being, he found no publisher. Appleton's wrote back: "great clearness and force," but "very aggressive;" Harper's, "revolutionary", Scribner's, "not interested."

Though penniless, George was determined to see it in print. He got work as a printer, a craft he already knew, and set type on his book at odd moments and after hours. He slapped in revision as he filled in the sticks, and at the last moment added the chapter "The Problem of Individual Life." It was one of the few books ever composed, at least in part, directly from the brain to lead type.

Three friends — Professor William Swinton, A.S. Hallidee, and Henry's brother — took the plates to Appleton's, which finally agreed reluctantly to bring out the work, royalty 15 percent.

The book attracted little immediate attention. The *Sacramento Record Union,* "a railroad paper," attacked his single tax doctrine bitterly. Newspapers in San Francisco, where George lived, largely ignored it. Later he was to say that San Francisco was "cold and barren, ruled by strenuous men too busy with mines and wheat and empire building to listen to prophecy." But the *New York Sun* gave it a full page review by M. W. Hazeltine. George's fame grew quickly. By August he was called to a post on the *New York Herald.* In his contributions, he applied his principles to the thorny Irish land question. In October, 1881, he was asked to visit Ireland and England to expound his views, to the annoyance of landholding Tories. His tour resulted in stormy attacks and frenetic applause. At times he was suppressed, threatened with arrest, but mostly was enthusiastically received.

Aided by European acclaim, the prophet on his return became more acceptable to his compatriots. Several U.S. papers, believing him to be a European, scornfully asked how any Britisher could be so cocksure about American farm problems, but they lavished more attention on him than they would had he been a homespun product.

George's ideas began taking hold of men in all walks of life. Horace Greeley, editor of the *Tribune,* now considered himself a single taxer. Thorstein Veblen pondered George deeply. In his boyhood, Robert La Follette read a dog-eared copy of one of Henry George's early books. *Progress and Poverty* became the bible of many a future Populist leader. It influenced the thought of Jerry Simpson, Hamlin Garland, and Ignatius Donnelly. Garland became an indefatigable single taxer. Simpson founded a single tax organization and was indebted to Henry George for his free-trade ideas. In 1890, after being elected to Congress, Jerry and four colleagues had George's *Protection or Free Trade* written into the *Congressional Record,* and 1,400,000 copies were distributed. Cordell Hull picked up some of his stubborn out-dated idealism from George. Single tax is still sacred to a million or so adherents around the world.

The theme of *Progress and Poverty* grew from the acorn of a chance remark into a full-bodied tree that was to spread its broad shade over the last two decades of nineteenth century American intellectual life. Lying on the deck of a top-sail schooner in the Puget Sound, George, then a penniless adventurer, was telling a companion that antagonism toward the Chinese was not justified (later he changed his tune), but the other argued that as the country filled up, wages would go down and the Chinese would become a problem. George was immediately impressed with the novel but not wholly sound idea, "that as the country grew . . . the condition of those who had to work for their living must become, not better, but worse." This unverified idea became the enduring central pillar of his economic critique.

He was born in Philadelphia in a back house on Tenth Street, September 2, 1839. In that year Adam Smith was forty-nine and John Stuart Mill thirty-four. Karl Marx had just polished off his twenty-first birthday.

His ancestors were English, Scotch, and Welsh. The name of one grandfather, John Valence, a well-known engraver, can be found on commissions signed by George Washington. George's father, who married Catherine Pratt Valence (after his first wife died), had been a publisher of religious books, but by the time Henry was growing up he had been reduced to a petty customhouse clerkship, with a salary too meager to support ten children.

Henry, the eldest son, was able to attend high school for only five months. Stern paternal religious observance plus poverty contributed to a restlessness that kept him on the go most of his life. Bizarre tales about missionaries stirred his curiosity about foreign lands. Unable to find work that would pay him more than $2.00 a week (in contrast to the Aladdin's lamp stories of fabulous riches to be picked off the ground in Australia and California), at sixteen he shipped before the mast on the "Hindoo" (for $6.00 a month), bound for Australia and India on "a shining sea of gold." No gold nuggets landed in his soon-calloused hands, but the weird enchanting sights jostled with narrower concepts learned at home.

The family's parting gift to him had been a Bible; and when, on

December 3, 1855, his vessel headed up the Hooghly branch of the Ganges to the ghats of Calcutta, a letter from his mother told delightedly of the new religious revival sweeping the United States. It aroused his impatience. Religious fanaticism, he observed, befuddled and crippled human beings.

After his return, the parental cage proved doubly irksome. He found himself in heated argument with his mother about slavery. With his father he clashed hotly over the freedom to come and go. Inability to get a job added to his touchiness. For a while he worked in a printing shop, learning to set type, then presently earned more than customary as a scab printer. Soon he had to ship on a dirty coal boat to Boston and back. Daily it became more difficult to find work. To a friend he wrote (in September of 1857, a depression year), "The times here are very hard and getting worse every day, factory after factory suspending and discharging its hands. There are thousands of hard-working mechanics out of employment in this city; . . . among them . . . your humble servant."

If only he could get west to the gold fields! When the "Shubrick," a government lightship, was announced as bound, via the Straits of Magellan, for permanent duty on the Pacific Coast, George wrote to a Pennsylvania congressman and was lifted into seventh heaven on being informed he was to be a steward at $40.00 a month. The boat almost went down in a storm but eventually pitched across the bar into San Francisco Bay. George jumped ship.

He lived with a cousin, went broke, and worked his way north before the mast to Vancouver to get to the Frazier River gold rush. A wild-goose chase — and he had to work his way back to San Francisco. Still in the quest of gold, he tramped off to the Sierra Madre and suffered two months of hard labor and unhappy vagabondage.

He obtained various short-time jobs, frequently as a printer, but usually lost them because of violent quarrels. For purely social reasons, he joined the Methodist church, a sorry comedown for a staunch Episcopalian family, but his mother, overjoyed at any sign of religiosity, wrote him a rapturous letter.

Life remained extremely difficult. September 15, 1860, he wrote his favorite sister: "How I long for the Golden Age—for the promised Millennium, when each one will be free to follow his best and noblest impulses . . . when the poorest and meanest will have a chance to use all his God-given faculties. . . ." "To obtain wealth is my principal object in life," he commented to a friend.

To his parents, who thought theater-going of the very devil, he wrote that he had sat in the gallery "among the gods" at the old American Theatre to see *Richard III*. On a new drop curtain was depicted an imaginary overland train to California. The audience surged to its feet and shouted itself hoarse. But the hysteria left George cold. He recalled morosely the topsail schooner conversation — "wages will go down."

Actually, the first spade of earth for the railroad was not turned on the Pacific end until three years later at Front and K Streets in Sacramento, railroad promoter Governor Leland Stanford wielding the shovel. George saw the ceremony.

With four others, he started the *Evening Journal* and kept up an unequal fight until his clothes were in rags and the toes of his shoes out. The completion of the transcontinental telegraph permitted better-heeled papers to bring in spot news and put his venture on the rocks.

In his darkest moment, with only "two bits" in his pocket, he married, against her family's wishes, pretty, intelligent, high-spirited Annie Corsina Fox, then only eighteen. They scraped together fare to get to Sacramento, where he found various printer's jobs. Their life remained precarious but joyous for years to come. Asked by a friend when his wife did her seasonal cleaning, George replied, "We don't clean house, we move."

In 1859, George had been bitter that the pro-slavery party had swept the state. In 1860, he cast his vote for Abe Lincoln. He was thrilled by the 1863 Emancipation Proclamation. He proclaimed himself a free man — if raising children and frequent joblessness,

[21]

meager living to the point of abject poverty, could be called freedom. His second child was born a few days after Appomatox, at a time when for three months they had been living on only twenty-five cents a day. His wife, through the haze of her pain, heard the doctor say to the nurse, "Don't stop to wash the child; he is starving. Feed him." George rushed out and begged five dollars from an unknown passerby on the street.

He got some things published. His most successful piece was "On Profitable Employment of Time" — time being his greatest asset at the moment. He helped promote a workingmen's paper and in 1865, jobless again, received a few dollars from the *Alta California*, the leading West Coast paper, for several brilliant pieces on Lincoln's life and assassination. Then he dashed off with a filibuster expedition to help Juárez fight Maximilian. The money from any articles he wrote for *Alta* was to be turned over to Annie. He seemed convinced this would provide enough for her and the children to survive.

His escapade was short-lived. The expedition was halted by an American revenue cutter, and imprisonment was threatened, but the case was finally dropped.

George busied himself founding a Monroe league in support of the efforts to throw out European invaders. He got a job in the state printing plant at Sacramento, which he held for several years.

His life seemed to him too prosaic, and he signed up for the National Guard, but the hard dusty drills with dummy guns did little to feed his ideas of plumes and glamor. He got out at the first opportunity.

He worked as a printer for the *Sacramento Daily Union* and also wrote for it under a *nom de plume,* "Proletarian," a word which did not inspire the hostility it was to later. After a typical quarrel with the foreman, he returned to San Francisco, where he put up at the Old Oriental Hotel. After odd jobs, alternating with near starvation, he went to work in the composing room of the new *San Francisco Times.* In his spare time, he wrote editorials and by June, 1867, was lifted out of manual labor to be managing editor at $50.00 a week. A third child was born.

He began writing articles for *Overland Monthly*. They appeared alongside the work of Bret Harte, Mark Twain, and Joaquin Miller. For his first piece, he got $40.00. Increasing population, he wrote, produced more poverty, and he set forth his first groping ideas about rents, wages, and margin of production. He showed an "ever stronger concern for the working classes."

For a few weeks he became managing editor of the *Dramatic Chronicle*, then tied up with the new *San Francisco Herald*. The owner and editor, John Nugent, sent him east to try either to get the paper admitted to the Associated Press or else to establish an independent news service.

It was a hard journey, first by stage ("a four-horse mud wagon"), then by train. On arrival in January, 1869, George wrote to the *New York Tribune*, attacking the Central Pacific and the Wells Fargo Express for excessive rates and careless handling of newspaper mail. The railroad had been built entirely by the people, therefore the high rates were wholly unwarranted. The Central Pacific, enjoying enormous political power, was already influencing conventions and managing legislatures and had representatives in both houses of Congress.

He opened a press office in the little office of the coal business his father had started in Philadelphia, but the telegraph company refused to take transcontinental code messages from a Philadelphia bureau. George moved to New York, whereupon Western Union upped his rates but lowered those of his competitors. He called on Vice-President McAlpine and denounced this "most outrageous breach of faith which had been procured by by the underhand workings of a ring," but he got nowhere. The incident deepened his determination to fight injustice.

Before leaving for San Francisco he wrote an article for the *New York Tribune* against the admission of more Chinese immigrants. He vented contemptible opinions of them as a race, showing the cheap prejudices that a decade later were to flower into three horrible days of burning, pillage, and murder in San Francisco's Chinese settlement.

The workers in San Francisco hailed Henry George and his opinions with delight. But the papers, "controlled by the railroads and interests wishing cheap labor," attacked him. George replied, "Root the whole American race [sic] in the soil, and all the millions of Asia cannot dispossess it."

He got an anti-telegraph monopoly bill introduced into the state legislature, helped found the American Free Trade League, and ran unsuccessfully for Congress on the Democratic ticket (he had voted for Grant the year before). He was penniless again, but the governor made him editor of the *Transcript,* a small paper across the Bay in Oakland which was fighting a subsidy to the Central Pacific Railway.

While horseback riding through the new residential hills of Oakland — his usual exercise — he asked a teamster the value of lands there. "One thousand dollars an acre!" George had never had that much money in his life. He recalled his old conversation on the topsail schooner. "Like a flash it came to me that . . . here was the reason of advancing poverty with advancing wealth. With the growth of population, land grows in value, and the men who work it must pay more for the privilege."

He was invited to take charge of the *Sacramento Reporter* for a fair salary and one-fourth the stock and was made Pacific Coast agent of a new press service to fight the Associated Press "monopoly," an effort now possible because of the opening up of the rival Atlantic and Pacific transcontinental telegraph line. But within a year the railroad bought out the *Reporter,* and George found himself back in San Francisco, unemployed.

He wrote a pamphlet in favor of laissez-faire economy. "Government should be reduced to a minimum." Government subsidies to railroads and other corporations were contrary to the democratic principle that forbade "the enrichment of one citizen at the expense of another." Subsidies led "to waste, extravagance and rascality," were a means of "plundering the people."

He became secretary of the Democratic state convention and ran for the legislature. His defeat, he claimed, was due to the gigantic power of the railroads.

He set to work on *Our Land and Labor Policy, National and State.* With the rapid dissipation of public land and the railroad "steals," all available areas would be given away by 1890. This anticipated the 1890 census report and Frederick Jackson Turner by twenty years. In California, many individual holdings exceeded hundreds of thousands of acres; a strong horse could not travel across one of them between sunup and sundown. But land is the storehouse, the creation of God; its value is not an element in the wealth of the community but merely represents an unequal distribution of wealth. Actually, the value of the land consisted in the power ownership gave to appropriate the product of labor. "Where rents are high, wages . . . are low." Monopoly increased land values and decreased the value of labor. Such monopolization had reduced 374,000 English landholders in the middle of the last century to 30,000 in the nineteenth century. Small farms had gone into large estates.

According to Ricardo and Malthus, the value of land should be determined solely by the advantage it possesses over the least advantageous land in use. George pointed out the difference between this "real value" and the fictitious speculative value.

Land monopoly was furthered by the existing tax system, which permitted the man holding 100,000 acres to pay taxes that amounted to a fraction of those paid when the same land was divided among 50 holders. Land should be given to actual settlers in small quantities and a land tax established that would not bear down on production and yet be easy to collect. Land prices would fall; speculation would receive its death blow. "Imagine this country with all taxes removed from production and exchange!" With the confiscation of land rents, the great monopolies astride the bottlenecks of economic freedom would vanish.

[25]

George's ideas were derived from direct observation of western population growth and the fencing off of free acres. Although by the time of his later *Progress and Poverty* he had read most of the classic economists, his concepts were arrived at independently. In this particular tract, he had been influenced chiefly by his personal observations and by Bisset's *Strength of Nations*, but had not even heard of the Physiocrats, until a lawyer friend told him his ideas had been anticipated a hundred years earlier by French economists. He was never irritated by the charge that he had made no startling discoveries. To an English critic, he retorted that truth is eternal, neither new nor old. The important thing was that it be reiterated in the light of contemporary experience.

In this book, he crossed the old school of liberalism with New England transcendentalism — Locke plus the theory of the sacredness of the individual. His ideas flowed in the channels of Jeffersonian idealism and Encyclopedist "natural rights." By personal observation and meditation, he had recreated part of the thought of Harrington, of Marx's economic determination, Mill's unearned increment, and the Physiocratic concept of natural order — meshing them into one sovereign remedy for American land concentration. His basic axioms were: the right of a man to the produce of his labor and to use "as much of the gifts of nature as may be necessary to supply all the wants of . . . [his] existence."

In 1871, he and associates started the *Daily Evening Post* and made it so pungent it became a growing concern; then they sold out. The new owner made it a more conventional paper, circulation vanished, and George and his friends took the enterprise back at a song. He upset the apple cart generally. He personally drove out of the city the brutal keeper of a house of correction who had threatened to shoot him. He attacked the lynching of a rich farmer who had shot a woman in the back, but pointed out that the lynching was due to the fact that the courts, because of the farmer's wealth, were going to free him. George jumped with both feet on the chief of police for his gambling interests and unearthed a school-supply scandal. He lashed at evils with a "whip of scorpions." George became a patriarchal figure as he rode to his office in a deep Mexican saddle on a tan-colored mustang rarely groomed properly.

In June, 1872, he headed the state delegation to the national Democratic convention in Maryland, where he supported Greeley (whom he visited) and attacked Grant's carpetbag administration of the South.

Hard times were cracking the financial and business prosperity of the state — the tail end of the depression-hurricane of the '73 panic began hitting the West Coast. Drouth had destroyed the grain crop, cattle died, the gold yield fell off, and the Nevada bonanza silver mines began to peter out. In 1875, San Francisco suffered its own Black Friday. Overnight, the empire of W.C. Ralston, the great bonanza king and banking czar of the Pacific Coast, was caught on the spit of bankruptcy and basted brown by the treachery of his most trusted lieutenant, William Sharon. Ralston swam out to sea and vanished, and Sharon took over his mines, his banks, his swank Palace, and his Grand Hotel, where he installed mistresses. Ralston's palatial Belmont estate and six-horse tallyho were sucked into Sharon's maw. People promptly rewarded his duplicity by making him United States Senator.

Deep resentment was abroad. Even prominent people were beginning to seek out the causes of financial collapse. George was asked to lecture at the University of California, where the famous geologist, John Le Conte, was President. It was hinted George might get a professorship. Overjoyed, he told a friend that college teaching was the most satisfactory profession he could attain to. But George's paper had exposed graft in the erection of North Hall on the campus, and in his 1877 address there he uttered words that barred him then, as they would today, from a seat in a leading institution. Every kind of weapon, he said, had been used "against every effort of the working classes to increase their wages or decrease their hours of labor." Freedom was proclaimed for capital, but what substantial promise was there for the working man save that he should refrain from raising children? — outspoken language at a time when unemployment and labor agitation were causing alarm. George was asked by the city to deliver that year's Fourth of July oration at the old California Theatre. A little man with a golden beard, alone on a vast stage, he talked abstruse economics in poetic breathtaking phrases. He warned that republican government was still only an experiment. Republican institutions had worked well enough under the early social conditions of the republic — cheap land, high wages, and very little distinction between the rich and poor, but when population became denser, wages low, and a great gulf separated rich and poor, republican government would break down. Wealth "concentrated in the hands of a few corrupts on one side and degrades on the other. . . . In the long run no nation can be freer than its most oppressed, richer than its poorest, wiser than its most ignorant." He finished with a purple apostrophe to liberty.

Not personally immune from the speculation he denounced, he gambled in mining stocks, was caught short, and had to take Senator Jones of Nevada, a wealthy Comstock Lode man, into ownership. Jones soon called for his money, and George lost his paper. For a while he filled a semi-sinecure as state inspector of gas meters, which gave him time for working on *Progress and Poverty*.

Industrial depression, social disorders, and war abroad provided plenty of footnotes for his opus. The Desert Land Act now made possible further gobbling up of the public domain. The last really great westward push of settlers was causing fresh Indian troubles. Custer's force was trapped and massacred. The Nebraska legislature was rocked with disclosures of bribery and embezzlement. Jay Gould was physically attacked in Stock Exchange Place by Major A. Selover. James G. Blaine, confronted by the Mulligan bribery letters, shouted down critics, but the smelly record barred him from the Presidency. In Georgia, the evil convict-lease system, maintained by the Democratic Ring, was being investigated.

On May 17, 1877, former President Ulysses Grant sailed for

Europe on the "Indiana" with wife and son, leaving behind him a stench of misgovernment that still reeks through the pages of American history. But his departure was accompanied by a chorus of praise from the newspapers of the North. Shortly after he left, great strikes swept the country. June 21, 1877, the first of the Mollie Maguires was hanged, and July 1, a Baltimore & Ohio Railroad strike resulted in riots, train-burning, and deaths. Federal troops were sent into 12 states. Disorders took a toll of at least 200 lives, and property losses were estimated at $12,000,000. Henry Ward Beecher, in his $20,000 a year New York pastorate, hastened to assure everybody that a workman could easily raise a family on $20.00 a week, but many workers were not paid that much, and he himself was soon engulfed in an adultery scandal.

In Chicago, the police invaded a meeting of furniture workers in Turner Hall, then attacked a public meeting in Haymarket square, employing billy-club tactics that culminated in the bomb tragedy and the May 1 public hangings of innocent "anarchists" that shocked the world and created a permanent international commemorative holiday.

The *Chicago Tribune* (deep-mired in politics run by "gangs and stabbers") was advocating putting strychnine or arsenic in food given tramps, and decorating lamp posts with "communistic carcasses." Prominent Chicago citizens presented a Gatling gun to the city to shoot down strikers. That year there were more than 18,000 business failures.

In California, Barbary Coast thugs, the unemployed, labor unions, and all the riffraff of San Francisco took out their frustration on the poor Chinese (brought in to work the mines and build the railroads for the Big Four, whose mansions towered on Nob Hill), beat them up, stole their property, murdered them, burned them alive in their washhouses and shops, until vigilantes, armed with federal weapons and aided by funds from magnates trafficking in coolie labor, put the violence down.

[29]

The Sand-Lots labor agitation began, whipped up by the sten-torian oratory of stout, blunt-featured Dennis Kearney, an Irish dray-man from County Cork, via the Bowery, who led a parade with banners: "We want work, bread, or a place in the county jail;" "Down with the Chinks." One windy day Kearney led his ragged hosts up swank Nob Hill to denounce the Big Four. "The monopo-lists," he shouted, his restless dark eyes aflame, his stubby hair bristling, "who make money by employing cheap labor had better watch out. They have built themselves fine residences on Nob Hill and erected flag staffs upon the roofs. Let them take care that they have not erected their own gallows."

Kearney was jailed, but local officials, frightened by the storms of protest, freed him forthwith. To the consternation of long-intrenched job-holders, Kearney's new Workingman's party carried county after county. "The rich have ruled us and ruined us," said one proclama-tion. "We will now take our own affairs into our own hands. The Republic must and shall be preserved and the workingmen will do it. Our shoddy aristocrats want an emperor and a standing army to shoot down the people." Kearney's party held the balance of power in the new state constitutional convention, which drafted a document that was hailed by some conservatives as the end of the American system, but the railroad lawyers smiled and, until the time of progressive governor Hiram Johnson, fifty years later, kept on running the state with the same arrogant lack of consideration for the public, the workers, or the passengers.

It was in this troubled moment of snarled social relations that George started *Progress and Poverty,* a propitious moment for a serious study of economic ills of life. For George personally, no moment could have been less propitious. His sinecure had ended. He was jobless again, another child was on the way, and food was often lacking. By the end of the year, though scarcely eating, he was $450 in debt.

But there is no record that Annie Corsina Fox, who eloped with him when he had only twenty-five cents, ever complained. She had even acquiesced gracefully, though tearfully, in his absurd filibuster exploit. Convinced of his genius, she spurred him on to finish his book at all costs. Geniuses are notoriously ill-mated, but apparently no genius was ever more fortunate in his marital companionship than George. Half-starving, he plugged away at his great work. Hard times continued through 1878, and the plight of the farmers continued to agitate the nation. The Grange had reached its peak, had temporarily restrained railroad abuses, was now declining, but the militant Farmers' Alliance was gaining ground, promoting political mugwumpism in unexpected places.

With such ferment all about, George fought hard to concentrate on his writing. He took time off to organize the Land Reform League of California and earned a few precious dollars lecturing for it on wages, rent, and land, under the title, "The Coming Struggle." He assured his audiences that just as the battle against chattel slavery had ended successfully so would that against wage-slavery. "I tell you the glow of dawn is in the sky. Whether it comes with the carol of the larks or the roll of war-drums, it is coming — it will come."

He also took time out to organize the free public library of San Francisco and served as a member of the original board of trustees of what has since become one of the finest city and county libraries in the country. He was nominated to the state constitutional convention by both the Workingman's and Democratic parties, but, though receiving a larger number of votes than any one else on his ticket, he was defeated.

Finally, by mid-March, 1879, *Progress and Poverty* was finished and sent off on its long quest for a publisher.

No man, declared George, has a right to more land than he can use himself. The value of land, he insisted once again, depends upon society, not upon landlords; the unearned increment should be expropriated: "widespread social evils . . . everywhere oppress men amid an advancing civilization." From the fundamental injustice of land-ownership flowed all the injustices which distorted and

[31]

endangered modern development. It condemned the producers of wealth to poverty and pampered the non-producer of wealth in luxury; it reared the tenement house alongside the palace, planted the brothel behind the church, and compelled the state to build prisons as fast as it opened new schools.

He had the passion of the reformer plus the gift of scientific analysis. But except for elementary notions of monopoly, he grasped little of the significance of the new age of steel advancing with such gigantic strides. He never fully comprehended that monopoly of machinery, transportation, patents, banking, and control of currency could also result in improper exploitation. Thus, he largely avoided problems of money and currency, soon to be set forth by a brilliant young contemporary, Henry Demarest Lloyd, the scourger of Tammany and the Chicago gangs. George never truly appreciated that land is only one element in production, distribution, and consumption, only one of the toll bridges where pay-meters could be located. The land increment he wanted confiscated was due, however much the hair-splitting, not merely to increase of population but also to improvements upon property — buildings and industry. A single tax to rectify all economic abuse evaded the basic fact that he would be taxing such improvement, even though penalizing speculators.

It was Thorstein Veblen, among the great American theorists, who pushed George's argument to its logical conclusion that "all land values and land productivity," including the "original and indestructible powers of the soil," were a function of the industrial arts, that the concept of unearned increment applied to all capital goods.

Nor did George envisage, any more than did the young Marx, that, though the American worker and farmer might later receive an ever smaller portion of the wealth produced, better techniques, improved machinery, and greater ouput, would, in spite of any injustice, improve the standard of living for the bulk of the people. Despite serious depressions and the exceptions of southern share-croppers, dust-bowl victims, and Negroes, the availability of civilized comforts for most has expanded since George's day. He did not foresee that this expansion of the standard of living, however wasteful and unfair, might well continue — except for folk caught in stagnating pockets — so long as national resources were not exhausted, so long as foreign markets existed or could be artificially created by gold-buying or such wartime palliatives as lend-lease, rearmament, or other means of destruction of surpluses so employment and production could be kept at peak levels. By these and other artificial prosperity methods, the country has lived and prospered for seventy years. Until waste and war cut more deeply into our natural resources — and even then this may be long offset by new scientific discoveries — George's critique will have little general appeal. He failed to see that his panacea might not be the only means, or even a sufficient means, to offset end-century trends. Similarly, he failed to see the influence of the rise of great farm and labor organizations, the effects of consumer power on government, and various other ameliorative factors that were to modify the overall picture.

Many Alliance and Populist leaders, though others were ardent single taxers, soon saw that George's ideas would not get the farmer out of his immediate bad fix, might even make it worse. In April, 1889, Jay Burrows, President of the Northern Farmers' Alliance, pointed out in detail the inefficacy and dangers of George's proposals. Indeed, the application of his principles — without the correcting of other abuses — would have ruined the Middle Border farmer beyond all hope, for, despite his economic difficulties, he was part of the acquisitive system he was fighting and was actually saved from utter ruin by it.

Even when seriously engaged in farming, the early owner was imbued with prevailing speculative fever. President Timothy Dwight of Yale, who traveled widely through the country, pointed this out vividly early in the nineteenth century. In the 1830's, Alexis de Tocqueville, one of the keenest observers, wrote: "It seldom happens that an American farmer settles for good upon the land

[33]

which he occupies, especially in the . . . Far West, he brings land into tillage in order to sell it again, and not to farm it; he builds a farmhouse on the speculation that . . . by the increase of population a good price may be obtained for it."

If increasing population had not made land dearer, had it not created a demand for farm products, the farmers would not have had so large a market or credit or the occasional high prices that brought them windfalls. True, in the eighties farm product prices started on the downgrade. Markets were glutted or contracting, tenantry on the increase. But if it had not been for the land monopoly practiced by the railroads, the cattle kings, the insurance companies, and great corporations, the middle western farmer could never have gotten the big mortgages by which he lived, and prices likely would have been even lower.

After the Civil War, farming was rarely a paying occupation. The farmers lived not so much off the products of their land and labor, but *off the unearned increment of their land* (in the beginning often a free government homestead). This was the very evil George abhorred, but without its reward the small farmers could not have survived.

Thus they had gotten by, less by farming than by gradually consuming the social values created by increasing population, land monopolies, and industry. They had lived by eating their own tissues, their capital, by access to the "fictitious" speculative values George deprecated, by mortgages.

In short, the middle western farmer was kept going by being a small capitalist as well as a producing laborer. To have struck him down as a small capitalist — George's theory — before he had safeguards for proper recompense for his toil, would have been disastrous, even though he was being squeezed both as a proprietor and as a laborer. These were ironical immediate aspects, which the single tax enthusiasts did not explore.

As to long-range results, George, of course, had the better of the argument: "small land owners do not profit by the rise in the value of the land; on the contrary they are extinguished." Twelve percent mortgages, high freight rates, middlemen, and rigged prices saw to that.

However dear land might become (or however cheap, theoretically, with a single tax), nevertheless currency fluctuations, transportation monopoly, market controls by speculating middlemen (so vividly described in the novels of Frank Norris), the relatively high prices of fertilizers, implements, clothing, and manufactured goods, protected by tariff walls, as compared to farm products, would still have blocked rural prosperity.

George put his finger on many evils, saw them clearly, but his theory and therapy were oversimplifications. The problem and the remedies needed were more complicated than he envisaged.

Even so, his analysis of American society, much of which is still valid and pungent, was brilliant. He was one of the first great prophets of America. No man ought call himself educated who has not read him. He was the first to foresee clearly the fate that would overtake much of rural society.

In any case, he made an enormous contribution to the forces of freedom. He was always fighting for human rights and future ideals. Unlike his more learned fact-hunting contemporaries—though many were better known and more honored — George had no interest in busily gathering string for the nests of corporate power, no interest whatever in providing paint to polish the walls of existing palaces of injustice, no desire to provide convenient alibis for brutal exploitation. He sought clear-eyed for truth, and thereby built a solid edifice for society and for the human soul. He did for economics what Tom Paine did for politics. *Progress and Poverty* pushed economics back into the democratic current. He sought "to humanize the gloomy science," and did. His greatness is still little appreciated. He does not shine in school and college texts.

But with his facts about farm ownership, his profound analysis of current agrarian questions, directly or indirectly he penetrated the thought of all America. For decades his ideas were a major factor

[35]

in this country's thinking.

His work cannot be properly appreciated apart from the great farmers' revolts of the eighties and nineties or the Wallace New Deal. The effect of his writing was to be far greater than indicated by the more sectarian single tax organizations that sprung into life and still flourish. He still has a large organized following throughout the world; his adherents today are more numerous than during the years he lived.

George fought on through the years for his ideas. In 1883, he said, "In every essential land differs from those things which, being the product of human labor, are rightful property. It is the creation of God; they may be increased illimitably. It exists though generations come and go; they in a little while decay and pass again into the elements. What is more preposterous than that the tenant for a day of this rolling sphere should collect rent for it from his co-tenants, or sell to them at a price, what was here, ages before him, and will be ages after him? What more preposterous than that we, living in New York City, in this 1883, should be working for a lot of landlords who get the authority to live on our labor from some English king dead and gone these centuries? What more pre-posterous than that the present population of the United States should presume to grant to our people or to foreign capitalists the right to strip of their earnings American citizens of the next gen-eration? What more preposterous than these titles to land? As Thomas Jefferson said . . . 'the earth belongs . . . to the living.' "

George's long political battles in California and his later-day campaign as candidate for mayor of New York were exciting foot-notes to a busy intellectual life. He never lived in an ivory tower. His tent was ever pitched in the marketplace. His feet trod the broad highways of contemporary events; he jostled elbows with his neighbors at every step. Not his political activities but rather his great contribution to the economic thought of America, his influ-ence in shaping the thought of millions, the impulse he gave to the democratic alliances of rural America — these have built his true and lasting monument.

For the printer-editor and author had a touch of the fine old craftsman in him. He belongs with the *primitivi,* naive, honest, a bit crude, but strong and full of shining light. His ideas had grown, in part, out of the smears of inkstained aprons, of messy type, of lead liners. His thoughts were closely tied to the actual manual labor of setting them forth before the world; they were linked with sweat and callouses. His was a vertical edifice, its pillars set in the mines from which came metal, the fields from which came food. Its sills rested in the composition room and it held within it the clank of presses. The wires of the international news services hooked on to the eaves; the pulsing daily life of his times throbs through every room of his intellectual mansion, and the whole edifice converged to the great dome of human freedom and justice he planted there. He was both a working journalist and philosopher. Both talents benefitted thereby, both were strengthened. Only three or four other Americans can claim a comparable place of importance in world literature and thought.

III
THE GILDED AGE,
THE GRANGE,
AND KELLY

The battle of the farmers, which was to have the nineties for its testing ground, had been brewing ever since the Civil War. In 1868, the bosses of the victorious war party, busily looting the South, began looting the whole country. Overriding faint southern and western protests, they rammed through the national convention, amid patriotic cheers, the nomination of General Ulysses S. Grant.

He was pledged to the repayment of bankers' greenback war debts in gold from the U.S. Treasury. Gold was the great symbol of the day. Of gold was the final spike driven in the first transcontinental railroad, exactly five weeks before the General took over the Presidency — almost as though that high office were a personal prize of war. Grant and his Congress performed dutifully. Gold became the one metal with which war bonds would be redeemed. The National Bank and Debt Act provided that war bonds and the $1,000 bonds bought up two years previously with bargain-counter greenbacks would now be paid in gold — a vast steal.

Even conservative John Sherman of Ohio (though he soon got

in line with banker plans) considered it a shameless raid on the people's money. "Our bonds do not state that they shall be redeemed in gold. That is not part of the contract. Our soldiers and sailors who . . . saved the Union were paid in greenbacks. . . .Why . . . should the money-lenders . . . who bought our bonds at cut-throat discount during the war be singled out from all other creditors and be paid par in gold? . . . Financial panic and disaster are sure to result."

They did — that year, and still worse from 1873 on. For years this "credit strengthening" act, so applauded by academic economists, brought more deflation and accelerated the ruin of the small American property holder and the farmer, South and West. It came to be known as the Great Public Crime. In a few more decades, Cleveland would be selling more bonds to buy gold to pay out gold.

As early as September, 1869, the two pirates, Jim Fisk and Jay Gould, were in a position to attempt their famous and infamous corner on gold. They bribed high government officials and relatives of the President, and "No President" — John Bigelow remarked — "was ever got in the family way so soon after inauguration." He had not heard of the later Roosevelts and the Kennedys. A. R. Corbin, Grant's brother-in-law, a slippery eel of sixty-seven years, his arm deep in the stinkpot of high finance, served as "jackal for this pair of lions." In Corbin's house, President Grant secretly consulted with Gould, a "dark, thin, fragile man like a serpent." Gould and Fisk took Corbin, Grant, and his daughter to Fisk's opera house. The two lions also took the wooly-headed Grant off on a boat trip on Fisk's Fall River line.

Fisk, a former "country peddler of low instincts," clad this day in a flamboyant admiral's uniform, piped the President aboard with full honors. After dinner and cigars and champagne and French brandy in copious amounts, great matters were discussed, specifically, the Treasury's gold supply.

Soon, memorable Black Friday, when gold rocketed up to over 162, then plunged to the price of clay, rocked the nation's financial structure to the foundations. Men clawed and wept and killed themselves, firms went into bankruptcy. The country went down the chute into the Panic of 1873. Yet it took several more decades for public opinion to rally — unsuccessfully — against the gold plundering. That people revolted at all was due to the growth of farmers' organizations.

The greatest early champion of rural democracy was Oliver Hudson Kelley. Though now well-nigh forgotten, he deserves a big niche in the American hall of fame. On the broad foundations he laid rests the whole edifice of civil and economic rights and political progressivism in this country. Almost singlehandedly, he altered the whole structure and outlook of American life. This proves how dreadful can be a lone man with one big idea.

When the Minnesota Territory was organized, Kelley took up a claim among the Chippewa Indians forty miles northwest of Minneapolis, only two hundred miles from the very headwaters of the Mississippi, and hard by the forgotten village of Itasca in what was to become the town of Elk River in Sherburne County.

Drouth drove him to the wall, and he took a petty government job in Washington. There he worked out an immigration plan to help Reconstruction, got the ears of higher-ups, and in 1865 President Andrew Johnson — a believer in the yeomanry and not the carpetbaggers who would soon knife him close to the death — commissioned him to report on agricultural conditions in the conquered southern states, where military and political skulduggery made it difficult to secure reliable information.

Kelley traveled through Virginia and the Carolinas, visiting rice and cotton plantations. He found a ruined land, where agriculture was broken, debt piling up, deflation bringing bankruptcy, and the farmers becoming the "lien law slave of the merchant." The trend toward mortgaged farms, disinheritance, and wasteful and miserable share-cropping was setting in. The South was developing into the vast rural slum it later became. Appalled, Kelley observed and pondered deeply.

While he was on his tour, it was rumored that northern troops were to be recalled. Panic-stricken northern politicians, carpet-baggers, and speculators stampeded out on the first train, and Kelley wrote a friend that not politicians but fraternity would restore peace and abolish sectionalism. It was the deliberate policy of northern capitalists, he observed, to depreciate property in the South. Only the true alliance of the people, North and South, could offset this grab-bag policy. It would be a good move to start a secret society of agriculturists to restore kindly feeling.

In ruined Georgia and Tennessee, his idea grew mountain-high, continent-wide. "I remember comparing the Mississippi and its tributaries to such a national organization and its subordinates."

"I long to see the great army of producers in our country, turn their eyes up from their work; stir up those brains now mere machines, get them in motion in the right direction; make them discard their old almanacs and signs of the moon; and just imagine what a volcanic eruption we can produce in this age. Everything is progressing. Why not the farmers?"

His report was duly filed to gather dust, and he had to take a job as a minor post-office clerk. But his dream really was as big as the Mississippi. He buttonholed everybody, corresponded far and wide with whomever showed any interest.

In Washington, he communicated his hopes to other government workers, especially to his fellow Masons, William M. Ireland, Chief Clerk in the Post Office finance office, and Reverend Doctor John Trimble, Jr., a Treasury Department employee. Every evening after work, he hauled Ireland up to his room in the United States Hotel for a "cheerful smoke," and to make plans. With Trimble he went to Boston to see Kelley's niece, Carrie A. Hall, who had encouraged him from the start. Among other helpful suggestions, she proposed that women be given full membership. This in itself was a revolutionary step, and it was to change women's role in American life from then on. Kelley went on to plan the previously described degrees and rituals for women.

He sent out his blueprints for the proposed organization and was grateful for any suggestions that seemed wise or appropriate. "What name?" Kelley asked Anson Bartlett, a North Madison, Ohio, farmer. "Lodge" seemed too prosaic. Farm, Vineyard, Garden, or something of that sort would be more appropriate. Other names suggested were Knights of the Plow, Knights of the Flail, Knights of the Sickle. The irony of these feudal titles never struck them. The correspondence over names — "temple" for "hall" — and details of ritual went on: "childhood, manhood, prime of life, old age, prepare ground, planting, harvest . . . bud, blossom, fruit, fall, leaf . . . laborer, vinedresser, gardener, husbandman."

Presently, Kelley suggested the organization be called the "League of Husbandry," and the lodges, "Granges," a word he had taken from a name of a novel being advertised. Grange was "pure old English, used by older as well as recent writers and poets, in the sense of a farm-stead or rural residence." "Why not call the order 'Patrons of Husbandry?'" asked Bartlett. "Original at any rate." He had hit the nail.

Kelley planned to have four degrees, representing the four seasons. Over the next two years he worked over the details, filling in each little cranny of his soaring castle. "With the vast amount of talent that can thus be united," he wrote a correspondent, "we shall be able to get up some degree that will surpass in magnificence of language and tableaux, anything now in existence. . . .While in Masonry there is much that is speculative, there will be in this Order little else but operative features. It will not call the members' minds from their work, but every tool they touch upon the farm in their daily labor will call up some good thing they have learned in the lodge." The first degree examination might be based on a month's study of natural history, a second degree on chemistry. The leading officers could be Master Overseer, Chaplain, Steward, Assistant Steward, Gate Keeper, Secretary, Treasurer. Ceres, Pomona, and Flora would be lady officers. He worked out installation ceremonies, the "lectures and charges" for the degree work.

[43]

The lodge would be elaborately decorated with evergreens. "Be on the lookout for appropriate songs," he wrote Bartlett. "Cowper's poems would furnish some magnificent and appropriate language in the ritual . . . In the degrees, pile in the songs. We want the attendants of Ceres, Flora and Pomona to be mostly females, and to constitute a glorious chorus." He visioned celestial graces, not dumpy toil-worn farmers' wives. "Get the *Intelligencer* of today," Bartlett answered, "and read, cut out and preserve, the poem on the last page entitled the *Sword and the Plough*. It seems written expressly for your order. It is very exquisite."

Every "Vineyard" should have a library of at least fifty volumes. Every member would get a newspaper at reduced rates, along with crop reports, which were not otherwise available those days. There would be a fair every fall. Afterwards, the exhibits would be given to the poor. The organization should set aside money to lend to distressed members.

Boys and girls should be admitted so they would not get disgusted with the limited outlook of farm life. Clergymen would be admitted gratis, but no congressman could join. The organization might cooperate with the government, but no Grange officer would be allowed to hold a government position.

Within twelve months they would number their brothers in millions. With a hint of glee, he added, "Presuming half the agricultural population are firmly bound through this order, where will our political demagogues find supporters?"

As a pressure group it would bring about the appropriation of a million dollars and the creation of a full-fledged agricultural department. The government could then send out free lecturers with scientific knowledge — "the best talent" — to the farm groups.

Had he foreseen that this moderate step would require over thirty years to accomplish, he might have been discouraged. But like all prophets, he found himself depressed merely by his inablility to reveal all the shining glory of his vision to those he desired should share it.

But he was also a practical common-sense man and kept the

proposed program down to simple externals, with an eye on the basic needs of the farmers. They showed, he wrote, a lack of energy in favoring progressive methods. Except for a few reaping machines, farming was still carried on as in generations gone by. "Of the science of agriculture, the natural laws of government, the growth of plants and kindred subjects of pleasing and vital interest to farmers . . . once they turn their attention to them . . . 90 percent . . . were totally ignorant." They disdained "bookfarming," and in one western state only one in every 230 inhabitants took a farm paper. Something was wanted "to produce an excitement which when once created we can throw on fuel and increase the flame."

Kelley wrote Bartlett with an accent of prophecy — "Save every scrap of manuscript you write. For should we build a magnificent Order, you and I can be ready to write the history."

Soon Kelley brought another Mason, Superintendent of Parks and Grounds William Saunders, "an intelligent and thorough Scotsman," into contact with Ireland to discuss things. Saunders was afraid of the secret features, but agreed, while on a trip to a St. Louis pomological convention, to sound out reactions.

Many, he wrote back, had found the Grand Idea acceptable.

Another interested Post Office employee, Dr. Lowrie, made sketches of regalia and emblems. Kelley suggested a wide sash over the shoulders, an apron of skin with the hair on it and with a pocket, and that they use farm colors.

For the state Granges, silver trimmings; for the National Grange, gold trimmings. 'We should have lots of fun in that, including a picnic feast at the close of it . . ." In a letter to Bartlett, he included a bit of ritualistic verse:

> Learn to toil, and gaily sing
> All flesh is grass, and grass is king.

Bartlett wrote, suggesting a bell be used instead of a gavel. Kelley replied, "Your design to use a bell instead of a mallet is

[45]

new. A facetious brother suggests that the Master blow a horn. He says they are common on farms. Imagine the Worthy Master blowing a fish horn to call up to receive the Chaplain's benediction. It would make Gabriel blush."

Kelley took almost childish delight in all such mumbo jumbo. Everything had to be perfect. He had an almost Dantesque vision of hierarchy, the vision of a harmonious and happier world, in which every man would have his proper place, his duties and privileges. His ritual was merely that utopia in miniature — a symbol of his larger concept of contented and properly functioning human beings, all harmoniously interrelated in a great and good nation.

On November 1, 1867, Kelley had three hundred circulars printed (on credit) at Polkenhorn's on Seventh Street, and mailed them out. He got back mostly enthusiastic replies and, on November 15, sent out a formal call for his Washington friends to assemble at the office of Park Commissioner William Saunders for the purpose of "organizing an Order of Agriculture in the United States." This was accomplished in two meetings, and December 4 became the formal date of the founding of the order — there "in the little brown building . . . standing embowered in the trees of Four and a Half Street and Missouri Avenue." So was the Patrons of Husbandry, the Grange, born, and the founders became the first national executive committee, Saunders chosen Grand Master. Its motto was *Esto Perpetua* ("Let it Endure Forever"), and it still flourishes throughout the land, though now chiefly as a small-town social organization. But it still maintains extensive cooperative undertakings.

To try out the ritual, Kelley got together a subordinate Grange made up of government clerks, Potomac Grange No. 1. It met January 8 in a room on Ninth Street. There Kelley set forth the methods and purposes of the proposed organization and tried out the ritual he had devised. His earnest enthusiasm sometimes drew smiles. He was slightly rustic in appearance, with slanting, tired-looking shoulders, a large jutting beard lighter than his receding hair, combed straight back from a smooth domed forehead. He had large sad eyes and an ever-wrinkled forehead. He was the fifth child of a Boston tailor, where he worked as a drug clerk. Later, in Illinois, he became a newspaper reporter, and in Iowa a telegraph operator. In 1849 — he was twenty-three — he took up land in Minnesota Territory, earning part of his living as an Indian trader.

There, at the new Potomac Grange, the ritual was revised to seven degrees, the highest being Demeter, "a continuation of an ancient association once so flourishing in the East." February 14, he wrote McDowell that the following Wednesday the Ladies of the Grange would receive the first degree, and the meeting would have a splendid quartette. Later he was to append a disgusted footnote of advice for Granges. "Quartette clubs are not reliable for music. The one referred to did wonders the first night, but they never got four together afterwards. One usually has a cold or is out of humor." But the Potomac Grange of white-collar workers, fired by Kelley's enthusiasm, secured a nice well-furnished hall with a piano, and prepared to simulate a farmer's club. By the end of March, the local had been built up to fifty members.

At this late date the memorized ritual sounds horribly pompous. Imagine horny-handed farmers' wives of the Middle Border getting up clumsily to mouth such high-falutin' jargon as "Anciently, I welcomed the manumitted slave to freedom. To me he sacrificed his flowing locks, and I crowned him with the liberty cap. So, freed from the ignorance and selfishness of the outer world, I now welcome you to the liberty of our Grange, and the free-will labors of our accepted husbandry. In return . . ."

But very likely the ceremonies had to have the stilted starch of the epoch. Actually the order, with its multiple secrets, must have opened many windows of poetry to the tired and toiling men and women of the far spaces beyond the reach of most contemporary cultural influences — as yet having little access to scientific knowledge, no rural free delivery, no daily newspaper, no books no radio, no theater, no contacts except for occasional hard buggy or wagon trips to distant centers. There were few fairs, and even church-going was often impossible because of bad weather and gumbo roads.

If his vision of a vast army of farmers was to be realized, Kelley had to strike out across country and organize. At the moment, the Great Order consisted of only a few petty bureaucrats in Washington. He called the national executive members together in a special session on March 28, 1868. They voted him a salary of $2,000 a year and traveling expenses, "same to be collected by him from subordinate granges." Officers of the national Grange were not to be responsible for any payments, but Potomac Grange No. 1 gave him "a generous" farewell "feast" in a gaily decorated hall. Several associates did guarantee future payment of his hotel bill — the organization was also still in debt for its printing bills — and raised about $40.00, with which he paid necessary expenses and bought a ticket to Harrisburg, Pennsylvania.

He said good-bye to Saunders. "Here I am ready to start."

"Start for where?"

"I have bought a ticket for Harrisburg and stop there the first place. I propose to work my way to Minnesota, organizing Granges."

"Have you got any money?"

"I have about $2.50 of Grange funds, but intend to pay my way as I go."

In a pleasant way, Saunders said, "Well, you are a fool to start on such a trip."

"Can't help that; fool or no fool, you shall hear from me, and I'll make the Order a success or burst."

Saunders himself did not shell out one red penny, but Kelley modestly and optimistically recorded, "Probably no one less fitted for the work could scarcely be found. I have no oratorical powers, and only a slight knowledge of how to manage. . . .However, I felt that a strong force remained behind to back me, and send words of cheer as I would progress." Naïveté could hold no brighter candle to his own enthusiasm. Those left behind had no vital interest, and the Potomac Grange promptly failed to meet.

Kelley had been given "a letter of credit" (not money). Though "very handsome," this recommendation proved "of no particular value." In fact, his greatest obstacle proved to be "the assertion that . . . [the Grange] was controlled by government employees." "Pluck" and "perseverance" he soon found to be the most valuable assets in overcoming obstacles.

Arriving at Harrisburg, he looked up a correspondent and met several gentlemen with whom he had "pleasant conversations." Sunday he spent in his room, probably with some pangs of loneliness. Monday, three interested persons paid him $15.00 for a dispensation, but the sponsors had little to do with farming, and the meeting that evening was failure. No Grange could be organized. "There was a skeleton in the closet" — Kelley does not say of what nature. "My first lesson," he added ruefully.

His $15.00 carried him a bit further. "Tuesday at 3:00 P.M. April 7, I left for Penn Yan. It was snowing. I arrived at 2:30. . . .Six inches of snow."

"Wednesday, April 8, I took horse and buggy, and drove to Wayne, where I had a hearty welcome from Brother McDowell [his long-time correspondent]. . . . Severe snow storm set in . . . kept me there three days."

"As I was . . . . leaving, McDowell said, 'Kelley, you have taken upon yourself an enormous task, but do not get discouraged; every good cause must always have a martyr. You will make a good one for this.' . . . He gave me $50.00 and cheering words."

Kelley's attempt to found a Grange at Penn Yan proved another failure, but at Fredonia, New York, where he arrived April 15, Brother Moss, another correspondent, helped him start a "lively" Grange. "This was the first regularly, organized Grange where every member paid his fee, and we may give Brother Moss credit

[49]

for being the father of the first genuine Grange that lived, breathed and had a being." He moved on to Ohio, where he saw Bartlett. Part of Kelley's success was a result of his eagerness in welcoming suggestions and giving due credit for them. He always downgraded his own importance and ideas. His only concern was the success of the order. En route he received many valuable ideas about protecting the farmers. Farmers were preyed upon by fake fertilizer companies, by seed salesmen claiming fantastic yields, by venders of useless or defective mechanical equipment, patent pain-killer agents, rain-makers, and religious dervishes of all sorts. Two well-known swindles were worked far and wide, the "lightning rod" racket and the "Bohemian oats," the latter, alleged to have a stupendous yield, catered at $10.00 a bushel. Against such exploitation there was only one remedy, education, but no means existed to spread proper information, for Washington was too much concerned with plunder to give heed to farmers' needs. One new friend suggested that subordinate Granges should test out machinery and products. The National Grange could then issue a certificate to the inventor or proprietor — a sort of early consumers' research — to prevent worthless merchandise being foisted upon gullible farmers. In Ohio, George H. Blackslee, of the *Ohio Farmer,* told him that if the Order would protect the farmers from patent-right swindlers, it would be popular — and save Ohio farmers $500,000 annually.

Thus, little by little, he saw ever greater possibilities, and he wrote McDowell, "Between ourselves it will be an organization that will in a few years' time, rule in this country."

Two days later, from Columbus, Ohio, he wrote Bartlett that several correspondents whom he had met wanted him to "make as officers of our Granges . . . farmers and not outsiders. . . . Be cautious who you have at the head of the Grange in Wellington. *Confine it to farmers at the start,* else we may have trouble. . . ."

To McDowell he wrote, "I am getting my hand in. Wake up D'Ascoli's ghost, and get some funds. . . . This Order. . . .will . . .

sweep the country from the present race of politicians. There is nothing else that can restore peace and quiet between North and South.

"Every kind of monopoly is now at work grinding the producer. . . . You are at the head of an Order that will in four years' time be the most prominent in the land."

In Chicago, H. D. Emery of the *Prairie Farmer* had a group ready to be organized, and Kelley moved on to Madison. From the train he wrote McDowell, "I shall reach Madison with $3.00 in my pocket. If I start a Grange, it will be $15.00 more — just enough to land me at home, dead broke. Now laugh, for I am laughing, and well we may. We have a big order started and there is a future in it. *Success is certain.* . . .Men in New York with thousands of Dollars at their command ought to be willing to donate liberally to the cause. . . .Try and smoke them out."

At Madison he met another party with whom he had corresponded. "From the reception he gave me, and the assurance that his immense wealth and influence would carry the town, I did think he could swing the State. I felt sanguine of a grand finale. . . ."

At the evening meeting, as various persons came in, Kelley's friend whispered, "That's the president of our bank." Another was "the mayor of our city," etc. "This is the class of people I associate with."

But when Kelley said "money," these very important folk proved skittish. "You would have been amused," he wrote, "to see some of them creep out of the room. . . .They said the Order would be of great advantage in country towns, but not in *Cities* like Madison (1800 voters). . . .No matter . . . nothing but a shower; it will clear up by the time I reach Minnesota." Kelley asked his wealthy sponsor for a personal loan of $15.00. The latter flatly refused, and Kelley had to get help from the local Masonic order.

After a day's wait at Prairie du Chien for the boat, he reached St. Paul, May 1, 1868. It was eleven months since he had seen his family. There, he received a reply to a gloomy letter he had sent

McDowell from Madison. "Don't give up the ship. We are all battling in a glorious cause so let the fight rage on, and ever." Very "consoling," remarked Kelley sourly, "to a fellow without a round of ammunition."

He asked the National Grange to have the ritual key printed. He had to write it out laboriously in long hand for each new grange, some thirteen pages. In reply he received a whining letter, the first of many such, from Ireland, pestering him about petty bills.

"What to do I don't know," wailed Ireland. "They all come to me as I am Treasurer. . . . What am I to do? . . . The landlady is also stirring us for hall rent." How could Kelley expect cooperation?

But Kelley was encouraged by good news from another correspondent who had founded a grange at Newton, Iowa, and enclosed $15.00 for the dispensation and instructions.

Kelley sent the $15.00 to pay off his Madison debt and wrote Ireland that if any money came in to apply it to bills.

"I will do all that a human being can do, only have faith; stand by and work boldly; we will come out right. My dear brother, you must not swear when the printer comes in. You will never have half the anxiety about the work I had during the winter, in getting the Ritual and Constitution ready. When they come in to 'dun' ask them to take a seat; light your pipe; lean back on a chair, and suggest to them that some plan be adopted to bring in twenty or thirty members, and thus furnish funds to pay their bills."

He wrote McDowell about the lack of initiative in Washington, the inability to comprehend the work the Order could accomplish. "If they expect you and I to run the machine, why let's do it. . . . For an adviser it will be more to my interest to look to you than to them. . . . They are surrounded with the peculiar atmosphere of government . . . official position there makes a perfect slave and tool of a man. He loses all ambition for everything but an increase of pay. . . ."

A few days later he wrote again: "All hands at Washington have

quietly sat down, leaving all the work for me to do. . . . I thought
I had done pretty well during the past month, but they seem to
think I ought to have raised enough to pay my own expenses
and square up all the accounts at Washington. It is really laughable.
Here is an Order we have started, and $150.00 will clear every
cent of debt; yet they do not seem inclined to make any exertions
to secure membership enough to liquidate the sum."

Repeatedly Kelley berated both Ireland and Trimble for letting
the Washington Grange go to pot. Finally, he got a soothing note
from Saunders saying, "You have done nobly," but Dr. Trimble
was sharp: "It is not pleasant to have the United States Hotel man
come up to my room to dun me — the first dun I ever had here.

"I know nothing, absolutely nothing, about the Order here, and
am not able to take any part in the matter. . . . So you must not
hold me accountable for inaction here. I have nothing to do with
the active or actual work of the Order. Please bear this in mind.

"I give you unbounded credit for masterly efforts in trying to
seduce me into active participation, but, like impeachment, it fiz-
zled. . . . Your trip was a success . . . but — 'aye, there's the rub,' the
note at the United States Hotel isn't paid."

Kelley asked his Washington friends for more manuals. None
were sent. Moss of the Fredonia Grange wrote to Washington,
as did many others. Their letters went unanswered. Moss, complaining to Kelley, asked if he had taken the National Grange
with him when he left.

Kelley had to tend to his farm, but he instructed his daughter,
July Welkin Kelley, in the ritual, and in June went to Sauk Rapids
to get a Grange in motion, the first in Minnesota.

To McDowell he wrote, "I have but seventeen manuals. There
are 900 copies in the hands of the printer at Washington but suppose he will not let us have them until his bill, or part of it is
paid. . . . I shall certainly have an edition printed here. . . . We
must issue another address to the farmers. The circular is all very
well for educated persons, but it will not take much with the

working classes. We must . . . convince them that by supporting the Order, they are to be benefitted in many ways. . . . I am determined as long as you stand by me, to push ahead. The laboring men of this country must be organized."

He kept appealing to Washington for a copy of the Harvest Grange bylaws there and for fifty manuals so he could organize. Also he kept appealing, in letter after letter, mostly unanswered, for songs that Brother Grosh was selecting before Kelley had left Washington.

He finally stirred a reply out of John Thompson (a lecturer who never lectured) that he was sending on the bylaws and that he had twice called on Grosh for the songs. "Unfortunately for the Order as well as for us individually, with the exception, perhaps, of Brother Saunders, we are poor and cannot get money enough to get ahead to take the manuals out of the printer's hands." He was glad, however, to send Kelley encouragement, "Heartily and fully, but silver and gold (or greenbacks) have we none." He complains of the hotel note. The hotel was after them at short intervals.

"It vexes, worries and annoys us, and puts us out of humor. I hope you will relieve us from the vexation and embarrassment by sending the money to pay the balance, which is thirty-nine dollars."

Kelley replied in a most discouraged vein. His own farm was under an old mortgage that kept his spirits "in perpetual eclipse." He was in debt, and the National Grange debt on top of that, paltry though it was, "served as a nightmare." As for the hotel bill, which Manager Bean constantly pressed for payment, "The only consolation I have is that Bean's calling upon you keeps me fresh in your mind; to be cursed by an old friend is better than to be forgotten. I suggest the Granges use black and white Beans for ballots. . . . The assistance that I want from the National Grange is, that they take some measures to establish working Granges elsewhere, and not leave it all for me to do."

He followed this up with a stern letter to all the officers.

"When I left Washington three months ago, you all said the Patrons were a success. I felt encouraged; I presumed the interest shown would be kept up by you all. There were in Washington at least thirty or forty interested . . . You have not added a member since I left; but sat down to see what I was doing, watching my progress, and looking to my labors alone to pay all bills and keep the thing running. . . . I am not in a very pleasant situation [and] trust you will be lenient. . . . I have accepted the position of associate editor of a small paper here, with a brother patron, and we are determined to help the work. I have added this extra work for the good of the cause, and have no remuneration for it . . . all my efforts will avail nothing, if . . . they learn there is no interest taken by you. . . . You have a good thing — a big thing — if only you will be active."

He urged them to write up the Grange, to get the members of the Potomac Grange to organize other Granges, then it would not be long before they would see "money in the treasury."

He also suggested a shift in outlook; the Order should oppose monopolites. The farmers at the moment did not so much need education as "protection." "Now is the time to sound the keynote of the Order. *Sound it loud* . . . it will take. . . . Faith will remove mountains. . . . Come down among the people; don't stay up among the politicians. If you hit the point right, you will sweep the West. You must get into the farmers' pockets to reach their hearts, and a lively palpitation there invigorates their minds. . . . Mark my word, there is a revolution growing among the people, and if you strike the right chord . . . the Patrons will be a power, and you yourselves at the head of it."

But for all his brave words, the treasury, as he remarked to McDowell, was so empty that a five-cent stamp would need an introduction.

July 9, Kelley wrote Brother McDowell that he had been to Owatonna to the state Agricultural Society meeting, and the idea of the Grange had been received heartily. But he had to go home that afternoon to attend to his own affairs. "I am in a stew all the time. Have to hire a man to attend to my work in my absence, and I cannot be long enough in a place to get a Grange fairly at work, for all are not ready when I get there. Am short of funds, and do not see how I can accomplish anything with credit to myself or the Order. We must have some capital to work on. . . . Do find someone to help us financially, or else we will have to give up, and I cannot bear to think of that after working as hard as I have."

McDowell agreed to pay for getting a few manuals. Kelley wrote him promptly, "My wife has a block of twenty lots in a town in this state which we got two years ago, intending to keep them as an investment for the children, but we must have funds to set this order ahead, and it will be a safe investment to make use of them for a little while, at least. If you can raise any money by mortgaging these for eighteen months, you have full power to do so. . . . Mrs. Kelley . . . is beginning to have faith in our work."

Years later, he remarked, "Thus closed the month of July, the darkest in the history of our Order. . . . If all great enterprises, to be permanent, must necessarily start from small beginnings, our Order is all right. Its foundation was laid in *solid nothing* — the rock of poverty — and there is no harder material. . . . Hard friction is necessary to sharpen diamond grit."

The first grit was of granite. Casper Grange was founded, with Miss Mary Russell, the "first white child born in this town," as a member, and paid in $15.00. Presently a Grange was established in Minneapolis. It included the name of J. S. Pillsbury, the wealthy miller, political ramrod, and future governor — not quite in keeping with Kelley's frequent admonitions, but it was all hard sledding, and he had to clutch at any aid from any quarter.

"I am in a perfect ferment all the time," he wrote Washington. "Send me those songs without delay."

Ever faithful Moss of Fredonia wrote to thank him for manuals and the bylaws and to ask for songs. "Perhaps you are to be the martyr . . ." he said cheerfully. "Ancient Orders used to look to the East for light, but 'Westward Empire makes its way,' as we are looking that way now for our President, perhaps light for the oppressed 'Laborer,' 'Cultivator,' 'Harvester,' and 'Husbandman' may come from the West. I hope you will make a blaze that will shine out on the Eastern horizon, which will equal the prairie fire . . . If I was twenty years younger, I should like to throw my whole soul into it; but infirmities of age deter me somewhat." Kelley, at least, would live to see the blessing of the Order to the toiling millions.

In August, Kelley's niece, Miss Hall, came west to help. In contrast to the aloof skepticism of his wife, she proved a tower of strength.

He was working hard to get friendly material into farm papers and had found columns open to him in papers in Chicago, Columbus, Cleveland, and St. Louis. In Minnesota — so he reported to his slothful Washington friends — all the daily and weekly papers had agreed to publish material.

August 17, he wrote to Ireland: "I am pretty well used up; have been on the tramp all the week." He had had printed 1,000 copies of the constitution, and it was being reproduced in full in prominent papers. "You all continue quite dumb. I get no replies to my letters to you. You will jump, by and by, as if you had sat down on a hornet's nest. If I have got to run the institution alone, all right. There are men taking hold of it here who do not play with their work."

He wrote McDowell that he had decided not to mortgage the lots. His wife was not enthusiastic, and why should he risk his own patrimony when the Washington group was so apathetic? The National Grange was a farce, he would report to McDowell only. "If we outsiders are compelled to run it, I guess we have the vim in us to do so. . . .Want of funds is the only detriment, not only in doing the work of the Order, but, being cramped in my family matters, makes it very embarrassing."

Even so, he kept on prodding the indifferent Washington clerks and sent Ireland clippings of the growing newspaper publicity.

He finally got 20 manuals out of Saunders, although McDowell had paid for 60. A portion of the secret work, as well as 500 circulars, he had printed locally. The Order, he said, had to be "advertised as vigorously as if it were a patent medicine."

Though everything still seemed dark, Kelley's indefatigable work in so many directions was at the point of flowering. He had written so many letters from Itasca that the local postmaster's salary was increased from $4.00 to $20.00 a year, and, before he left there, to $75.00.

At the end of August, he met Colonel Dan A. Robertson, who started a farm paper and helped him organize North Star Grange No. 3, on the stage of Ingersoll's Hall in St. Paul.

The colonel, who had retired to a farm near St. Paul, told Kelley the Grange had to be a fighting organization. Bad times had hurt the farmers worse than anybody; low prices, outrageous freight rates, high prices for farm machinery, this plague of burned articles. Kelley listened and nodded. Robertson helped him revise the circular to simplify and strengthen it by presenting a more ambitious program; the dissemination of knowledge about crops, prices, markets, transportation, purchasing, employment, the merits of new machinery. The Order was to protect "by all means available, the farming interests from fraud and deception of every kind. . . .

"We desire the agricultural societies shall keep step with the music of the age and keep pace with the improvements in the reaping machine and the steam engine."

Grange pronouncements became increasingly militant against railroad and corporation abuses. Kelley was getting the real pulse of the farmers.

On September 21, he wrote McDowell that the Washington group was still silent, only a dun from the printer there. Colonel Robertson generously paid for 200 manuals to be forwarded by express. They did not come. "I do not know how I should behave if I had no vexations."

Fortunately, the St. Paul Grange was enthusiastic. It rented a hall and put out $200 for furniture. Its members acted "like human beings."

Kelley finally wrote McDowell on October 5 that he would reprint the manual at the Pioneer office and sell it to the Patrons at a small profit. He would make all reports henceforth to McDowell as Priest of Demeter.

However, his constant prodding, the signs of favorable newspaper publicity, and echoes from other sources finally impressed Ireland, and on October 3, he called a special meeting. "The National Grange," he wrote, "will hereafter take an active interest in your work and respond promptly to your call." The songs asked for so many months before had at last been hunted up, but Ireland did not send them.

Saunders also wrote that Kelley must be worn out with anxiety. He enclosed a resolution, praising Kelley for the advances made in Minnesota.

Colonel Robertson commented: "We understand all about this National Grange. When we see you, we see all there is of it."

On January 4, 1869, Kelley went to Maple Plain to start the Order there. He found a new town of a dozen unfinished houses, among stumps and embryonic streets. The new group was organized in a room 12 feet by 16 feet and furnished with only a cookstove and bed.

This success set his enthusiasm spinning. "By the great Horn Spoon, if any of you have a doubt about the Patrons come to Minnesota and see for yourselves." The Maple Plain Grange had "set the ball in motion in the Big Woods, and there is no stopping it. Everybody is bound to be a patron." Other towns were making inquiries. "A few such letters," Kelley wrote, were enough "to send me up in a balloon inflated with seventy pounds of pure joy to the square inch. . . . We have a big work before us, and a fire is now kindled that will burn in this country for all time. . . . Give me *printer's ink* and I can control public sentiment on this continent."

[59]

Kelley gathered together the masters of eleven Minnesota Granges — some came over 100 miles at their own expense — and organized a state Grange. "A big success," he wrote. The Order was now rolling.

An annual meeting of the National Grange was held in Washington, January 25, 1870. By then Granges reported were:

Minnesota	40
Illinois	3
Iowa	3
New York	1
Ohio	1
Pennsylvania	1

By January, 1871, the State Grange of Iowa was organized. By the end of the year, there were 130 Granges in 13 states.

The whole West was stirring. Nationwide hard times and governmental corruption brought still more members in. During January, 1872, the State Grange of Indiana was organized, and by the end of the year there were 1,074 Granges scattered in more than half the states of the union. The movement was snowballing rapidly now, and Kelley's correspondence and publicity had grown so great that often four express wagons were lined up at his door day after day.

Official Washington pricked up its ears. Commissioner Watts of the Bureau of Agriculture called a national agricultural convention. He derided Grange proposals and attempted to hold the proceedings down to innocuous matters so loved by politicians. But delegate Colonel D. Wyatt, head of an important conservative farm organization in North Carolina, jumped over the traces with a scorching talk. The convention was completely ignoring the wants of the farmers, and he praised the realistic program of the Grange. His remarks were omitted from the published proceedings, a typical bureaucratic boo-boo, and Wyatt angrily swung the 10,000 members of his organization into the Grange.

James Dabney McCabe, in his *History of the Grange* (1873), declared, "The influence of the Grange in elevating the farmers socially is already apparent. . . . It brings together the farmers of a neighborhood, old and young, men and women, and if it did nothing more, it would not have been established in vain." New ideas were exchanged; something was carried away to think about during the week — the best crops for given lands, the best methods of cultivation, sometimes social and moral questions. "It is impossible," wrote McCabe, "for the farmer to leave his business for a month in the summer and spend the time in recreation. . . . His purse is rarely long enough to pay the expense of such a vacation. But he can spend a day between planting and cultivating, another before harvest, and a third when the grain is stacked; and the Grange, taking advantage of this, either invites those of neighboring townships to a basket picnic, or accepts an invitation itself. A day is spent in some pleasant grove; there is speaking and music, and perhaps a little dancing, and the farmer goes back to his field better prepared for his work; some of the marks of care are smoothed out of his wife's face."

As depression spread, new ideas were making inroads the country over. Kentucky was being plagued by northern suffragettes, dubbed "Jerushas" by the *Georgetown Weekly Times*. It called upon the members of the Kentucky legislature to marry the "fussy old Yankee girls and convert them into sensible women."

In New York, two noisy, beautiful, well-heeled suffragettes, sisters Victoria Woodhull and Tennessee Clafflin, were making a big scandal by advocating and practicing women's rights and free love. They exposed the home-breaking exploits of Reverend Henry Ward Beecher by praising him for his extra-marital sexual freedom. They had had notable court brushes with Anthony Comstock. At a convention in the Apollo Theatre, to which were invited "all male and female beings in America," Victoria was nominated for the Presidency of the United States.

Each year now, non-veteran voters were being added to the registry lists, and the nomination that year of Horace Greeley,

[61]

editor of the *New York Tribune,* for the Presidency by liberal Republicans and Democrats indicated "the slow emergence of civilian distaste [of] arrogant and corrupt domination by victorious soldier-officers, serving as tools for predatory wealth."

In Minnesota, Greeley was backed by Ignatius Donnelly; he was supported by most of those who later led the end-century third-party movement. The Greeley revolt was "sentimental and literary," lacking wide appeal, but it was a symptom of what was coming.

The Grant machine of War-Republicans and victorious veterans was still too powerful, and so, in spite of wholesale federal corruption, the great electorate sent Grant back in as President for another four stodgy, plundering years, a period of criminal graft, hard times, panic, and wreckage.

It was a wild, get-rich-quick era, an era of "rusty souls," of gilded ostentation and ruthless speculation. Grant had a wide-eyed awe of wealthy tycoons and had become their dupe. Dutifully he helped carry out their schemes for self-enrichment. Officialdom wallowed in graft and debauchery in scandal after scandal. William S. King of Minnesota, former Congressional postmaster, became involved in a bribery scandal on behalf of the lush Pacific Mail Steamship subsidy and fled to Canada. The Credit Mobilier and the Union Pacific, the bribing of Senators by Oakes Ames, the venality of Vice-President Schuyler Colfax and of Grant's own family and intimates, the Wall Street corner on gold, the District of Columbia real-estate grab, the Star route grab, the Indian posts grab, the Sanborn contracts and the hurried resignation of Treasury Secretary Richardson, the attempted Santo Domingo grabs, the back-pay grab, the delinquent-tax grab, the revenue evasions and briberies by the Whiskey Ring (which had financed Grant's 1872 campaign), the bribery and resignation of Secretary of War Belknap — these and other sensational disclosures rocked the nation for years.

There was also a crop of local exposés, for instance the bribery of legislatures for Senate seats, the customary method of filling up the august national upper chamber. Such an exposure in Kansas sent the venerable Senator Pomeroy into retirement and saw the emergence of the caustic and brilliant but unprincipled J. J. Ingalls to a long political reign, until, in turn, a similar exposure and the rising tide of Populism defeated him in 1890.

The year 1872 ticked on in mounting tension. The financial uncertainties, the tightness of money, the restriction on currency and credit, the deflation of the benefit of inside speculators, the recurring scandals, and the repercussions of the European wars were like the blowtorches of a wrecking crew. The year ended with a record of 4,000 business failures, totalling $121,000,000, real money, those days.

The panic of 1873 poured more oil on the flames of discontent. In September, in the rain of the gloomy day of the nineteenth, brokers lurched along Wall Street, dazed by the spreading news the the financial house of Jay Cooke and Company had failed — Jay Cooke, the invincible, Jay Cooke, the bold Civil War financier, "the pirate of clever propaganda," the name above all others that symbolized unswerving success. The nemesis of his grabs when the boys in blue and the boys in gray were marching to their rendezvous with death had caught up with him. Now newer, younger, more ruthless men gave him the squeeze and battened on his carcass — they "found no heart, and the kidneys and liver were tough."

But even in the very midst of the depression, the patiently laid banker-schemes to control the monetary system moved forward. Silver was dropped from the list of coins minted by the United States Treasury — "the Crime of '73." This greedy foolishness raised up a whirlwind in the West.

Crop failures added to general national bankruptcy. In 1874, grasshopper plagues crippled the Middle Border and returned to devour crops in '75 and '76. Wheat was worth only forty-two cents; corn, ten cents; eggs, five cents; butter, nineteen cents or less a

[63]

pound; undressed hogs, two and a half cents or less. Many folk abandoned their farms.

Fannie McCormick, who knew frontier life intimately and in the nineties became head of the Women's Alliance, gave the picture in *The Kansas Farm*. Sod huts and cabins, women cooking over stoves made of "tin wired together in a cylinder with two holes in it and a tin cover; sunflowers, snakes, rattlers, buffalo wallers; wolves stealing chickens; skunks; dreaded prairie fires that burned up the crops, often also houses and people." She describes 1874 as a dry year that gave only half a crop, hot winds sweeping over the land. The temperature was 116 degrees in the sun and 106 in the shade. People were starving, and charitable folk in the East sent out clothing and provisions. Women and girls went around in sewed-up flour sacks, the only garment to conceal, in part, their nakedness. Even the Santa Fe railroad "loaned" some wheat.

A dark cloud appeared. People cried "Rain! Rain!" but it was grasshoppers. The pests devoured everything. They ate not only the crops, but stripped the trees. They came into the houses and chewed up the lace curtains — anything that had any starch. Fannie's cashmere dress was eaten down the front, when and where she does not state. They buzzed up the sleeves, into the teakettles, into the plum butter. They were swept up in dustpans. Even Santa Fe trains stalled on slippery tracks. "The engineer would stand in the cab looking as humiliated as a dethroned monarch." It was the end of a seven years' struggle for many, who could no longer meet their 12 percent mortgages, with wheat at only 40 cents a bushel.

"A mortgage bearing twelve percent is like a bed of quicksand; every struggle the victim makes only sinks him deeper down into it, until at last he is completely overwhelmed and swallowed up."

"A financial policy was being pursued by those in authority in the interest of the money-loaners, which cause money to be scarce, with rates of interest high." Years of contracting currency, the putting of the circulating medium into the hands of a few, threw tens of thousands of farms "into the claws of the loan companies. Men and women gave up the unequal struggle and started forth homeless, like cattle driven westward . . . abandoned the old homestead, and with trembling hands and bent forms, strove to endure again the hardships of making new homes in a new country."

In the typical bathos of the times, she described the sheriff's summons, as it affected Mary and John, a young farmer couple. "The sun shone, but they saw it not; the birds sang sweetly, but they heard no music; the tall grain waved gracefully and the flowers bloomed, but it brought them no gladness. Mary sank into a chair and seemed turned to stone; her face was white as marble and her eyes had a strange, cold look, not unlike death. Despair is like death; when hope is buried, the body might as well be . . . Men and women cannot succeed under like circumstances." The sheriff would sell the farm for half-value and would take horses and farm machinery to satisfy the unjust judgment.

"It has long been evident to earnest thinkers," wrote McCabe, "that the farmers of the United States are the most cruelly oppressed class of our community." Hard times now became Kelley's chief organizer.

Delegates from 1,400 Granges in 11 states at the national meeting, January 8, 1873, drew up a new constitution and installed Dudlie W. Adams, of Waukon, in northeast Iowa, as head of the state organization. He was soon to replace Saunders as the Grand Master of the national organization.

Adams was born in 1831 at Winchendon in the northern pine woods of Massachusetts, where his father ran a saw mill. They moved to a rundown rocky farm, and young Adams became the local school teacher. At twenty-one, he went west and took up a piece of wild government land at Waukon. At the time of his Grange leadership, he was a man of mighty body, with a vast bristly beard, luxuriant unruly hair, a prominent nose, and clear compelling eyes: "A man of great firmness and force of character, fertile in resource, possessing great tact, and above all . . . a practical farmer . . . thoroughly devoted to the interests of the class for whose benefit the Order was working."

[65]

His energy and talents, combined with those of Kelley, pushed the Order on to greater success, and during 1873, 22 new state Granges were organized from California and Oregon to New Hampshire, from Michigan to Louisiana, Georgia, and Florida. By the end of the year, new Granges were being organized at the rate of 1,000 a month, and the tempo soon quickened to over 2,000.

"With irresistible power the great wave has increased and swelled in volume until it has reached both oceans," wrote Ezra S. Carr in his history of the Pacific Coast Patrons. "It lifted the bowed head of the South; it included both sexes; it became a national educator."

In Minnesota, Ignatius Donnelly, fighting the railroads and political bosses, became Grange lecturer and spoke in nearly every place in the state. His Grange pamphlets were circulated by tens of thousands. "Wherever among the fullness of the earth a human stomach goes empty, or a human brain remains darkened in ignorance," he declaimed, "there is wrong and crime and fraud somewhere." The "battle of the age" was on. "Could the ordinary man retain his economic independence, or must he become the wage slave of the possessor of great wealth?"

He pulled the Patrons into politics. At the September 2, 1873 meeting at Owatonna, resolutions — probably written by him — denounced both old parties. A call for an "Anti-Monopoly" convention was issued.

A full state ticket was nominated. The new Anti-Monopoly party proposed to deprive private banks of the right to issue money. Federal greenbacks were to be made legal tender for debts and be interchangeable with government bonds. Donnelly, among other successful fellow candidates, was sent to the state senate.

The Anti-Monopoly party spread rapidly into Indiana, Illinois, Missouri, Michigan, Wisconsin, Iowa, Kansas, Nebraska, California, and Oregon. The political equilibrium of the most steadfast states has been broken, said the *New York Tribune*.

In the South, discontent was still channeled into the struggle to free the various states from vestiges of War-Republicanism, carpetbag, and "nigger" rule — slogans useful to home-grown gangs. But discontent also channeled into the Grange and enabled honest independent candidates to step forth. Dimly there was emerging the possibility of the establishment of a bona fide two-party system instead of a one-party system based on Negro-baiting and white rule. The Grange played a tremendous part in leavening sodden southern life. In Georgia, it sent Dr. William H. Felton, the wiry vitriolic Methodist preacher from the Bloody Seventh district, to Congress.

"Men talk of . . . improvement in business," he shouted from the backwood stumps. "Do you find it in the homes of the farmer . . . among the mechanics and wealth creators of the country? No, Sir! Absolutely the rich are growing richer and the poor are growing poorer from day to day."

Grange pressure culminated there in the Georgia railway-lease probe of 1876 — the findings, concerning not only the railways but every dominant politician, were so scandalous that every copy of the report was stolen from the statehouse. Thus the Grange made possible the later political revolt of fiery Tom Watson and in South Carolina of one-eyed "Pitch-fork" Ben Tillman.

In Missouri, so many Grangers found themselves in the legislature that it was proposed to organize a Legislative Grange.

The idea of railroad regulation, which Kelley had helped implant in the membership as early as 1871, took hold of the Grange in a big way. Everywhere the farmers were vocal about railroad abuses. McCabe declared that the lands granted by the government to various railway corporations made up "a total area of 198,165,794 acres, or about 300,000 square miles, far larger than any western European country."

In Minnesota, the true home-state of the Grange, the battle led directly to the doors of the highest railroad offices. At every session the state legislature had been lobbied, bribed, browbeaten, and pressed to pay defaulted railroad securities, "swindling bonds," as the Grange called them.

"In spite of huge grants," says Joseph Dorfman in his *Thorstein Veblen*, "estimated in 1873 by the Minnesota railroad commissioner to be sufficient to have built all the railroads of the state, freight rates were high and tending to advance."

In 1873, William Watts Folwell, in his *History of Minnesota* (volume III), wrote that the railroad commissioner declared that Minnesota grants to railroads in land, bonds, and grade-ways totalled in value, "not less than $51,000,000" — more than the whole value of the lines in operation. Yet, after giving the railroad barons their property, the Minnesotans still had to pay "unreasonable rates and suffer the discourtesies of arrogance."

Granger anger grew so vocal that the governor came out for voiding railroad charters, for railroad regulation, and for rates fixed by the legislature, not on watered stock, but on a reasonable basis. It was time "to take these robbing corporations by the scruff of the neck and shake them over hell." Grange laws were passed.

Railroad lawyers, land agents, business managers, lobbyists, and major newspaper editors tried to tear new laws to shreds. Money flowed freely. But after three years, the Supreme Court reluctantly upheld the legislature.

In state after state, railroad regulatory acts were being introduced — the so-called Granger laws. State railroad commissions were created.

In Illinois, the head of one railroad advised the farmers "to go home and slop their hogs and not meddle with things they could not understand." But Grangers were swept into office, and they passed a law fixing maximum railroad rates and minimum elevator charges. Here, too, it required a three years' court struggle to make the laws stick for a short while.

By the end of 1875, the National Grange had 30,000 locals and 2,500,000 members. Iowa, Missouri, and Indiana each had more than 2,000 local Granges. Illinois and Kentucky were runners-up with 1,500; Kansas with 1,300; Ohio and Tennessee each had over 1,000. The organization spread into Canada. Colored Granges in the South now purchased through white Grange exchanges and cooperatives.

Everywhere Grange cooperative undertakings grew more ambitious. Great buying and selling associations, handling millions of dollars, were built up. Louisiana sugar and syrups were bartered for northern flour, corn, and bacon. Grange grain, cattle, hog, and cotton pools were formed. Community grain elevators were established. In Iowa over half of all elevators came into Grange hands. Buying associations cut the price of headers from $325 to $150. A saving of $80.00 was effected in harvester-machine prices. Granger factories were started to manufacture rakes, mowers, steel plows. The Granger Werner was "the best harvester on the market." Warehouses, grist mills, pork-packing houses, bag and broom factories, brickyards, blacksmith shops, machine and farm implement works, cotton gins, cotton yarn mills, and canneries flourished. Grange leaders estimated that Iowa Cooperative buying had saved $365,000 for the members. New stores bore new Granger signs such as Pomona Threshers, Inc. on the tall wooden foreheads all across the prairie country. Transportation companies — rail and water — were built up. Granger homestead associations, land companies, and insurance companies did a thriving business. By 1875, according to Carr, not less than $18,000,000 were thus invested by the Grange, with a saving to each member of more than $100 annually.

During the first year in California, the Grange alleged it saved its 16,000 members more than $5,000,000 by breaking the market monopoly of wheat king Friedlander and his "ring." "Who will now say that the millenium is not near at hand?" exulted Carr.

But the year after, the Grange fleet of seventy leased vessels bound for Europe encountered damaging storms, and the banks withdrew all credit. Also the Grangers misjudged the market. Losses were great. So, after all, the farmers got "a knife in the ribs" from "the scheming speculators," concluded Carr.

Undaunted, the Grange went into the banking business itself, erecting an impressive establishment at California and Leidensdorff Streets in San Francisco. A huge business center was maintained at Market and Fremont Streets.

The California Grange was also watchful over public affairs. At its second annual meeting in Stockton, October 6, 1874, it exposed the shady manipulations of the Board of Regents of the University of California, under the thumb of the state banking and bonanza king, William C. Ralston. Granger pressure brought about scientific farm research at the university and eventually led to the creation of one of the finest, most progressive agricultural colleges in the world.

The California Grange also broke new ground in curbing the railroads. Its educational efforts led to the development of the Workingman's Party in the late seventies and the calling of a constitutional convention that liberalized the legal structure of the commonwealth.

Such efforts, plus social contacts, changed the farmers' outlook throughout the nation. "Nothing more picturesque, more delightful, more helpful," wrote Hamlin Garland, "has ever arisen out of American rural life." The exalted spirit of the new organization was revealed by the address of Worthy Master Adams at the 1875 Charleston convention. After speaking to the point on transportation and currency problems, he closed with an eloquent purple passage:

"From the snow-clad hills, the flowery vales, the golden shore, and prairie lands, we meet together by the historic palmetto. Not as nomads who gather at the shrine in obedience to sentiment do we come, but as chosen representatives of the fraternity, whose object is the moral and material advancement of the great industrial interests of the great republic. . . . The work has spread from ocean to ocean . . . This uprising and organizing of a great and scattered interest has not a parallel in the history of the world. . . . It burst upon us with the suddenness of an erratic comet, yet promises to remain with the brilliancy and permanency of the sun."

The Grange had found the farmers of the nation "unorganized, isolated, unrecognized, weak, plodding, and their voice, virtually unheard in the councils of the land. Today they are organized, united, strong, thoughtful and duly respected and recognized as one of the great powers to be. . . . We have . . . stepped upon the mount and caught the glimpse of the promised land. . . ."

The struggle had just begun. Great wealth still held the citadel, and monopoly would not be given up without a struggle. "We must keep our ranks full, our faith strong, our work pure, and our actions wise."

Actually, the Grange had now reached the peak of its growth. Its expansion had been too rapid, its sudden wealth too overpowering. The leaders feared the cheering multitudes they had gathered together, petty power politics caused factionalism, and chaos crept in. Soon accusations were levied concerning high salaries and the conduct of national officers. The angry Illinois Grange distributed its $50,000 surplus to the individual vineyards. In many places meetings were abandoned. Minnesota lost 32 lodges.

By 1880, practically all the Grange grain elevator enterprises had been wiped out. Other business failures followed, due partly to mismanagement, but also because of hard times and the pressures exerted by railroads, distributors, middlemen, and hired politicians, fearing the loss of profits or power. Machinery companies dumped products below cost to crush Grange establishments. Constant lawsuits were brought for the infringements of patents — any peg on which to hang costly legal action.

But more serious than any business trouble had been the rise of the Greenback party. Farmer energies deflected into political activities meant less enthusiasm for the Grange. Many Grange members were unwilling to be weaned away from Republican or Democratic allegiances, so partisan disputes marred the previous harmony. By 1886, although 30 states were still represented in the national convention, the total membership was probably under 200,000, less than one-tenth of what it had been a decade earlier.

With Grange decline, the railroads recovered quite a few lost positions. State supreme courts often reversed themselves, and Grange railroad rates and regulatory acts, previously upheld after long legal struggles, were cast into limbo. In time, regulatory governmental agencies were taken over by railroad attorneys. The Grange had shot its bolt.

But for a decade the Grange was the dominant force in rural

[71]

America. It forever changed the contours of American life—in every way for the better. It was, of course, too full of lofty moral platitudes. "God," "charity," "the development of a better and higher manhood"— such pious generalities were ever to the fore in its declamations. It set forth a long list of moral principles such as "Work hard and buy less." But its real success lay not in competition with Protestant revivalism but in its attack on the corporate evils of the day. It helped heal ugly sectionalism and curbed postwar corruption.

For the first time the Grange brought American farmers out of their long rural isolation and made them an integral part of the nation. It forced the government to institute rural services. It broke ground for political reform and the growth of aggressive popular organizations that would eventually make the basic Grange demands part of the law and custom of the land.

It greatly influenced such future leaders as La Follette, Altgeld, Donnelly, Bryan, Jerry Simpson, Hamlin Garland, Tom Watson, Davis Waite, Ben Tillman, Weaver, Peffer, and Van Wyck; also Hogg, Nugent, Kearby, and Davis of Texas — all great names in the progressive movements of America.

In his *Autobiography*, La Follette declares: "As a boy on the farm in Primrose Township, I heard and felt this movement . . . swirling about me; and I felt the indignation which it expressed in such a way that I suppose I have never fully lost the effect of that early impression. . . . It was the first powerful revolt against the rise of monopoly, the arrogance of the railroads, and the waste and robbery of public lands."

In spite of the decline of the Grange, it still flourishes on a national scale, though in many places only as a small-town club, not a farmers' organization, and is still a grass-roots force for democracy. It was invited to send advisory delegates to the San Francisco World Security meeting in 1945. It still has three million members. It still runs many cooperative enterprises. In 1942, the Grange League Federation of New York State alone did a gross business of $110,000,000. Nationally, farm cooperatives, many stemming from early Granges, did $12,400,000,000 in 1961. Pretty good compound interest on Kelley's $2.50 and his tribulations.

Kelley, at loggerheads over political action, to which he was opposed, undermined by backdoor scheming and apparently false charges of dishonesty, left the organization in a huff. He packed off to Florida, where he invested all his savings in a real estate boom and lost everything. He came back to Washington to knock at the door of the Grange.

By then several of his earlier lackadaisical Washington associates were in the saddle, riding an organization grown wholly respectable. The crusading days were over. So was Kelley's usefulness, but the order and his old friends showed gratitude and voted him a life pension. To the end of his days, he remained highly venerated by the membership.

Kelley really had done a great work. This somewhat naive but dogged visionary Irishman who set forth courageously like a modern Don Quixote, with only a few cents in his pocket but a great conviction in his soul, welded together for the first time the rural citizens of the nation. In a few years he built up one of the most powerful democratic organizations ever to appear in the land. This single man, more than any one else, sired progressivism and democracy in rural America. It was the first organization of national scope to bring women into community and public activities and make them aware of economic, social, and political problems. Despite Kelley's bitter efforts to keep the Grange out of politics, he was the true father of the Anti-Monopoly party and the Greenback movement. From the foundations he laid came the later Farmers' Alliance and the Populist movement, both so fruitful for American democracy. His efforts are the fountainhead of the whole post-Civil War movement in behalf of political and economic freedom.

Though mentioned in very few public-school texts, though one will not find his name either in Webster's unabridged dictionary or the *World Almanac*, Kelley deserves a lasting place among the great apostles of American independence. He was a builder of the American ideal of popular liberties.

IV
MACUNE AND
THE GREAT ALLIANCE

Unlike Kelley's great organization, the Southern Farmers' Alliance, soon to become more powerful than the Grange had ever been, was never carefully blueprinted. It came to have a ritual, grips, and passwords, but like Topsy it grew out of human needs in a remote corner of Texas. It was truly grass-roots democracy.

In Lampasas County, in 1874, a little group of farmers met in schoolhouses to discuss their needs and what was wrong with the nation. Some were Kansans, driven from their home state when they lost their lands to the railroads. These little groups gradually came together, first in the north-central frontier counties and finally in 1878 in a Grand State Alliance.

It sought to protect settlers against shyster land-claims often based on old Spanish titles; it assisted in the capture of horse and cattle thieves. As cattle raising gave way to farming and cotton raising, interest shifted, and it came out against high railroad tariffs, the loan merchants, the gouging middleman. It, too, built up cooperatives to help farmers buy implements cheaper and to market their products.

By 1886, the organization had grown powerful. That year at the Cleburne convention 84 counties and 2,700 sub-Alliances with 100,000 members were represented. The resolutions adopted required the organization to labor for the agricultural classes in a strictly nonpartisan spirit. The language was flowery: "The brightest jewels . . . it garners are the tears of widows and orphans, and its imperative demands are to visit the homes where lacerated hearts are bleeding to assuage the suffering of a brother or sister, bury the dead, care for the widows and educate the orphans." The program called for higher taxation on lands held for speculation (in echo of Henry George), for the prohibition of alien land-ownership, no dealing in futures, adequate taxation of railroads, new paper-money issues, and an interstate commerce law.

The strong spirit at Cleburne was Dr. C. W. Macune, then thirty-five years old, a self-educated lawyer, doctor, and, lately, Texas farmer, who was made Executive Secretary and put in charge of the Alliance Exchange or cooperative businesses. He looked like a good-natured Irish bartender, with twinkling clear dark eyes, a healthy-sized portly moustache, a strong jutting chin, his hair plastered well forward to cover his extreme forehead baldness. He was born in Kenosha, Wisconsin, May 20, 1851. His Scotch-Irish father, a blacksmith and Methodist preacher, died of cholera en route to California when Macune was only a year old. His mother took him to Fremont, Illinois. At ten he quit school to work on a farm, but drifted to California, then Kansas, finally Texas.

Well-read, he could write and speak with authority, had considerable wit, and great personal charm, but was too much of a compromiser to please some, and not always ethical in money matters.

As head of the Alliance, he embarked on a vigorous program of nationwide expansion into other southern states, where the farmers had never recovered from the Civil War and its marching boots, and were now being trampled anew by the inroads of northern finance and ugly persecution by large southern plantation owners, themselves squeezed by northerners and loan merchants. The prolonged misuse and impoverishment of the soil, which the farmers themselves, because of ignorance or lack of resources, had helped bring about, did not help. A spirit of revolt over intolerable conditions was rapidly spreading. Macune's first important move was toward Louisiana, where in a few short years a strong Farmers' Union had been built up.

In the fall of 1884, Farmer Tetts said, "I met brother Samuel Skinner on the streets of Ruston, Louisiana. He had just sold his short crop of cotton for a short price, and was feeling none the best over the prospects for another year. I had also disposed of my crop, and found that my receipts did not meet my expenses. We decided to take some steps toward organizing the farmers for mutual protection and assistance. . . ."

At a meeting on March 10, 1885, at Antioch church, Lincoln parish, nine persons joined and took the oath. Members were accepted from a wide territory. Tetts himself had to ride fifteen miles to attend. Soon groups sprang up all over the parish, "owing to the enthusiasm of the members and the undoubted necessity for some relief."

The first mass parish meeting was held in Vienna in July. Tetts was made secretary and two lecturers were named. The constitution adopted was largely a replica of that of the Texas Alliance. The ritual of the defunct Grange was reduced to one degree— "very impressive . . . [it] did much to keep our meetings interesting."

Tetts wrote pieces for *Home and Farm* and hundreds of private letters. At a state meeting, called for October, 1885, four parishes were represented. The Alliance soon spread into other southern states.

The Texas Alliance sent Brother Evan Jones to Louisiana to talk over federation. This was achieved in October, 1887, at a Shreveport, Louisiana, convention, where nine states were represented. Among the delegates were noted farmer leaders such as S. B. Alexander and black-bearded Colonel Leonidas L. Polk of North

Carolina, soldier, legislator, reconstruction leader. As State Agriculture Commissioner he had advocated an agricultural college and a state department of agriculture to help diversify crops and promote livestock raising. Soon he realized that the plight of the farmers went beyond what mere technical assistance could remedy.

He was born on a poor farm in Anson County, North Carolina, April 24, 1837, the only child of a second marriage. Orphaned at the age of fourteen, he received only a common school education. But in 1860—then only twenty-three—he was elected to the state's lower house. The following year, though but a lukewarm supporter of Secession, he enlisted as a private in the Confederate army and saw active service. After the war, he was again elected — as an "Army candidate" on a veiled anti-carpetbag platform — and specialized in agricultural problems.

In 1886, he started the weekly *Progressive Farmer*, built up a state-wide farmers' organization, and the following year was appointed to the newly created post of Agricultural Commissioner.

According to M. Scott Morgan, in his *History of the Wheel and Alliance*, the first Alliance group — the "Ash Pole Alliance" — was founded in Robeson County, April 30, 1887, and spread rapidly. Polk soon swung his own organization into the folds and helped organize a state Alliance at Rockingham, Richmond County, under the presidency of S. B. Alexander, a man of great standing in the state. The following year the Alliance counted 42,000 noses. A moving orator and writer, at Shreveport Polk was made Vice-President of the new united body.

Macune, chosen President, told the assembled delegates, "This body is the first organization of the real cotton-raisers ever inaugurated to assist the poor man. . . . The price of that staple is not equal to the cost of producing it." The members "must stand shoulder to shoulder in one solid phalanx till the effort is crowned with victory. . . . The future prosperity of this movement is . . . in your hands. . . ."

Two Texas Alliance organizers entered Georgia in 1887 and "touched a match to the tinder of discontent . . . almost immediately the state was aflame," said C. Van Woodward in his *Tom Watson*. "Hundreds of 'lodges' sprang into existence, each with its 'lecturer,' organizers rode all over the state; dozens of papers and journals were founded or changed their tone and adopted new slogans; great quantities of reform literature were distributed. In less than three years, 134 out of 137 counties . . . sent delegates to a state convention." Over 2,000 lodges had a membership of more than 100,000. In one year the Alliance saved Georgia farmers over $200,000 in fertilizers alone. Cooperatives, gins, stores, and warehouses sprang up all over the South.

Macune next set to work to draw in the powerful Arkansas Agricultural Wheel as part of the Alliance.

According to Nelson A. Dunning in his *Farmers' Alliance History*, the Wheel had been started in 1882 by schoolteacher W. T. McBee and eight farmers in his schoolhouse near Des Arc, Prairie County, as a secret organization with ritual. Its purpose was to provide its members with knowledge of the theory and practice of agriculture. "No machinery can be run without a great drive wheel. . . . Agriculture is the great wheel or power that controls the entire machinery of the world's industries. Had it not been noted by Prophet Ezekiel in Chapter ten, 'The Wheel, he saw worked as it were, with the regularity of a wheel within a wheel and, it was said in my hearing, O Wheel, and so we hear it [possibly chapter 10, verse 12]?"

The distress of the people caused the Wheel to grow rapidly, remarks Dunning. The farmers believed its teachings to be wise. It would "burst both political parties into atoms and scatter them like a star dust throughout the universe."

"What gave rise to the Wheel?" asked W. W. Tedford, one of the founders. "*Monopoly*. A monopoly that wants to buy the earth, and with it the souls and bodies of the people who inhabit it." Flour was selling at ten dollars a barrel, meat at twenty cents per pound. Merchants, holding mortgages, controlled the weighing, measuring, and pricing of goods and produce.

[79]

The state constitution later adopted at Goff's Grove in 1883, where delegates from forty counties gathered, stated, "The general condition of our country imperatively demands unity of action . . . to foster agricultural and mechanical pursuits, encouraging the toiling masses, leading them in the road to prosperity, and providing a just and fair remuneration for labor, -a just exchange of our commodities. . . ."

The farmers, said the preamble, should raise "less cotton and more of their own meat and bread," diversify their crops by planting corn, wheat, oats, and grasses, and thus "increase demand far beyond the actual supply, securing better prices, and holding the stock of provisions from the greedy paws of merciless speculators." All monopolies were "dangerous . . . tending to enslave a free people and subvert and finally overthrow the great principles pursued by Washington and his glorious compatriots."

"There is a God, the great Creator of all things. . . . He created all men free and equal, and endowed them with certain inalienable rights, such as life, liberty and the pursuit of happiness," and "any power that tended to restrict or circumscribe any class of our citizens in the free exercise of these God-given rights and privilges, is detrimental to the best interests of a free people."

At a special get-together on October 15, 1885, at Greenbrier, the Wheel, then having 462 sub-Wheels, combined with another early Arkansas organization, the Brothers of Freedom, with 650 local organizations. Joint membership was 40,000.

The press attacked the new order violently, so it grew more rapidly than ever. The word "White" was dropped from the eligibility clause, and separate Colored Wheels were organized. Soon Missouri, Mississippi, Alabama, Kentucky, Texas, and the Indian Territory had state Wheels. Organizers were at work in the Indian Territory, in Georgia, Virginia, and Michigan.

The first meeting of the National Wheel, by then 500,000 strong, was held at McKenzie, Tennessee, November 8, 1887. President Lance C. McCracken, a fierce eager man, told of the history and

[80]

the phenomenal growth of the Wheel and Brothers of Freedom. "One cause is [due to] the chartering of so many corporations, which have no souls, and never did, . . . that have received and are receiving, from both State and national governments, privileges which individuals do not receive" — among others the Standard Oil Company of the East and the Cotton Seed Oil Company of the South and West.

"It has been claimed that competition is the life of trade. Competition is the greatest enemy that the American wage-earner has to contend with; not only competition among themselves, but . . . with foreign labor, the laborers having been landed here by shiploads under contract . . . on the other hand competition has ceased to be a factor with the moneyed men of our land."

One reason for the farmers' difficulties was that nearly 80 percent of the United States' total exports were farm products, and farmers had to sell to a free-trade country, Great Britain, but had to buy what they needed in a high protectional tariff country. Instead of increasing the cotton area, as in 1885, farmers should reduce it about 30 percent. The farmers would receive as much for 4,500,000 bales as they did now for 6,500,000. "There would be fewer mortgages . . . and we should be independent, as we by right should be."

The convention adopted a fourteen-point statement. The Wheel was to protect them from the shameful abuses that farmers and mechanics were suffering at the hands of arrogant capitalists, powerful corporations, and the seemingly insatiable greed of dishonest creditors. The public land was to be reserved for settlers only — not another acre to railroads or speculators. The public debts should be repaid rapidly, by operating the mints to full capacity in coining gold and silver. National banks were to be abolished, and treasury notes instead of bank notes issued. No speculation in futures was to be tolerated. Other demands were for a graduated income tax, prohibition of immigrant foreign labor, abolition of convict contract-labor system, and the direct election of officials of the national gov-

[81]

ernment. Tariffs on raw materials for manufacturing should be removed. Duties should be levied mainly on luxuries. The government should protect the Chickasaws and Choctaws of the Indian Territory in their inalienable rights and prevent railroads and other wealthy syndicates from overriding the treaties for their protection. Education of the masses by a well-regulated school system was advocated.

By July 25, 1888, the organization had become so powerful that it was allowed to meet in the Hall of Representatives in Little Rock. By then the state organizations had strong Roschdale stores and such other cooperative undertakings as a tobacco warehouse at Fulton, Kentucky, cooperative mills in Missouri, and a department selling farm implements.

It was high time, Macune believed, that the Alliance and Wheel be combined. The two organizations met simultaneously at Meridian, Mississippi, on December 5, 1888. The Wheel had delegates from 8 southern states and from Wisconsin. The Alliance, with 10,000 sub-alliances, 800 county alliances, and a membership of 400,000, sent delegates from 12 states.

Macune told them: "The perpetuity of our system of government must be largely affected by our success or failure." The farmers were the largest, most conservative class of citizens, the greatest producers, the permanent, stable, and solid class, on which the prosperity of all others depends.

"We have two classes of anarchists [the bugaboo word of those days] in this country: one the avowed anarchists, who oppose all law and order, and the other a blindly selfish class, who would loudly disclaim anarchy, but advocate conditions that so surely sap the vitals of productive labor, that the result is ten times more productive of anarchy than all the agitation of the avowed anarchists . . . The evils now afflicting agriculture had been developing for years, consequently no spasmodic effort and no single idea were adequate. Let the order be the great school of truth, in which, by a thorough exchange of ideas, all may be truly educated."

[82]

At the joint session in the courthouse, a single organization was created with the name Farmers' and Laborers' Union of America, though it remained known chiefly as the Southern Alliance.

The first Colored Alliance was started at Houston, Texas, December, 1886. Thanks to the indefatigable work of white Baptist minister R. M. Humphrey, within two years it grew into a strong national body, the National Alliance and Cooperative Union, with a million members, and had large and successful cooperatives. As time went by, it cooperated with the white Alliance and utilized white cooperatives and other facilities, but according to William Dubose Sheldon in his *Populism in the Old Dominion,* in some states, for example Virginia, it had no relations whatever with white order.

Unlike the Wheel, the Southern Alliance stayed mostly below the Mason-Dixon line. Other organizations sprang up in the North, because of drouth and hard times, and, according to Dunning, because of Greenback teachings about specie resumption and currency contraction.

The first Northern Alliance was organized by Milton George in the office of *Western Rural,* Chicago, Illinois, April 15, 1880, as Cook County Alliance, No. 1.

George had taken over the *Western Rural* as a mortgage holder to save his investment and bought a small farm to establish his status as a true farmer. Particularly incensed over railroad abuses, he denounced the free passes by which legislators were "bribed." The railroads were "starving" the farmers.

The second Alliance chapter was organized by Jay Burrows, a former Granger, in Filley, Gage County, Nebraska. Within a month, claimed the *Western Rural,* a hundred locals had been chartered, and within a year, over a thousand. Burrows became the moving spirit in the whole Northern Alliance.

He was born in Chautauqua County, New York, worked as a newspaper man, and fought for four years in the Civil War under Sheridan and Custer in the Shenandoah Valley.

[83]

Soon membership of 24,500 was claimed, largely in Nebraska, Kansas, and Iowa, and at the third national meeting at St. Louis, October 4, 1882, 100,000 members. Enthusiasm ebbed, and in 1884 and 1885 no national meeting could be called. But hard times and the drop in wheat prices drove farmers into the ranks again. The order spread to Colorado and Minnesota, and a Territorial Alliance was started in the Dakotas.

The Dakota organization protested against the new state constitution drawn up by Henry Villard, President of the Northern Pacific. According to Paul Fossum in his *The Agrarian Movement in North Dakota*, he told the farmers that Alliance efforts were a "piece of unwarranted outside meddling." They laughed angrily in his face.

At the Minnesota state convention in St. Paul, the indefatigable Ignatius Donnelly dictated the multifarious platform, which, among other things, proposed government ownership of some transcontinental railroads and public control of the remainder.

At the seventh annual meeting at Minneapolis, October, 1887, six states and one territory were represented. Milton George was made a life member, and Jay Burrows of Nebraska, President. Strong resolutions were adopted: "We recognize in these troubled times the need of appealing to the higher nature of men, that they may seal anew their belief in the holiness of self-sacrifice and the meanness of greed. . ."

Burrows moved to Lincoln, Nebraska, and started the influential *Weekly Alliance,* soon famous for his scathing editorials. He was a hard, bitter man.

The order continued to grow in Iowa, Nebraska, Kansas, and Minnesota, and became influential in Illinois, Wisconsin, Michigan, and Missouri. "Never in our history has there been such a union of action among farmers as now," wrote Milton Park in August, 1890. The order had then close to 2,000,000 members; Kansas alone had 130,000. By November, 10 states had been organized, 5 others were being organized, and many locals were scattered among other states.

[84]

Another large northern farmers' group was the Mutual Benefit Association of Illinois. In the fall of 1882, each of five neighboring farmers of Johnson County brought a load of wheat to market. The buyers refused to take it, claiming the market was too unsettled. The farmers believed this was a scheme to fleece them. A wire to the city market revealed that prices were rising, and they telegraphed for a freight car. The incident became the talk of the neighborhood and led to the formation of secret clubs. The organization quickly became statewide, and by 1888 a Mutual Benefit Association Printing Company was formed.

By then, 200,000 members were claimed, and at the November 1889 meeting in Mt. Vernon in Southern Illinois, rapid and permanent growth was apparent. Strong cooperative enterprises and insurance companies had been built up. The Association demanded equal and exact justice for all, special privileges to none, the abolition of all monopoly, the suppression of all trusts and combines limiting production, and the repeal of all class legislation. Otherwise, in a nation "of millionaires and paupers, of plutocrats and slaves, government by and for the people" would soon perish.

Another organization drawing close to both Northern and Southern Alliances was the powerful Knights of Labor, led by Terrence V. Powderly. The K. of L. antedated both the Grange and the Alliance, having been founded as a secret order in Philadelphia in 1869.

Traveling in Europe, Powderly had met a tailor in London who had given him pamphlets, among them the *Communist Manifesto*. It had contained, he said, "pretty much everything I had thought out for myself, and I used it largely in the preparation of the Declaration of Principles of the Order." Soon press and pulpit accused the "tea-pot" society of gruesome communistic and incendiary plots.

In 1878, it changed into an open organization and held its first annual convention in Reading, Pennsylvania. J. R. Sovereign became Grand Master, and was succeeded by Powderly at the

[85]

1879 convention in Chicago. The organization claimed 700 locals and 52,000 members. By 1885, 110,000.

The K. of L. Declaration of Principles stated: "The alarming development and aggressiveness of the great capitalists and corporations unless checked, will inevitably lead to the pauperization and hopeless degradation of the toiling masses." Industrial and moral worth, not wealth, were the true standards of industry and national greatness. It sought to secure the workers the full enjoyment of the wealth they created.

Public lands, the heritage of the people, should be reserved for actual settlers, "not another acre for railroads" or speculators. All lands held for speculative purposes should be taxed to their full value.

In October, 1886, 800 delegates attended the General Assembly in Richmond, Virginia, representing from 500,000 to 800,000 members.

By then a disastrous strike and internal feuds over craft unionship had weakened the organization, cracking it down the middle. When the head of the Colorado K. of L., Joseph R. Buchanan, refused to oust craft unions, Powderly drove him out of the organization. Among groups ordered to withdraw was the International Cigar Makers' Union, headed by a little Jewish-Dutch immigrant, Samuel Gompers, of the rising American Federation of Labor.

But the K. of L. was still the largest workers' group, and Alliance leaders, particularly Macune, hoped for a merger of all farm and labor organizations in the country, and all were persuaded to hold their national conventions in, or send representatives to, St. Louis in December, 1899.

There assembled were the Southern Alliance, the Colored Alliance, the Farmers' Mutual Benefit Associations, the Northern Alliance, and the Knights of Labor. On reduced round-trip railroad fares came representatives from every corner of the Union and of every shade of political opinion — Democrats, Republicans, Greenbacks, Union Laborites, Anti-Monopolists, Prohibitionists, Suffragettes. It was the first and the greatest reunion of its kind in the history of the nation. If the various organizations could be united, it would be the largest organized body in the country.

This great gathering was for Dr. C. W. Macune the great climax of his life. In ten years he had come to lead millions, he had become a mighty power in the land.

Macune established headquarters at the luxurious Hurst's Hotel in the finest suite in the city, a resplendent place of red plush and mahogany, where shoeshiners, valets, waiters, brass-butlers, bell-boys, porters, and barbers were almost as numerous as the guests, and quite as busy. His quarters were crowded with the great and near great: Colonel L. L. Polk of North Carolina, one-eyed "Pitchfork" Ben Tillman of South Carolina, who roared out profanity and wit, scorchy young Tom Watson of Georgia, the hero of the poor farmers, white and Negro.

His talk to the farmers was racy: "You were born on plenty and spent your childhood in plenty . . . then you lost your homes. The sheriff's red flag was planted at your front gate. You and yours took down the family pictures from the wall, picked some favorite flowers from the graveyard, and took your weary march into the strange cold world. You walked the roads looking for work. I have done it, too."

From his year's crop, by the time the tenant farmer buys a mule and guano, pays up his store account, he "hasn't enough left to buy a bottle of laudanum, and not enough cotton to stuff his old lady's ear."

To Macune's suite came the notable sage and orator Ignatius Donnelly of Minnesota. There came the Kansas cyclone, Mary Ellen Lease, who had once done washing for fifty cents a day, had raised four children, and had become a successful lawyer. As a platform speaker, with her splendid voice, her tall, slim, taut body, her imperious queenly carriage, her quick extemporaneous oratory, her swift cutting wit, she was unequaled.

Then to St. Louis came one-legged Henry L. Loucks of South Dakota, where he was a power who would help install a Populist

governor. "His long narrow beard was in and out of Macune's suite."
There, too, appeared "Calamity" Samuel Weller, congressman from
Iowa; tall Davis Waite, a bitter puritan from Colorado; bright, little,
bouncy Anna Diggs, alternately of Kansas and Colorado; big Civil
War veteran James Weaver, of gold-rush fame; and big, bearded,
puff-mouthed, William Peffer, editor of the *Kansas Farmer*, soon to
be Senator.

The Southern Alliance delegates, two hundred strong, assembled separately at Entertainment Hall in the Exposition Building
at 10:00 A.M. to listen to speeches of welcome by the governor and
mayor and replies by bushy J. H. McDowell of Tennessee and
A. J. Streeter of Illinois and the Northern Alliance.

Keynote speaker, Southern Alliance President Evan Jones, told
of the "wonderful growth" of his order in the past ten years. It was
destined at no distant day to embrace all farmers, all the laborers
of the world to protect them from the encroachment of rings, trusts,
and soulless combinations.

All the wealth of our nation flows from the land; to its proper
and just distribution is owed the prosperity, contentment, and happiness of the yeomanry, a class upon whom all nations must greatly
depend for strength and support.

Said Jones: "During the greatest prosperity of Rome, almost
eighty-five percent of her population owned titles in land . . . she
was founded upon a rock, and was mistress of the world; but
. . . through the monopolization of her lands by the few, through
unjust legislation, the homes were wrenched from the hands of the
masses, and when the dark death-ford was reached, upon which
civilization was to die, less than two percent of the people controlled
the land . . . about fifteen hundred men controlled the wealth
of the world.

"Today in America millions of acres of her fertile lands, bought
by the lives and efforts of our forefathers, which should have been
held sacred for homes for their posterity, have been squandered
upon railroads and other corporations . . . millions more are owned

[88]

by domestic and foreign syndicates. . . . a large percent of our homes and controlled by domestic and foreign syndicates. . . .a large percent of our homes are hopelessly mortgaged, and about fifty percent of our sons are tenants. But give the people homes — theirs to improve, theirs to cultivate, theirs to beautify, and theirs to enjoy — and our grand republic will stand as the acme of modern civilization and national greatness. . . ."

Macune, who followed, told the delegates how in a short time the entire cotton belt had become well organized. The same protection had to be brought to other agricultural regions. In 1867, the cereal crops of the United States had aggregated 1,250,000,000 bushels worth $1,250,000,000; by 1885, the crop had increased to over 3,000,000 bushels and brought in *less* than $1,250,000,000. In a single hour, instructions from one office could depress prices 50 percent.

The Alliance was the complete opposite of a political party and had to remain non-political, yet it had to exert the pressure necessary to attain its goals. "Party speaks to prejudice, and depends on partisan hatred for power to perpetuate itself." A party platform was "constructed with the highest modern art . . . to pander to the prejudices of every section . . . terms as to mean one thing to one man and the opposite to another. . . . Our strength lies in an entirely different and opposite direction."

The land committee reported that of the 5,000,000 farms in the United States, 1,280,000 were rented — a 25 percent increase in 10 years. "It was peculiar that producers had grown poorer . . . The cold, hard fact stares them in the face that they are not only not living as well as they should . . . their farms are gradually slipping from their grasp." A land aristocracy and tenant farmers were being created as in European countries. Farmers did not average 50 cents a day.

The mortgaged indebtedness on the farms and homes of the people was "not less than $16,000,000,000," and at eight percent per annum an annual tribute of $1,280,000,000 was being paid "to

[89]

Shylocks." This vast sum "exceeded the value of the entire wheat, corn and cotton crops of the United States for one year." Other forms of indebtedness, public and private, swelled the above sum "to more than $30,000,000,000." Since "the annual increase of all agricultural interests is less than three percent, it is only a matter of time when the eight percent annual tribute will absorb all the land in the country."

It was demanded that the government allow the free and unlimited coinage of silver or the issue of silver certificates against an unlimited deposit of bullion. Certain banks were to cease to be United States depositories. Instead, in every county that offered for sale during one year $500,000 worth of farm products — including wheat, corn, oats, barley, rice, tobacco, cotton, wool and sugar — a "Sub-Treasury Office" must maintain warehouses or elevators necessary for the careful storing and preserving of agricultural products to be sold at auction within twelve months. Against this agricultural gold hoard the government was to issue certificates of deposit showing the amount and quality which the farmers could borrow at 1 percent interest, legal tender paper money equal to 80 percent of the value of the products.

This was the famous Sub-Treasury Plan, of which Macune was the major author. It has an echo of the large central warehouses, bursting with produce, set up in Bellamy's Utopian *Looking Backward*. It was similar to the much narrower program put into effect by Secretary of Agriculture Henry A. Wallace fifty years later. Had it been adopted in 1889 it would have saved millions of farmers from losing their farms. Under Wallace it benefited large land corporations more than small farmers or farm workers.

December 28, 1889, the *National Economist*, edited by Macune, hailed the Sub-Treasury Plan with the headline:

EUREKA! KEY TO THE SOLUTION OF THE
INDUSTRIAL PROBLEM OF THE AGE

The question of the amalgamation of the orders came up. The

easiest sailing appeared to be with the Farmers' Mutual Benefit Association. But unwilling to submerge the identity of the Order, its leaders agreed only to mutual cooperation.

A faint effort was made to unite with the Colored Alliance. The *Topeka Advocate* remarked, not very grammatically: "Once having established conditions wherein self interest is enlisted on the side of justice and fair-dealing with the Negro, the path of progress and advancement is thenceforth straight and clear for him. . . ." But racial prejudices were too great to admit Negroes into the same locals. Joint efforts were agreed upon but never formally adopted.

At the Knights of Labor gathering, Powderly, impressive with his broad forehead, tear-drop eyeglasses, and bushy, curled moustache, told how the English used to jail workers for conspiracy who joined a labor union and ship them off to Australia, but since 1875 the coercive laws had been wiped out and unionism was completely legal, whereas in the United States men who dared to join a union were thrown out of their jobs.

"The farmers," he went on, "have resolved to stand by us. Let us resolve to stand by them, make their cause our cause everywhere and in everything. When they are assailed, we are assailed and should resent it. . . ."

Though the K. of L. endorsed the entire Alliance program, consolidation was not feasible. Labor needed many things the farmers' environment did not call for and vice versa. But their respective Washington legislative committees would work in concert to push desired laws. Neither would back any candidate who did not support their joint demands. The Alliance did open its membership to "mechanics" and thereafter always included the K. of L. membership as its own.

"The agreement made with the Knights of Labor," said an Alabama farm spokesman, "added much strength to the movement and gave it a standing among a class of people who had hitherto been inclined to doubt its motives and methods. This compact has stood the assaults of both old political parties."

[91]

But Macune's real desire was for a fusion of the Northern and Southern Alliances. Messages, messengers, and prominent figures flew back and forth between the headquarters of Macune in the Hurst Hotel and those of Jay Burrows at the Planter's Hotel, where the 75 delegates of the Northern Alliance were meeting.

The difficult points at issue were:

1) The secrecy of the Southern Order.
2) Negro exclusion by the Southern Order.
3) The acceptance of non-farmers as members by the Northern Alliance.

Nor did the Northern Alliance wish to accept the official southern name, "the Farmers' and Laborers' Union." They suggested instead Farmers' Alliance and Intellectual Union. The southerners readily agreed.

Considerable progress was made in resolving the other differences. The southern Alliances agreed to leave Negro membership to the decision of each state. They even agreed, if reluctantly, to admit Negroes to the Grand Council. But they were stubborn about retaining secrecy. However, they suggested that in the future secrecy be adopted only gradually. This proposal was accepted by the Kansas and North and South Dakota delegations, but most other northerners drew back, particularly those from Iowa and Minnesota. One Kansas farm editor called southern proposals just another "rebel yell."

There was not full identity of purpose of farmers of the two areas. Though the platforms of both organizations were practically interchangeable, the northerners were more concerned with farm foreclosures, wanted railroad regulation and preferably government ownership. Also, they were more inclined toward political action. whereas the southerners were mostly fanatic one-party Democrats.

But failure to amalgamate was chiefly due to Burrows, still bitterly fighting the Civil War. His deep antagonism toward the South made him distrust the more brilliant, volatile, and adaptable Macune, especially as Macune, a fine politician, and Polk of North Carolina, not Burrows, would certainly head up any united organization. A stubborn rule-or-ruin man, who crushed and got crushed, Burrows was unable to step gracefully into a larger arena where he might have to subordinate himself to others.

In the end, the only thing achieved was a willingness by all to work together on specific beneficial proposals.

After the St. Louis failure, Macune moved boldly into the North to capture the farmers there and set up Southern Alliance groups everywhere. He pushed rapidly into the Pacific Coast states, into Colorado, Indiana, Kansas, Illinois, the Dakotas, Minnesota, Ohio, Pennsylvania, and New York. The *National Economist* gained an enormous nationwide circulation, larger than most news magazines of today. Soon President Polk was able to say, "We took the farmers and laborers of the North and of the East and of the West by the hands, and today we are trampling sectionalism under our feet."

The Sub-Treasury Plan was the spearhead of the new effort. Macune had the Plan drawn up as a bill and introduced into both houses of Congress. Much literature was sent out, precedents and similar foreign legislation were gathered from every possible source. The project aroused a furor. The old parties fought it bitterly, and the politicians went wild with rage over "the innovation," as they termed it. "We don't want any more states until we can civilize Kansas," said the *New York Evening Post;* "Scheme to level the Rockies," *St. Paul Pioneer Press;* "The Farmers' Alliance wants pawn tickets; and though its chiefs do not know a mowing machine from a mulberry grub, they want the earth," *Philadelphia North American.*

But petitions from "the back country," with tens of thousands of names, letters, and resolutions, poured into Washington until both the old parties became alarmed and confused.

The bill was stalled in committee, but Congress had to remain in session late, so when the politicians reached home, they found the hard-working Alliance thoroughly entrenched. They made every effort to divide the organization on this same Sub-Treasury Plan, and in Texas partly succeeded. Elsewhere, they stubbed their toes. The Sub-Treasury Plan had become the great rallying cry of the Order.

Political action became increasingly important. Northern Republican politicians shied away from Alliance demands, so farmers put up their own candidates. In the South, control of the Democratic party by the "Jeffersonian Democrats" — the Alliance — became the issue. In Texas, they were read out of the party, in Alabama, forced out. But candidate after Democratic candidate pledged himself to Alliance principles. Some governors were called Alliance men.

Reform meetings in the West "were the largest political gatherings ever seen on the continent. . . . The effect of this political contest," said Dunning, "will go down to future generations . . . a deserved rebuke to old party methods, and a rugged notice that conditons must be changed." Such was the year 1890. In 13 years, Macune had built up a powerful organization of 4,000,000 members.

The Alliance prepared for a great 1890 Convention in Jacksonville, Florida. It was rumored a new national third party would be launched. Macune was bitterly opposed to this. But that was the way the tide was running, and soon the tide would overwhelm him — and the order he had set in motion.

V

KANSAS
CRUSADER

No mere mechanical survey of the growth of the Farmers' Alliance can give an idea of its importance to the millions of farmers who rushed into the ranks. The Alliance was a crusade; it had its marching songs, war cries, and principles. Its buying and selling cooperatives gave the farmers reliable goods at lower prices and disposed of farm products at better prices.

"One would have to go back to Medieval Europe, on the eve of the first Crusade for an emotional situation comparable," declared Hacker and Kendrick in their *The United States Since 1865*. The Alliance crusade was a religious experience, its meetings had the hysteria of camp meetings and revivals, but it had more meaning, more individual freedom, was stentorious with parades, placards, burnings in effigy, music, and high-jinks. One Georgia preacher said, "The Alliance was born in heaven." Senators saw it "taking the place of churches."

Tom Watson said of the Alliance program: "It is sacred to us because it gives hope to our despair; gives expression to our troubles; gives voice to our wants. Our wives have knelt and prayed for it. Our children have learned to love it. Not a church in all the land where God's blessing has not been invoked upon it." Even thirty years later, at the age of sixty, after he had become a miserable race-bigot, he still felt the glow of those times: "What radiant visions lured us toward the future! What noble deeds we would achieve! What fame and influence would be our reward!

"Were conditions wrong? We could right them. Were laws bad? We would make them good. Were the weak oppressed? We would crush the oppressors. Were righteous principles enchained, like captive maidens in the olden castles of feudal lands and lords? We would put on the bright armor of chivalry, ride forth to rescue and smite the dungeon door with the battle axe of Lionheart."

In Virginia, the Alliance was slow in getting under way, but by 1889, 35 counties in central Virginia were organized under the leadership of Colonel Gabriel T. Barbee; by 1890, 96 out of 100; and enthusiasm mounted as Alliance lecturers took advantage of "cotehouse day," when a large portion of the male population gathered about the county courthouse. It was a monthly ritual — usually on a Monday — and became the most important event in the farmer's humdrum existence. There, on the badly trampled green, the Alliance leaders harangued the tobacco juicers, telling them how they themselves could bring about their release from "the insufferable thralldom of a worse than Egyptian bondage." The enthusiasm took hold of the flour-barrel cliques of the crossroads stores and invaded neighborhood churches. Old "bankers and brokers, lawyers and bar-keepers were excluded from Alliance gatherings." The crowds steadily increased in size.

Lawn parties and dances and summer encampments were arranged where farmers and their wives, daughters, and sweethearts could "enjoy an outing just as the monopolists do at the seaside." Spring and summer, big picnics with basket dinners were held. The spirits of the "brothers and sisters" were enlivened by bowling-green games of ninepins, of bean bags, and by pistol shooting.

[96]

Songs and recitations were staged. Lectures were delivered. Sometimes, says Sheldon, Colonel Polk came across the line to speak.

Farmers' institutes and fairs were held. The personal welfare of members was looked after, sympathy and help extended in moments of trouble, as when the daughter of Brother and Sister Smith was in "a critical state through having a watermelon-seed in her windpipe." An "evangelical fervor marked the entire agrarian crusade" in Virginia, wrote William Dubose Sheldon in his story of Populism in that state.

In December, 1889, Colonel Beverly, a rich planter and conservative gentleman, said of Alliance enthusiasm, "life-giving-hope-inspiring . . . this union comes and wafts its way joyfully northward, and God grant that it may drive back and melt out the wintry cloud of distress and oppression and give us instead the heaven-sent rays of prosperity and independence."

Everywhere in the South and West the Alliance dramatized its struggle and stabbed its hoofs-and-horns adversaries with sharp vivid epithets: "The crime of '73," "the silver conspiracy," "gold bugs," "the railroad Tzars," "the Wall Street octopus," "the plundering plutocracy," "the cold blooded money-trust," — epithets that amused and alarmed eastern sophisticates, and also homegrown William Allen White.

It was a battle royal against a hydra-headed monster called MONOPOLY. Soon enough, the Alliancers found that the flesh-and-blood heads of the monster they wished to decapitate had teeth also. In Texas, Alliance men could not get jobs; the merchants and middlemen fought them; banks foreclosed their mortgages; the railroads hauled their campaign opponents free. The official organ of the Georgia Alliance observed that "in many . . . towns there has been manifest secret but bitter and most vindictive animosity against the Alliance movement, and every scheme possible has been resorted to to bring it into contempt or ridicule."

All this was reflected in the statistics of farms lost to mortgage holders, the rising percentage of tenancy, the appearance of migrant

[97]

labor, problems accentuated by the rapid telescoping of several eras. The United States came to the end of its free land-resources at the same time that industrialism began to establish roots. Either event would have ruptured the social fabric of any country. Taken together, they constituted a great revolution, the effects of which are still felt, the end of which is not yet in sight.

From the start, the Alliance men, then the Populists, posed the question of whether the wealth of America should be monopolized in the hands of the few or whether economic freedom should progress along with political freedom.

In a short time, the Alliance farmers became the best-informed citizens in the land. Men hitherto doomed to isolation now came into close contact at regular intervals to discuss not only farming methods but also the state of the nation. Their newspapers sprang up by dozens, by scores, by hundreds in state after state. As early as the 1887 Shreveport meeting, the Alliance had voted to establish a national publication. Specifications: "Not less than a four page, seven column paper, issued weekly, and devoted to the circulation of official news and the interest of agriculture, and the general dissemination of the true principles of political economy, strictly non-partisan in politics and non-sectarian in religion; to be a clean and neat paper of high moral tone, such as will be a source of true education to the youth, of emulation to those in active middle life, and of congratulation and comfort to the aged."

The first issue of the resulting *National Economist*, under Macune's editorship, appeared in Washington on March 14, 1889, "making its bow with no flourish of trumpets or ostentatious display." It was not to be a "showy publication." No attempt would be made to purvey current news. It would "appeal to reason and judgment and seek to educate in the principles of society, finance or government rather than to relate the visible effects of the violation of such principles." There were only two classes, the producers and the non-producers. Vast enterprises sought to befuddle the taxpayer. Agriculture was the basis of all true prosperity. The paper proved to be solemn and dignified, with weighty articles on economics and detailed items concerning state and local alliances, particularly their cooperative and business activities, which by then represented an annual turnover of more than $10,000,000. From Mississippi, Harry Tracy reported that the state business exchange was selling $700 worth of goods daily, direct from manufacturer to consumer. The Alabama exchange had $150,000 cash reserves. On February 25, 1889, Doctor J. A. Mudd had organized the first Maryland Alliance at Piscataway.

The March 30 issue criticized Andrew Carnegie's statement in the *North American Review* that trusts should cause no alarm because they were a passing phenomenon. Competition "being supreme must triumph." An argument unworthy of its author! The trusts were making the rich richer and the middle class poorer, and the effects were permanent and deplorable.

The *Southern Mercury*, the organ of the Texas Alliance, also became a notable publication or national importance.* Alliance papers went into the hands of every member, keeping interest alive and creating a common point of view.

---

*Also famous were:
   Polk's *Progressive Farmer*, North Carolina
   The Vincent Brothers' *Non Conformist*, Wichita, Kansas
   Barber County Index, edited by Musgrove, later by Leon Eli Beals
   Weaver and Gillette's *Iowa Tribune*
   E. B. Cummings' *Ruralist*, Huron, South Dakota
   Waite's *Aspen Union Era*, Colorado
   Southern Alliance Farmer, Georgia
   Rural Messenger, Petersburgh, Virginia
   Vidette, San Diego, California
   Liberty Banner, New Mexico
   McDowell's *Weekly Toiler*, Tennessee
   Farmers' Alliance and the *Dispatch*, Florida
   Colonel Randolph Harrison's Virginia *Alliance Farmer* and his
       Rural Messenger
   Herbert Pierson's *Virginia Sun*

In addition to newspapers, the Alliance published pamphlets and books by such outstanding authors as Donnelly, Dunning, Morgan, Weaver, Watson, Polk, Tracy, Davis, Peffer, and Emery. The revolt attracted the typical intellectual fringe. Benjamin O. Flower, publisher of the *Arena* — "an epic departure in liberal thought" — opened his columns to articles on free silver, the Farmers' Alliance, single taxers, muckraking, and spiritualism. Hamlin Garland, a confirmed single taxer, became its literary light. In 1889, he published a single tax propaganda story in *Harper's Weekly*, "Under the Lion's Paw," and brought out his novel *A Prairie Heroine*. He also wrote articles for the *Standard*, Henry George's New York paper.

Long before Carnegie turned philanthropist, the local Alliances gathered together libraries. Homes that had known no books except the Bible and the almanac came to have pamphlets, novels, and impressive tomes dealing with the Alliance and with economic problems. The Alliance distributed hundreds of thousands of copies of Bellamy's *Looking Backward* and his *Duke of Stockbridge*, the fictionalized story of Shays' early rebellion. Their papers advertised, and often sold with subscriptions, works by Thomas Jefferson, the spiritual godfather of most alliances; *Caesar's Column* and other books by Ignatius Donnelly; Senator Peffer's *The Way Out*; Weaver's *Call to Action*; Cyclone Davis' *Political Revelation*; William H. Harvey's *Coin's Financial School*; the writings of Tom Watson; Tracy's and Scott's works on the Sub-Treasury Plan; Thomas M. Norwood's novel, *Plutocracy or American White Slavery*; Richard T. Ely's *Taxation in American States and Cities*; N. A. Dunning's *Philosophy of Price*; James F. Hudson's *Railways and their Abuses*; Lloyd's *Wealth versus Commonwealth*; Henry George's book on the tariff and his *Progress and Poverty*; *The Riddle of the Sphinx*, by N. B. Ashby (a leading Bellamy Nationalist). Worn copies of these and numerous pamphlets circulated from hand to hand, and were quoted in season and out.

Those who read Bellamy learned that the inhabitants of his Utopia could not understand why the men of '87 "came to entrust the business of providing the community to a class whose interest was to starve the community. The wonder with us is, not that the world did not get rich under such a system, but that it did not perish outright from want." "The whole state" of Virginia read *Coin's Financial School.* Everybody read Donnelly's *Caesar's Column.* "The Alliance people of Georgia are reading and thinking," said Morgan — a typical comment.

Alliances were especially urged to buy Cushing's *Rules of Order* and the *National Economist Almanac,* full of statistics and arguments on farm problems. They were told to send off for government publications.

Every Alliance had its own "lecturer," a member required to inform himself properly about current problems and pass his knowledge on to the members. Members, in turn, had to prepare informative papers. Each county Alliance also had one or more lecturers and organizers, and each state Alliance and the National Alliance sent out speakers. The local folk vied with each other in entertaining those from afar. It was an honor to put them up.

Rural dwellers were thrilled and dazzled by the range of new contacts; fresh vistas were opened up, the doors flung wide upon the world. All this built up experienced leadership, created good platform orators and a vast following able to understand those who came with information and ideas. They now demanded bona fide arguments rather than "old style hollow flagwaving oratory, filled with sobs and breast-beating passages that had been the stock in trade of post Civil War politicians." Old party politicians woke up to discover that his poorest constituent was likely to know more about national problems than he had ever considered it necessary to learn.

It was one of the greatest intellectual ferments in the history of America. Rarely has the American democracy taken such spontaneous overall interest in public affairs. Nor was it any New Deal or Great Society regimentation. It was not imposed from above by means of censorship, funneled propaganda, and the superior wisdom of bureaucrats. It was out of the grass roots. It was free. Born of personal initiative and hope, it brought to life valuable latent individual talent in nearly every hamlet of the land.

The most hard-working, self-sacrificing Alliance men were the organizers, carefully chosen, specially trained, and bound by sacred secret oaths. There were hundreds of them, in almost every state in the Union. They traveled by the highways and byways, whatever the weather, the hardships, or the state of their pocketbooks. Many threw their whole lives into the movement and, like the religious circuit riders of old, journeyed hundreds of miles to the remotest corners through dust and sun, sleet and cold, to organize new Alliances and bring the farmers together.

Such a type was S. M. Scott of Kansas. He was born in Clinton, Ohio, near Sabina, on September 15, 1855. When he was five years old, his father moved to Sinking Springs, Highland County, and opened a hotel. In 1869, the family moved to Dayton, Ohio. Young Scott got no schooling but worked as a carpenter until by 1876 he had earned enough to take a commercial course at Miami Commercial College.

Borrowing money to get to Indiana, where his brother had large contracts, he worked there from May through September, 1877, then journeyed on to Kansas and took up farming. In March, 1889, he joined the Southern Farmers' Alliance. He was anxious, he said, to help better the condition of the farming and working class, regardless of race, color, or previous condition of servitude.

As an executive chairman, he arranged the July 4 Alliance celebration in McPherson County, near the center of the state. Nearly 5,000 people turned out with music and banners and marched behind a steam thresher with a band on top of the separator. Scott later remarked, "This day is long to be remembered as . . . the date which the farmers of McPherson County spoke to the world that they were equal to the occasion. From this day on, the farmers seemed to be proud of their occupation."

Scott was asked to come to state Alliance headquarters at Burton, Kansas, to take the examination to qualify him as an organizer. That was on December 14, 1889. The position demanded that he eschew liquor and be a person of high moral integrity. The examination quizzed him on all Alliance activities, its constitution and its principles, his knowledge of arguments to convince prospective members. He met all requirements and was assigned to organize Osborne County in north central Kansas.

Scott returned home bursting with enthusiasm. Putting his farm work in order, he arranged for a meeting of farmers at Willow Dale, four miles north of Alton. Bidding goodbye to his wife and his little son Lloidie, he set out on January 2, 1890, on a 160-mile buggy drive.

Late that night, after 40 miles of travel, he reached Claypooles and gave the Alliance signal at the home of a fellow-member. Before daybreak he was well on his way again. "The moon was still casting her silver light on the waters of Smoky River, which lay to my left, while in the distance could be seen the bluffs frowning all their majestic beauty."

He made good time to Smoky River ford but had to break ice to get across. By noon he had covered thirty miles to Ellsworth. He got off again at one o'clock, following alongside the Union Pacific Railway, and reached Bunker Hill just before dark.

Early the next morning, he crossed the Saline River at Suckers and drove to a point 4 miles north of Luray, where he had dinner. At Covert, 18 miles farther on, he found that the neighbors there, made enthusiastic by the Alliance paper, the *Kansas Farmer*, had just formed a local. People everywhere were ready to go, but did not know where, he remarked.

He came provided with printed posters and hand circulars, needing only to have the place and date filled in, viz.:

[103]

STOP AND READ
FARMERS

There will be a free lecture on the aims and objects
of the Farmers' Alliance and Cooperative Union of
Kansas at _____.

Come one, come all over sixteen years of age — and
hear a lecture you cannot afford to miss. The un-
equalled growth of this order warrants us in saying
that before another year rolls around we can boast of
the strongest organization in America.

Ladies are especially invited. Don't forget the date.

S.M. SCOTT

After a full day's drive, he reached Alton, on the South Fork
Solomon River, where he gave a talk on education and discussed
forming an Alliance. His listeners expressed discouragement over
the record of the Grange, which had once "reaped in the sheckles."

"The Grange," Scott told them, "was a splendid organization, but
the farmers made the mistake in allowing every one interested in
agricultural pursuits to join . . . They had all classes, the merchant,
the lawyer, the doctor, the banker, the railroader, and worse than
all, the professional politician, a cancer to any community or body."
The Alliance was strictly a farmers' group; no residents of cities
and towns being allowed to join.

He spent his first night in a warm sod house near Alton. "The
sod house ought to have the premium. This house, I presume,
was about 16 x 30 feet, two rooms plastered on the sides, with the
roof boards for the ceiling resting on a large log through the center;
on these boards were magnesia spalls, which we used to call marl
in Ohio. This makes the best roof, as it runs together and forms a
solid mass.

[104]

"The walls and ceilings were as white as snow; flowers were growing in the windows, which reminded one of spring. . . . Imagine my surprise when we retired for the evening when I found . . . half the amount of covering on the bed. . . I had been in the habit of using."

An impromptu meeting was called to order in Medicine near Pleasant Valley. Twenty men braved a heavy snowstorm to attend. One doubting Thomas asked, "Does any man know positively that the gentleman present is S.M. Scott?" And another put in: "Boys I make a motion that a committee of three be appointed to investigate this man's character, and if we prove him to be a fraud, we'll hang him on the Alton Bridge."

"Very well, don't trust me," responded Scott, "I'll trust you." He proposed that the money for the charter be deposited with a reliable member until their parchment and books arrived.

One then said, "Well, boys, it only costs us fifty cents to find out whether this is really genuine, so I am willing, if the balance are, to try a whack." Some, however, had no money. Others backed off. But finally eighteen "made up their minds to take a journey into the dark recesses of the Farmers' Alliance and view the goat as he really is in his worst temper" — phrases referring to the initiation and ritual. The two who failed to sign up were asked to leave. The hilarious proceedings that followed were not completed till about 2:00 A.M.

Scott went home with two "brothers," but they broke a wagon spring in the ruts and did not arrive till 4:30 — "about the time the chanticleer was chirping his morning lay." He got little sleep, for he had to drive back to Covert, 31 miles away.

There a storekeeper feared the Alliance would do away with his profits. He confessed that in order to cover the losses from bad accounts he added 30 percent above his regular profit to his prices.

"Well, I'll be damned," broke out a farmer on Scott's left.

The Alliance, Scott told them, would put its business on a cash basis, and thus the farmers would get the benefit of this 30 percent. Eighteen paid their fees. The rest were excused, whereupon several more hurriedly joined.

Scott had found that if he got the minimum number of twelve to sign up, it was better to stop his appeals, organize, and start the secret initiation. Usually a good share of those excluded would hurriedly change their minds rather than be shut out. This particular evening the initiation ceremonies were interrupted by rowdy boys, who had to be chased off.

At Roundmound, fifteen joined up as members; the rest were excluded. When the door was closed in the faces of non-members, one disgruntled "fine-haired gent . . . thought he would scare the goat, so he stoned the school house."

Scott returned "to Brother Hall's," where a meeting was assembled, and 24 people were initiated into the secret work. The gathering did not break up until 4:00 A.M.

The next day it was already sundown when he set out on a 25-mile drive over rough country to Willow Creek. He lost his way and went 2 miles beyond his destination. A rival farm organization was already in existence, but he signed up enough people for an Alliance.

. "The night was cold, the air was crisp, consequently our goat was a little frisky; he seemed to take exception to the color of one of the brother's hair," remarks Scott, in high fettle over his continuing success.

As a result of snow and cold Scott came down with the grippe but filled his appointment at Center, 6 miles from Brother Peters', where he was staying. It was bitter cold, below zero, but the house was well filled.

On occasions, he was discouraged. "Despondency at times seized my very nature when I contemplated the vastness of this work. What I would do was not to be carved on monuments of stone and wood, or tablets of silver and gold, but within the deepest recesses of men's hearts, never to be erased if my work was genuine; if spurious, it was to be for a season, then to be thrust aside with scorn and contempt, only to leave the recipients in deeper distress than when I commenced my work."

He received a telegram that his four year old son Lloidie was very sick. By the time he got home, the boy was dead.

"When I left home, Lloidie was in perfect health, chased my buggy as far as he could, then stopped and in his childish mirth said, 'Good-bye, Papa;' pressing his baby hand to his lips, and throwing kisses at me as long as he could see me."

Scott hurried right back to organizing. All the Alliances, having heard of his bereavement, draped their charters in mourning.

It was still the dead of winter. He had to ride all night in a storm to get to Royal on time. Often he traveled day and night, and gained a few minutes rest only by lying down at meetings when balloting or other routine business was going on. One group was called Cook Stove Alliance because he organized it in a school heated by an old cook stove. The lecturer of a new German Alliance was enthusiastic and determined. "Ve vas oll stuck in de Kansas gumbo; vont ve stick? You bet ve stick."

At Banner, Scott spoke from a buggy drawn up beside a millet stack. A railroader shouted, "To hell with the Alliance!"

"Is your name Jay Gould?" retorted Scott.

He had a good repertoire of jokes and stories to drive home his points. Some now seem rather "dumb," but they had the flavor of plains humor. Pat and August had an argument over a sausage so they each took an end, put his teeth into an end, and pulled. "Air ye reddy?" growled the Irishman between his teeth. The Dutchman said "Yaw" and lost the sausage. The railroad and commission merchants and so on were like Pat, whenever they got a chance they took all the poor man had. "The whole trouble has been lo, these many years, that . . . just because these dudes come around and make . . . some fine promises, we have said yaw, yaw, yaw, to everything, and we have always lost the sausage."

The farmers, Scott remarked, "seemed to think the Alliance had come to fight the merchant and . . . banker . . . [to] array itself against every other trade or profession . . ." This was false. "Grumbling and growling among the farmers on account of the other fellow's being prosperous . . . should not be, for we would be prosperous if we could." Farmers had their separate functions, and instead of abusing others for organizing to get what they wanted, they should learn to cooperate among themselves.

With facts and figures he told them how the railroads milked the public. "Why is it the railroads are allowed to issue watered stock to the amount of at least three times their cost and then fix their rates to pay interest on their fictitious indebtedness . . . ?" The railroads had destroyed St. Louis as a cattle center in favor of Chicago by a $15.00 rebate, resulting in a take of $3,000,000 from 1873 to 1879. In short, the railroads had stolen $600,000 per year from the cattle industry and had turned it over to these unscrupulous hirelings for the purpose of centralizing this trade in their hands. The profit of the dressed beef trust had been over $116,000,000 in eleven years.

Scott's general rules for organizing were:

1) Realize the importance of the work.
2) Be thoroughly posted.
3) See as few people as possible when calling on people to get meetings arranged. Do not enter into any discussion except at the meeting itself.
4) Carry your documents with you.*

---

*Among the documents he recommended, and this shows what a formidable arsenal the Farmers' Alliance lecturers and organizers carried around, were:
Federal Publications:
  State Department, Consular Reports 1889
  Reports of Commissioners to Central and South America
  Indian Affairs
  Territorial government

[108]

He was learning how to get results. The best way was to give first a lecture, then his organizing talk, and finally put the matter to a vote immediately, without debate. Farmers present, unprepared for such an association, merely aired old prejudices, stayed in the old ruts, and indulged in envy and spite. "Never give the audience a chance to make remarks. They have . . . heard one another time and again only to be further apart each time they meet."

After the lecture, the appeal, and the questions, a five-minute recess was allowed, with a temporary secretary at the desk to take the names of those deciding to join. Scott advised that upon securing five to seven applications, "Announce you have enough names to

---

Mineral resources
Department of Labor, 1885, 1886, 1887, 1888
Trees Department
Director of the Mint
Internal Revenue
Wool and manufacturers of wool
Revenue statistics
Internal Commerce of the United States
Instructions regarding national banks
Department of Agriculture, 1886, 1887, 1888, 1889 — statistical,
    entomological, microscopist, botanical, and chemistry reports
Navy Department
War Department
Cattle and dairy farming, consular
Laws relating to loans and currency
State Reports:
Commissioner of Labor
Secretary of State
Superintendent of Insurance
State Board of Equalization
Superintendent of Public Instruction
State Railroad Commission
Board of Agriculture
House and Senate Journals

The secretary of each Alliance was urged to send for these documents and make them the nucleus of a library.

organize . . . put up your blinds, keeping up a talk about some of your other work, say it is so much better for them to take the work then than any time in the future as they all assist . . . upon this occasion, while afterwards they would take it separately."

Time was allowed for the dues to be paid. But even if not a cent was collected, the signers were not to be given up. "Make them agree to safeguard you by promising to pay later."

"After these preliminaries, excuse those not joining, with the hope they will meet in the near future as Alliance brothers and sisters. If they are slow to leave, you have a pretty good show to get the whole house.

"Branch off on some story, get them in real good humor . . . [then] give another invitation to join . . . nine chances to one you will get them all."

The organizer should be fully prepared. "Have the secret work perfect so you will give it the same anywhere," Scott advised. "The brothers will follow you from place to place and they will notice any little mistake you make."

He preferred to start a new group with folk willing to join immediately. Such an Alliance always had a better chance of future success. Scott's methods were evidently reliable, for in less than three months he had rolled up a big score.

By March 28, he was able to call an Osborne County meeting at Prairie Hill. One hundred and twenty-three delegates, representing 1,448 members, came. Under the leadership of marshals, a procession of Alliances over 2 miles long, composed of 2-, 4-, and 6-horse teams, passed by. There were 5 bands, 26 large flags, and 29 banners. In all, 1,373 people turned out. Hundreds came on horseback. Thousands lined the streets and house-tops viewing the parade.

Important Alliance men addressed the reunion: bearded Judge Peffer (later Senator) and "Milkman" Ben H. Clover, President of the State Alliance (later Congressman). Scott spoke on gambling in futures, explained how the market was divided into Bears and

Bulls. About 5,000 men were engaged in this bargaining, and they determined the price of grains raised by the hard labor of the farmer. They tried to corner the year's crop, prices grew wild, but the farmer in no way benefited.

The reunion was enlivened by a barbecue and picnic, games and much music. From several thousand throats came the song "The Farmers' Beulah Land:"

> Oh! Farmers now the time has come
> And if you love your Kansas home
> You'll put your shoulders to the wheel
> An interest in our cause you'll feel.

Chorus:

> Oh! Peace and Love; Oh! God above,
> Come deck our banners as we move —
> For seeds will grow from what we sow —
> And move in one united band
> Until we free our Kansas land.

> So now we proudly take our stand
> And drive corruption from the land,
> We'll proudly wave our banner high
> And live in freedom or we'll die.

Fannie McCormick, in her *A Kansas Farm*, wrote, "The Alliance processions were often a beautiful sight, being anywhere from one to seven miles long. On the plains of western Kansas, they could be seen many miles, and looked like long trains. . .

"The writer, . . . with friends, stood . . . on the balcony of a hotel . . . in the western part of the state. We could see indistinctly in the distance a long line of wagons coming toward the center. Away to the right, and a little nearer, a long procession came winding over the great prairie. Off to the left . . . not far away, was a

[111]

procession with bands playing and flags and banners spread to the breeze. Taking a right-about-face we looked into the distance to see if any more were coming from that quarter . . . Someone brought a field glass, and . . . we could see a long line of farm wagons coming . . . from an adjoining county . . . [They] had started at midnight that they might be at the place of meeting in time to hear the speaking."

She described one procession: "A nicely uniformed brass band, next a carriage containing the speakers, then a wagon trimmed with evergreens containing a score of young ladies, carrying banners, and following them . . . one hundred people on horseback, all wearing handsome sashes, of either red, white or blue; all the vehicles belonging to one Alliance, then of another Alliance, and so on to the end. A large wagon had been transformed to represent a house with elegant furnishings and a finely dressed lady sat at the piano. By way of contrast, a house furnished after the manner of many farm houses with the farmer's wife and daughter at some of their tasks, created great merriment. . . . A mule, standing in a wagon, rode along in a procession with its ears laid back and its eyes flashing fire, as indicative of the state of mind of our Congressman's opponent. An old horse, about to die of general dilapidation was . . . placed at the tail of a long procession to represent the present condition of the two old political parties. Its ribs stood out in bold relief, and the backbone looked like the ridge of a house; its legs refused to follow in regular order as it wobbled along with its head lowered and tongue protruding. It was the embodiment of infirmity and exhaustion. One look made a person tired and confirmed the impression that if it did represent the state of the old parties their condition was certainly critical. . . . A huge header-barge packed with youngsters was labeled 'Over-production.'"

Alliance historian Dunning could write rhapsodically of the movement's destiny: "As well might we undertake to blot out the stars of heaven as to prevent the final triumph of this great movement. . . . The shackles it has worn so long will be stricken off, and the bands that have bound it to the chariot wheels of the oppressors will surely be loosened. The Alliance will yet prove [to be] the Moses that will lead the people out of their bondage and up to that condition which a kind Providence has vouchsafed to us all. . . . [and] will proclaim, in thunder tones, reaching from ocean to ocean: 'It is finished. Let the people go free.' "

Something of the meaning of the organization in emotional terms shines through a nostalgic reference in the *Monroe Bulletin* of 1896: "The greatest and best educator of the farmers was the Alliance which was founded on the broad principles of humanity and justice. It was a noble order . . . pure and lofty . . . peerless, grand, beautiful order. How we would like to hear its songs again. How we would like to see the bright faces and hearty welcomes of the brethren in council, sweet as the bees of Hermion and the oil that ran down Aaron's beard."

There were a thousand Scotts, those years of the eighties and nineties, who sacrificed themselves for the farmer's cause, who drove through the snows and the heat all the way from the Dakotas to Georgia, from the hills of Kentucky to the inland valleys of California. Their great crusade failed, but they helped build faith in the principle that Americans could shape their own destiny with their own hands. The spirit, the methods, hopes, and many of the aims of these hardy farm organizers are woven imperishably into the fabric of American life. That spirit may rise again some day.

VI
THE SAGE
OF NININGER

The great Jeremiah of the plains was dead. Three minutes past midnight on the first day after the first year of this century, that amazing Irishman of Minnesota, Ignatius Donnelly, "the Sage of Nininger," was stricken with heart failure, at the age of sixty-nine. He left a widow twenty years younger than his oldest son. For half a century he had valiantly tangled his lance of reform in the windmills of special privilege and was always back in the lists before his handsome bruises were quite healed. He worked hard for the Grange and for the Alliance. He organized four strong national third-party movements.

These years of atomic destruction and national peril have produced more than the usual quota of prophets of doom. In his day the florid Minnesota orator flew like a burning comet of exuberant verbal catastrophe across the troubled skies of mid-America. His Cassandra warnings of dire disaster gripped the hearts and minds of people shaken by an abruptly changing world, when the frontier rush was coming to an end and the nation was forced to seek new outlets — and new dangers — for its upsurging vitality. His busy life spanned four major epochs: that of the Westward Movement, the Civil War, the Gilded Age, and the Great Revolt. It ended right after the first thrust of the country toward world power — the Spanish-American War. He had seen the day of westward expansion swing wide, the westward stampede of the people, the country torn apart in civil strife, the dull postwar ruthlessness, the farmers' last-ditch fight, the hope of a true people's democracy, then saw the gates swing closed again. His whole life pivoted on the frontier movement. Before his death, though he never lost his excitement over the surging world about him, the new century had already swept past him in a great flood, leaving him aloft, defending the bulwarks far from the fray of the social conflicts ushered in by new industry and new power.

He began as a land-boomer, a founder of towns, a railroad attorney, with dreams, similar to those of youthful Henry George, of piling up a personal fortune. Hit by repeated failure, his town-building enterprises having collapsed and drouth and the grasshopper plague having put him out of business as a wheat-farmer, he evolved into an agrarian rebel, a foe of railroads, of the wheat ring, and the flour interests. Whenever his stomach was up against his backbone or the sheriff was peering in the windows, he sat down and wrote a book, and at least four of them were sensational best sellers, running into many editions — books which were to influence deeply American thinking for decades. One, *Caesar's Column*, was to inspire Jack London's *The Iron Heel*. Another, *Ragnarok*, had much the same thesis as the recent sensational *Worlds in Collision*.

Several of his books were reprinted in farm papers, one with a circulation of 4,000,000. Several official Farmers' Alliance papers used a sentence from one of his books — "Come, friends, let us reason together" — as their official motto.

He founded newspapers and flooded the country with his powerful pamphlets, read eagerly from Georgia cabins to Nebraska sod houses.

He had considerable success in politics, was many times a legislator, a lieutenant governor, acting governor, three times a congressman, a candidate for the Vice-Presidency, but it was as the leader of four third-party movements, as the leader of the hosts of revolt, that he excelled.

Above all else, he was a speaker and campaigner. Along with the Texas rebel, Cyclone Davis, and William Jennings Bryan, he was the greatest orator of his day, and he spoke far and wide across the country on politics, literature, religion, the currency. Along with Bryan and "Coin" Harvey, he was a free-silver advocate. He delivered side-splitting lectures on prose style and humor. "A memorable geyser of metaphors," remarked an admirer. "Whenever the Sage of Nininger bellows . . . the western multitude jammed the aisles," and he laid them out on the sawdust with laughter and with the belief that they had learned astonishing new truths. Once, when he was campaigning for the new anti-slavery Republicans, a cabbage was thrown at him. He held it meditatively in his hand, Salome-style, though scarcely with Salome's diaphanous grace. "Gentlemen, some Democrat has flung his head up here. I asked only for his ears, and lo, he has given me his whole head." His majestic rhetoric dominated the great Populist convention of 1892 in Omaha, where he roused the 1,776 delegates there to a storm of enthusiastic frenzy rarely equaled in any national convention.

Donnelly was born in Philadelphia, November 3, 1831, when Andrew Jackson was President. His father, an Irish immigrant, a graduate from the Jefferson Medical college, became a prominent physician. One of Ignatius' three spinster sisters, Eleanor Cecilia, published several score volumes of mystical religious verse. He studied law in the offices of a famous attorney and was admitted to the bar at twenty-one. After three years of Fourth of July orating, he declined the Democratic nomination for the legislature and set out for the West, temporarily parting from his bride, a grammar school principal and amateur singer, Katherine McCaffery, whom he loved deeply as long as she lived. "Both of us met with bargains," said Ignatius.

He headed for Minnesota, "the last toe-hold on civilization." His

[117]

story of his trip is vivid and witty. His moods ranged from the caustic, the bitter and contemptuous, to the enthusiastic and the exalted. Chicago, that year of 1855, was a "gigantic board yard . . . small, half-finished houses . . . dropped at random over the face of the dead flat prairie." The streets were quagmires, the dilapidated boardwalks dangers to life and limb. But the pretentious Hotel Young America was impressive; guests were waited upon by obsequious liveried lackeys, the beds would have done honor to royalty. But the fare, heralded on the gorgeous menu, with the names of many French dishes — an affectation he derided — consisted only of beef steak and lake snipe. He was a fastidious young man.

He crossed to Davenport, Iowa, over the first Mississippi bridge in the first train that ever ran to the western bank. "Here we are in the heart of the great West!" he exclaimed. "All is hurry and confusion; rapid growth is everywhere; millionaires are thick as whortle berries!" But the railroad beyond was in horrible condition; the rails, recklessly laid during fall and winter over the frozen ground, now were sinking into mud, and twice the travelers had to struggle through mire, baggage in hand, and board a new train to the next mudhole. It took a whole day to make 40 miles.

The stages were worse. Each morning the passengers fired off their pistols to be sure they were in working order. The drivers were "rough and impudent" and the road a morass into which their "four-horse mud-wagon" repeatedly sank. They had to get out in the ooze, which overflowed into their carpetbag boots, and pry the vehicle loose with the fence-rails the stage carried for such emergencies. The trip was a nightmare. As one traveler put it, "Swim the Missouri, wade, work your passage, skate, race around the world and come up on the other side, go to Purgatory and spend a month, visit the devil and stay a fortnight, even get to Chicago and pass the night, but do not take this line of stage."

The log-cabin hotels aroused Ignatius' ire. The fare of ham and doughy cakes substituting for bread cost the "outrageous" sum of forty or fifty cents a meal and were "flavored with uncompromising

[118]

impudence." They saw butter but once, a tiny specimen floating at the bottom of a dirty saucer.

"My bedroom was a loft, my bed a straw mattress; my overcoat served for a pillow, while the rain, trickling through the miserable roof, lulled me to uneasy slumber. . . ." Sometimes travelers were stuffed 3 to a bed, 24 to a room.

Nevertheless, he concluded, "this country is certain to become rich, prosperous and popular, but it is so desolate and bleak and the comforts of life all wanting." He was depressed by the lack of trees and boulders. "The winds roar and sweep over the land as they do over the ocean," often moving large houses bodily.

But when he took passage on the new "York State" up the Mississippi, his pleasure knew no bounds: fine meals, a beautiful cabin, a comfortable bed, polite attendance, and the fare for 400 miles was only $2.00.

"We have sailed into a new world," he cried rapturously. "We have left the flats, the morasses, the old coal fields of Illinois, Indiana and Iowa. Here are health, beauty and majesty."

He was thrilled by the "sight of the rapidly fleeting barbarian, which for so many centuries has held these beautiful lands in thrall." What he saw was a rag-tail old Indian, in leggings and stovepipe hat, moccasins and a cloth coat, pushing along in a bark canoe.

He soon exhausted all newspapers on board and found nothing else to read except the Bible. Lady passengers, impressed by his piety, asked him to preach to counterbalance the poker game at the other end of the salon. His persistent reading of the Scriptures provided grist for the grinder of his later oratory, for no man could go on the western hustings those days without ready ability to quote the Holy Writ. Donnelly was razor-quick with such quotations. Once, he lashed out, "and the ox knoweth his master, and the ass his master's crib."

Their vessel wheeled in among a tangle of steamboats below the bluffs and storehouses of St. Paul. The early-morning shadows

[119]

were still long on the velvet water, but drays and wagons were already busy on the levee. The travelers had reached the city of promise: the cynosure of all eyes, the new St. Louis, the youthful Chicago, the capitol of the newborn territory of Minnesota.

He liked the people, adventurers but intelligent men, though the rough newness jarred on him and he was upset by the high interest rates — 37 percent till maturity, 60 percent thereafter. "Shameless plutocracy! It would require years to give body and substance to such inflated speculation."

He and John Nininger, a fellow Philadelphian, paid $22,000 for 800 acres of wilderness river-frontage 30 miles southwest of St. Paul. Six hundred and forty-seven acres were surveyed into 3,800 lots, arbitrarily valued at from $100 to $500, but for the time being half were put on the market at $6.00. Plowed lines indicated streets, one of which was named Donnelly. Extravagant improvements were promised within two years: a free steamboat, newspaper, post office, gristmill, sawmill, stone hotel, eventually a railroad. Thus was Nininger City founded.

Ignatius built a large residence overlooking the Mississippi. Striding up and down the spacious veranda, he ejaculated ecstatically to his young wife, "Here I am, not yet twenty-six, and on the verge of a great fortune! How shall I ever be able to dispose of it?"

His hope did not seem unreasonable. St. Paul, starting with a few tamarack trading cabins, called "Pig's Eye," in a few years had become a metropolis of 10,000 people, with 12 hotels and 4 newspapers, 13 shoemakers and 17 tailors. In 1849, there were 14 lawyers, by 1855, 40! What greater proof of civilization and progress! Five-dollar lots had zoomed to a value of $4,000.

Nininger City, Donnelly claimed, was far superior. At the exact geographical center of Minnesota, the logical hub, and with a better river landing than St. Paul, it was destined to become the Chicago of the Northwest.

Donnelly was swimming the crest of a town-building movement

which had become an epidemic, a maniacal preoccupation. All along the river-landings town criers were yelling their wares, boosting this or that town as the greatest western city of the future. They sold gilt-edged stocks or lots from heavy parchment rolls, with elaborate drawings of imposing marble buildings and avenues where often there was only the grinning skull of a coyote or a buffalo. Senator John J. Ingalls was lured to Kansas at this time by "a chromatic triumph of lithographic mendacity."

All over the country elaborate prospectuses of such new towns were circulated, and stocks were peddled with the brazenness of later gold and oil and uranium frauds. Many a chambermaid dug into her stocking to exchange her savings for such pledges of Utopia and fortune. One Nebraska legislature facetiously introduced a bill to restrict new town acreage by setting aside 10 percent of the state for farms.

A similar torrent of eloquent advertising, persuasive letters, and talk sold lots in Nininger City to prospective settlers. Ignatius piled up quotations from earlier travelers about the fine climate, resources, and natural advantages of the new paradise: "The heathen mythology related of one who planted dragon's teeth," cried Donnelly, "and they grew up men, but it was reserved for the mythology of America with the same miraculous facility to raise not men but towns and cities!"

But the 1857 depression threatened to put his whole enterprise on the skids. To attempt to save the venture, he went East to try to sell lots and lure settlers to the great Nininger City. In March, he spoke rhapsodically at the Broadway House in New York. The future prosperity of Minnesota was assured by all the weight of centuries of migration and by God's own edict: "The same inscrutable Providence which stayed not the course of the frail *Mayflower* accelerates at this day the flood and current of which you are a part." The westward march began in Greece and Rome and England. Each empire in turn had been whipped by the Lord "with the scourge of religious persecution; He has stung them with the blight

[121]

of crowded poverty." But Minnesota, the future Utopia and the end of all man's sufferings, held forth its arms with hospitality and hope. In the East men were being fed in public soup kitchens; in Minnesota there were more jobs than men. Steady work all winter could be had for $2.50 to $3.00 a day, and the fare out was only $31.50.

But easterners who could scrape together fare did not often go to Minnesota, they hurried on to cheaper Dakota lands or to the Colorado gold-rush. "Pike's Peak or bust" became the new slogan and was often painted on the covered wagons as emigrants lashed their horses across the prairies to get in on the ground floor of the great land boom. All too soon many backtracked. The "or" was crossed out and replaced with "and."

Nininger City never passed the 500 mark in population, then declined. Soon the St. Paul-Hastings mail stage refused to swing out to the place, and Postmaster Louis Loichet had to struggle 3 miles through snow drifts carrying his mailbag on his back. Donnelly's newspaper, *Emigrant Aid Journal*, gave up the ghost. The specially built ferryboat, completely finished, its guard rails and deck-pumps painted, could not be paid for. Angry swindling charges were bandied about over the gilt-edged stock that had been sold to build the never-never St. Paul-Nininger railroad.

Donnelly lived on, almost without neighbors, in his big river-house, in the very center of his failure. Instead of selling lots, he had to plow up the property stakes and plant wheat; instead of being "the Moses of Nininger, striking the gushing rock, he was still a babe in the bullrushes."

Turning to politics, he ran on the crusading Republican ticket twice and lost. He went off and fought Indians. But at twenty-eight, after campaigning a thousand miles over prairies and wood-lands, he became Lieutenant Governor. His predecessor claimed election fraud and refused to vacate the office. The Republicans threatened to throw him out the window. Ignatius, who knew the famous story of the French defenestration, would not permit it. He afterwards remarked dryly, looking out at the hard ground below the window, "it did not seem like a good precedent to establish." He was reelected a second term, and during part of the Civil War was Acting Governor.

In 1862, he went to Congress instead of to war — the youngest representative in Washington. There he pushed the Garfield Bill to establish a national bureau of education. "The schoolhouses in this generation will prevent wars in the next," he cried, with unwarranted optimism. With floods of witty oratory, he favored an immigration bureau, agitated for reforestation, later on opposed Reconstruction abuses, and fought for an appropriation to feed Confederate veterans. He was an imperialist, always anti-British. American institutions should cover the whole North American continent, from "the thread of land which ties together the North and South continents . . . to the extreme limits of human habitation under the frozen constellations of the north." With the annexation of Alaska, British domination would "disappear between the upper and nether millstone." But not as he envisaged it, for Canada is still British in a sense; it is merely owned in good part by U.S. corporations.

He worked for generous railroad grants. In those great expanses, railroads were as important as population. Grateful companies cut him in, as they did most congressmen, on stock, a profiteering which was later thrown up at him repeatedly.

At the end of his third term, armed men kept Donnelly delegates out of the Republican convention. He had been attacking the "mill interests and wheat ring," and they spent $50,000, he alleged, to defeat him. He made three unsuccessful independent tries for Congress and the Senate. Secretly, he reminded Jay Cooke of past favors and asked unsuccessfully for aid in one campaign, promising to be a "firm friend and associate of the Northern Pacific Railroad Company," But to the voters, he was saying, "Whenever amid the fullness of the earth a human stomach goes empty or a human brain remains darkened in ignorance, there is wrong and crime and fraud."

He tried farming again. In exchange for his St. Paul and Pacific

Railway Company stock and mortgages, he secured several thousand acres in Stevens County, fenced it in, and built houses for himself and his two husky red-headed sons and their wives in what he called the village of Donnelly.

But he got in on the ground floor of the grasshopper plague, and the 1873 depression drove the houses of both Jay Cooke and farmer Donnelly to the wall. He blamed his latest failure on the robberies of the wheat ring.

The Grange farmer movement was at its apogee, and Donnelly became chief lecturer and visited every Minnesota county. His pamphlet, *Facts for Granges*, was scattered far and wide. "We can't look for a remedy in the Republican Party," its brains and its pocketbook were "in New England." The brains and pocketbook of the Democratic party were "in the reactionary South." Why not create a National Farmers' party? For the Grange to build solely a non-political organization was to make a gun that would do "everything but shoot."

At his call, more than a hundred delegates met at Owatonna to organize the People's Anti-Monopoly party. Donnelly sounded the keynote. "Children of Israel, Go Forward." His new paper, the weekly *Anti-Monopolist*, made open war on "plutocracy and wage slavery . . . Liberty must overcome all her foes or perish from the earth." Donnelly declared, and truthfully, that he had "enlisted for life in the great battle." He wrote no more beseeching letters to Jay Cooke or his kind.

The new party spread like wildfire, and Donnelly was elected to the Minnesota Senate. He introduced fifteen important reform measures, such as planting trees for windbreaks along public roads, farmers' credit, and so on. All were desirable, in a few years would be adopted, but he was howled down as crackpot. He was also attacked by a rural congressman, who himself had fled to Canada to escape prosecution for alleged graft, for taking money and stock while in Congress, for backing steamship and railroad companies, and for the appointment of Indian agents.

[124]

In 1876, he became chairman of the joint National Greenback and Anti-Monopoly convention in Cincinnati. He wanted to see "a party in which the poorest man who toils in the mines of Pennsylvania or the mills of New England will outweigh in consequence and importance Jay Gould or Cornelius Vanderbilt. . . . This is a people's country, and we need a people's party."

He was defeated twice for the United States Senate "by the flour interests . . . corporation bribery . . . [and] terrorism at the polls." This was his famous "Brass Kettle campaign." Donnelly charged that the "Wheat Ring," by fraudulently manipulating these brass grading devices, had "stolen" enough from the farmers to "pave the floor of all hell with gold."

Donnelly contested the second election. After two long and costly years, in which were compiled and presented 557 pages of printed testimony and 26 pages of facsimile handwriting, the United States Senate admitted he had won the election but refused to seat him on the flimsy pretext that one affidavit, of the many put in by his lawyer, was fraudulent. The $3,500 awarded Donnelly for expenses in presenting his case came nowhere near covering costs. The *Anti-Monopolist* folded up, and he lost his heavily mortgaged Stevens farm entirely. The sheriff was "peering in at every door and window. There was nothing left of me but the back-bone. I was pounding my head against the rocks. The very gulls had abandoned me." Had he expended the same amount of energy in behalf of the plunderers of the people, he wrote, he would have made "half a million."

He resolved to abandon politics forever and follow a literary career in his lonely Nininger house. He turned to speculations on man's peregrinations in the misty dawn of life. With a hodgepodge of fancy, pseudo-science, and mythology, he maintained that Plato's fable of Atlantis, the golden world beyond the Hesperides, was authentic. All the old stories of the garden of Eden, of Hesperides, the Elysian fields, the gardens of Alcinous, the Mesomphalos, Olympus, the Asgard, represented a "universal memory of a great land where early mankind dwelt for ages in peace and happiness." There the Aryan or Indo-European, Semitic, and Turanian races first rose from barbarism to civilization and overflowed into Europe, Africa, Asia, the Gulf of Mexico, and the Americas. They carried their sun-worship to Egypt and Peru. They gave the alphabet to the Phoenicians. His book, *Atlantis,* became a runaway best seller that ran through fifty editions.

Donnelly's next pseudo-scientific work was *Ragnarok, The Age of Fire and Gravel.* William Gladstone, British Prime Minister, read it, believed it, and wrote saying so. The book caused a national furor and ran into twelve editions. It begins with the disarming sentence, "Reader, let us reason together," later the motto of the official Farmers' Alliance journal of Texas, in which the story was run serially. The rich soil structure of north central United States, he claimed, was the result of a great "tiger" comet hitting the earth during an early geologic period. He painted a horrendous but magnificent picture of the crazy comet sweeping the earth with its great flaming tail, showering valleys and hills with many feet of stardust and ashes—all across Alberta and Saskatchewan, over North Dakota and Minnesota, on across Kentucky and Tennessee and the Great Smokies, into the Carolinas. The grass was seared, and compressed air crumpled mighty forests like matchsticks. The earth was a "lost child in the midst of a forest of wild beasts."

He piled up references from the legends of all primitive peoples to substantiate with folk memory the terrifying event. He reread Genesis "by the light of the comet." The findings of the geologists and anthropologists, the legends of the Incas, Egyptians, Greeks, Arabians, Norsemen, Chinese, American Indians, the words of Shakespeare, Byron, Aristophanes, Hesiod, Plato, Ovid, Orpheus, Garcilaso de la Vega, and the Bible — an incredible hodgepodge of vast erudition — are marshaled into battalions to storm the heights of the incredible.

"Is there not enough energy among the archaeologists of the

United States," he cried, "to make a thorough examination of some part of the deep clay deposits of central Illinois? . . . Cannot the greed for information do one tenth as much as the greed for profit?"

He was not hopeful. "The conservation of unthinkingness is one of the potential forces of the world. It lies athwart the progress of mankind like a colossal mountain chain, chilling the atmosphere on both sides of it for a thousand miles."

His moral was, "Put your intellect to work, to so readjust the values of labor and increase the productive capacity of nature, that plenty and happiness, light and hope, may dwell in every heart and the catacombs be closed forever, and from such a world, God will fend off the comets with his great right arm, and the angels will exult in heaven." Meanwhile his own plump arms were barely fending off the comet of personal ruin.

He set out to prove Bacon the author of Shakespeare's plays. *The Great Cryptogram*, based on an intensive study of the original Shakespeare folios and dedicated to his good friend, Barton Hanson, is a vast tome of a thousand pages filled with remarkable erudition— intricate mathematics, a thousand *Gold Bug* codes.

The great Shakespeare, tyrant of immortality and symbol of blind adoration, had to be dethroned. When battles failed in the present, rebel Ignatius created his own battles in the past and turned them into a storm of contemporary controversy. The world promptly divided before his prow. Friends praised lavishly. Enemies condemned.

"Venomous badinage," snorted a friend at the "large band of vacuous American reviewers who butted about in a blizzard of condemnatory inanities with flippant flapdoodle and rampant recalcitrance." All Baconians, he grieved, were inevitably "doomed to martyrdom."

Back in politics, with Greenback, Farmers' Alliance, and Democratic support, Ignatius was defeated for Congress by less than 1,000 votes.

He asked Cleveland for appointment as surveyor general, saying ingenuously he needed to buy books for his library. Unsuccessful in getting the next Democratic nomination for the legislature, he complained: "I have been beaten for Congress by the Hill-Kelly [Democratic machine] crowd, beaten for the surveyor-generalship, deprived of the slightest recognition by the Executive, read out of the party by the Democratic State Central Committee, defeated in my own county and even get daily cartooned by the Democratic state newspaper organ."

He headed thirty farmers to lay demands before both old-party conventions. The Democrats refused to receive his delegation, but the Republican convention seated the farmers on the floor and cheerfully wrote their demands into their platform. Encouraged, Donnelly boldly suggested he be given the nomination for the legislature. This, thought the Republicans, was going too far, so he ran as an independent.

Elected, he formed a bloc to combat the "wily politicians." Again, he became the most picturesque key figure at the state capitol.

At a Cincinnati convention, he helped pool a dozen reform groups into the Union Labor party.

A reform convention in Minnesota, commented the *New York Sun,* would be "like catfish without waffles in Philadelphia." He was nominated for governor. But he found little statewide support and, having no funds, withdrew. His fellow-workers branded it as a sell-out.

He worked hard to build up the Farmers' Alliance but was defeated for the presidency of the organization, then also for the United States Senate. He wrote another book, this time a novel.

After four editorial rejections, it was published in 1890 by an obscure Chicago house, as *Caesar's Column,* under the pseudonym of Edmund Boisgilbert, M.D., hinted to be a Chicago millionaire. It sold 700,000 copies and shaped rebel thought for a decade. He dwelt on the future marvels of the late twentieth century. His lively imagination foresaw television, hot-water heating, subways, elevated

[128]

railways, electric trains, moving sidewalks. He pictured aluminum dirigibles, stratosphere flying, 36-hour trans-Atlantic airflights with artificial mid-Atlantic Ocean landing fields, and great municipal airports. That for New York, approximately where La Guardia is today, was made by draining the East River. His airships were equipped with parachutes and parachute lifeboats.

The poor ignorant ancestors (the folk of 1888) drank alcohol, but in the New York of 1988 it was prohibited. A "vital watch" automatically selected the proper food for each person, and most men lived to be a hundred years old. Elevated glass-covered sidewalks flanked streets beautifully illuminated with vivid colors from the harnessed aurora borealis.

Here is the magical city of Ignatius' dreams, the city he had hoped to build but was unable, the Nininger City that never was. It is New York of the future, with 10,000,000 inhabitants, suburbs stretching to Philadelphia.

But New York was a doomed city, for its material beauties had out-distanced its spiritual light. Perfect air-conditioning destroyed all bacteria, but how about God's charity? demanded his hero, Welstein. Social justice was being wholly ignored.

The sad end of the New York Utopia was to be foreseen already in the existing "unhappy condition of society" of 1888, in which the "many are plundered" to enrich "the few." The face of labor grows sullen; the old tender Christian love is gone; standing armies are formed on one side and great communistic organizations on the other. "They wait only for the drumbeat and the trumpet to summon them to armed conflict."

September 10, 1988, Gabriel Welstein was stopping at the Darwin Hotel, an entire block on Fifth Avenue and Madison, between 46th and 47th. The elevators were as big as whole rooms. An automatic piano — a super jukebox — played "the trill of a nightingale" or "the thunders of a whole orchestra." The glass-covered hotel roof contained a tropical forest with birds of southern climes. Dinner was automatically served by a table rising into the room.

But Welstein was depressed by the hard greedy faces about him, for the land was ruled by Dictator Cabano. Welstein first saw lovely Estella being driven to the Palace to become one of Cabano's numerous concubines. She was the descendent of one of the founding fathers, but her family had sunk to low estate under the dictatorship. After hair-raising experiences, the hero saves her virtue, just as revolution bursts over the land.

Cabano is overthrown by the secret Brotherhood of Destruction, led by Caesar Lomellin, an early Capone, who became the new dictator in a revolt of unparalleled carnage. Cabano was burned alive, and the city was littered with dead bodies. "Burn 'em up!" Lomellin ordered. "Heap 'em all up and pour cement over them." Sixty thousand prisoners were flogged to build the gruesome column. In the ensuing battle against Lomellin's iron militarism, the whole world was plunged into flaming chaos and ruin.

Such was the dire warning Donnelly read to the rulers of mankind, the fate that would overtake this fair land if the rapine of power and plutocracy were not checked.

After hair-raising adventures with the secret police, Welstein and his bride escaped with friend to a remote vale in Uganda, Africa, where they put the noble Farmers' Alliance doctrines into operation and created an idyllic system of economic justice "like an Aztec legend" of paradise — and, of course, lived happily ever after.

Donnelly's next novel, *Doctor Huguet*, published in 1891 under the same pseudonym, was a tract against Negro persecution, though the picture of the chief Negro protagonist is far from pleasant. The souls of a white and black were transferred into their respective bodies — such soul interchanges were a frequent theme those days — with near-tragic consequences for all concerned, including the doctor's fiancée. Donnelly's moral was that Darwin's theory plus God provided the true philosophy for the new age. The Negro must "join with his white brethren to rescue the land from poverty and ruin."

By 1892, he was back on the political hustings, full of glorious renewed optimism. This time he did not wait for defeat to turn to literature. The new book, *The Golden Bottle*, was written on the Sage's knee in trains and humble western inns as he roared through the hurly-burly '92 campaign.

A tract, in the thin guise of a story, to explain and defend new ideas put forth by the Populist party, it envisioned the awakened hosts of the hinterland following the hero to the shining highways of a new American order and a new world order.

Ephraim Benegert, a poor Kansas farmer boy, "used to go in the night, and cry out in the open fields, under the stars, for God to come again on earth and make things right." Rising hungry from his straw pallet, he was given the secret of making gold from iron.

Ephraim freed his own family's farm from debt, then recovered that of his neighbor Hetherington, with whose daughter, Sophie, he was in love. The girl had gone to the big city where, from all reports, she had "gone wrong." "One thing money cannot do," declared author Donnelly solemnly, "It cannot restore woman's honor."

Ephraim bought up all Kansas farm mortgages and reduced the interest from "Banker Smith's 45 percent" to 2 percent over 10 to 20 years. Frightened merchants, doctors, lawyers, and clergymen shouted that he was "destroying business," that he was insane. Threatened with arrest, Ephraim fled to the big city.

He found Sophie in jail, her purity intact. The clothing manufacturer who had tried unsuccessfully to seduce her had had her arrested. "I have no friends," she told Ephraim, "the poor are always friendless." But Ephraim's gold soon remedied that.

With her aid, he founded the National Women's Association and a cooperative, which took over fifteen buildings—a model community with stores, bedrooms, proper workshops, reading rooms, libraries, and music halls. Again the never-never Utopian Nininger City.

Elected to Congress, Ephraim delivered a speech, the same speech Donnelly was delivering up and down the breadth of the land.

"A flood of debt, as huge as that of the water in which Noah floated, covers the whole land." The yeomanry are disappearing.

"Keep the land in the hands of the many," Ephraim cried. He urged that a post office be opened as a savings bank to lend money to the farmers and working men at 2 percent per annum. Paper money should be issued, $50.00 per capita (great applause). "Money was invented for man's use. Man was not created for money's use. . . . One farmer who raises a bale of cotton . . . has done more for mankind than all of Wall Street. . . . Oh, the sin and shame of it, that the real producers of wealth are crushed and degraded by the possessors of a couple of metals, with scarcely any intrinsic value, but rendered sacred by a prehistoric superstition . . . Let us relegate the worship of gold and silver to the region of witchcraft and spooks."

Ephraim's House Resolution for a people's money passed, but the agents of "money aristocracy," the Senate, the "King" called a President, and the Supreme Court could still annul the action. A bunch of lawyers, selected by the great corporations, sitting on a bench "with old women's gowns upon them," could set aside the will of the Senate, the President, and the People. This was "liberty with despotism in its belly." The "Declaration of Independence had been wrapped up in watered stock. . . . George Washington dead and Jay Gould living! God help us!"

When Ephraim's bill reached the Senate, "they clapped chloroform — called a committee — to its nose to stop any bawling, and it died peacefully and graciously."

"I GET MAD!" says the Kansas hero.

"I had not that amiable American frame of mind, the product of our high civilization, which patiently submits to gross injustice and looks around with a smile, for a compensating chance to steal something. I still had the flavor of Kansas mud on my boots and in my soul. . . ." If the men of 1776 had possessed "the cultured frame of our minds today, they would have regarded it as . . . insanity to think of going to war barefooted and in rags for eighteen years for a principle. They would have taken the money the Revolution cost and loaned it out at high rates of interest and wiped a lot of poor devils off the face of the earth and called it national prosperity. You couldn't have dragged them away from John Bull and his aristocracy with a yoke of oxen. They are [now] hungering . . . to get back into his embrace. They would rather be kicked by a duke than kissed by a genius."

Ephraim made enough gold to replace every debt in the country with 2 percent mortgages. Crime disappeared and the courts fell idle. Business and manufacturing flourished. "And men laughed and wondered . . . [how for] so many ages, mankind had permitted a few of their fellows to put snaffle-bits in their mouths and saddles on their backs and ride them to destruction."

Ephraim bought up vast tracts of land around a healthy site near Egg Harbor on the New Jersey coast, with a natural roadway for ships. He put up a great sea-water dam, "a salt-water Niagara," to manufacture enormous electric power. This was Passamaquoddy, half a century before it was attempted by F.D.R. and sabotaged by the Army and the Maine power companies. But for Ephraim it was a success, and he set to work to build a transcontinental *electrical* railroad with model cities enroute, each with free electricity, an eight-hour day, and not a single saloon, cities in which free souls eternally matched material splendor and perfection, cities set in broad smiling acres, where men toiled easily, unbeholden to "the railroad octopus, the loan bank, or monopoly." Tenscore shining Nininger City Utopias!

Using gold to "corrupt the corruptors," Ephraim was elected President. Civil war loomed, but he bought off everybody in sight. In his inaugural message, he declared America to be "united by a ligament to a corpse — Europe. . . . Europe today is an armed camp built up from the prostrate bodies of the producers. . . . Every worker carries a soldier on his back."

Believing him "mad," the European powers declared war. The Norwegians, Danes, and Swedes stayed neutral, but mighty armed forces gatheied in England, Germany, Austria, Russia, Spain, and Italy.

Populist Civil War veterans saved the day. Canada fell "like a ripe pear." Porfirio Díaz, the Mexican dictator, refusing to be reformed, was taken care of. With a flotilla of 300 vessels and a great force, Ephraim of Kansas, Commander in Chief of the Army of Liberation, established headquarters on the great steamer "John Adams of Massachusetts" and set out to subdue Europe, with sweet Sophie at his side. He led his army ashore at Queenstown.

IRELAND IS FREE! screamed the headlines. Sophie insisted that women's suffrage be established.

A manifesto was issued to the people of England, Scotland, and Wales. "We come not to enslave but to liberate you! I proclaim the republic of Great Britain." The old rulers were deposed. Ephraim landed on the Belgian coast with 200,000 men. As his hosts of freedom wavered in the critical Battle of Marburg, sweet young Sophie appeared on a white horse in a rift in the battle line and saved the day. Perfect Freudian and surrealist symbolism! Sophie was perhaps the girl Marian, whom Donnelly was to take as his wife a few years later. Wonderingly, he was watching Marian bud into womanhood at a time when his beloved wife Kate, desperately ill, was not expected to live.

To the Teutons, his hero swore: GERMANS — AMERICA LOVES YOU. "We do not come to oppress or subjugate you. We come to give all your people the blessings enjoyed by the inhabitants of the United States — education, liberty, fraternity, prosperity. Will you be free men or slaves? We will give every man in Germany a home, a farm, a house, a garden."

The battle opened, and Sophie went flying up and down the lines on her white charger. Victorious, the good Yanks went on to tumble down the tinseled czardom of Russia.

The Day of Jubilee was at hand. THE UNITED REPUBLICS OF EUROPE was set up. "Noble little Switzerland, mother of Republics, gave a ten mile square on Lake Lucerne, and Ephraim laid out a great city called 'Liberty,'" — the pure white columns of the European League of Nations, of which the lowly son of Kansas became the head.

[134]

The book concludes, "A new birth of religion is needed. Love God with all thy Heart." It was another best seller.

History has since imparted to Donnelly's rantings the golden seal of prophecy. The dust-covered novel, with its strange fantasy and childish propaganda, reads like a sour premonitory satire on the tragic career of Woodrow Wilson. Ignatius was merely a premature F.D.R. If Ephraim Benegert (and Donnelly) were crazy, as his critics said at the time, then Woodrow Wilson and F.D.R. were really crazy. In some uncanny way, Ignatius probed the deep nerve cells of growing national power. He goes crusading with blood and steel on European soil for righteous New Deal purposes three decades before it first happened, half a century before F.D.R. went over on another white charger. In Freudian dream fashion, Donnelly felt the red pulse of 1917 and 1941 and 1966.

Donnelly was riding the high tide. The best years of his long life coincided with those of the Populist party of the nineties. He was one of the chief founders. In Exposition Music Hall in St. Louis, under gala banners, he roused the gray-haired, rough-handed farmers and workers to revivalistic glory. "We meet," he said, "in the midst of a nation brought to the verge of . . . ruin. Corruption dominates the ballot box, the legislature, the Congress and touches even the ermine of the bench." The purpose of the assemblage was "to restore the government of the Republic to the hands of the plain people," to uplift mankind.

He was the hero at the great Omaha nominating convention of July 4, 1892, where his arms flailed above the heads of 1,776 delegates and 9,000 people.

"An astonishing gathering," he declared, ". . . without a single tool . . . of monopoly or robbery in its midst . . . not . . . a single representative of the rings which are sucking the lifeblood out of this American people [cheers]."

The Republican and Democratic conventions were ruled by stooges of railroads and millionaires and oil corporations. The delegates were "wriggling upon their vest buttons in base subservience [cheers]. . . . Where is Horace Greeley, Charles Summer, Wendell

Philips, Abraham Lincoln? . . ." he cried. "Point out to me a single friend of labor in those conventions, a single friend of the poor, a single friend of the mechanic . . . One hundred and sixteen years have given us from 8,000 to 30,000 millionaires, and one and a half million tramps, while the whole land is blistered with mortgages and the whole people are steeped to the lips in poverty. . . .

"This continent is the last great camping place of the human race. If liberty fails here, it fails forever."

Donnelly campaigned across the nation. The Populist candidates carried three middle western states, won strong legislative representation in twoscore others, put numerous candidates into the House and Senate, and rolled up the largest third-party electoral vote since Lincoln's day.

Donnelly fought on throughout the nineties with growing optimism. But like most people, he was sidetracked in 1896 by the Bryan currency issue, free silver coinage, and "a people's money." He opposed fusion, but finally helped herd his party into a sterile alliance with the Democrats and their battle against the "cross of gold."

He published a lively dialogue, *The American People's Money*, between a bright farmer and nitwit banker. The farmer overwhelmed the banker with proof of his extortionate misdealings and with sermons about planned currency, the righting of railroad abuses, economic wrongs, and the farmers' program.

Donnelly and the Populists went down the Democratic false trail of free silver. It was the end of the great People's party.

The silver campaign was lost. The gold bugs and the silk-hat boys led by Mark Hanna made William McKinley President.

Later, Donnelly, Tom Watson, and others tried in vain to save the wrecked People's party organization and make it hew once more to the original line of farmer reform. But by then the Farmer's Alliance had also crumbled. The farmer's revolt had been broken, not to reemerge until the Great Depression and the clumsy Wallace New Deal.

[136]

Ignatius was long dead then. After 1896, he turned from politics back to his literary pursuits. Age deepened his sense of defeat and futility. Again he was driven toward recondite erudition. But he was unquenchable, this florid tawny-haired man, and he was in love. Three years before, he had written a beautiful *In Memoriam* for his faithful wife Kate. Now he asked his close friend Hanson for the hand in marriage of his beautiful daughter Marian, more than forty years his junior, twenty years younger than the oldest of his big red-headed sons. Hanson, it was said, was rather sick about it, but Marian was enraptured, deeply in love also.

The new imperialism of the Spanish-American War was now stirring the pulse of the nation, and new industry was bringing the greatest prosperity in the history of the world, confounding all the prophets of disaster.

The world had swept by Donnelly. Inspired by his new young wife, he planned to reissue a revised edition of *The Great Cryptogram* and revive the Bacon-Shakespeare controversy. He was also planning a momentous opus on spiritualism. This time his literary projects were a mask for real defeat. In his prime he had been the great Jeremiah of the American epic. Now he was driven into hazy mysticism. Strangely enough, a number of Populist leaders turned to spiritualism as a panacea. The twentieth century was a world that the anguished prophet of the closing jaws of the frontier did not know except by prophecy.

Had it not been for his Catholic background, Donnelly at the 1900 Cincinnati convention would have been made standard-bearer of his shattered party instead of elderly Wharton Barker of Philadelphia. There were only 76 delegates (4 women) from 12 states, and they were mostly old tired bearded men, who had been Grangers and Alliancers and had seen their great hopes grow small through repeated defeats. Even half of these angrily left the hall, denouncing what they considered the further betrayal. Even so, as vice-presidential candidate, Donnelly campaigned strenuously. But he did not get enough votes to stuff in a squirrel hole.

[137]

Though for years considered a crackpot, nearly everything he fought for has become the adopted law of the land. Of all his prophecies, none bears the seal of destiny more deeply than the New Deal's storming of the battlements of the world in the name of democracy. The millions of copies of Donnelly's propaganda books paved the way for that. Let us hope that his horrible Cabano and Lomellin dictatorships fail to materialize. But these are still a few years away.

VII
THE GARLAND
OF THE NINETIES

One of the few writers who interpreted rural America during the nineties in strong human and social terms, and wrote some of the finest simple prose of the language, was Hamlin Garland. Notable writing was done during those gay stormy years of farmer bankruptcy, but none was closer to the grass roots than that of Garland.

These lowly aspects of. American democracy were not especially noted in a most significant study, published in 1890, entitled *The State and Federal Governments of the United States,* for it dealt largely with legal mechanisms. The peculiar importance of this volume did not become apparent until thirty-odd years later, when its author, Woodrow Wilson, emerged from academic insignificance to become the captain of the crew riding the great "Donnelly" flotilla eastward on the backwash of the closed frontier — to help stave off the latest thrust of the mid-European barbarians against the British empire.

Probably many of the 467 volumes on theology published that

year of 1890 had more immediate circulation than the works of Garland or of the southern professor. This was also true of a goodly number of the 1,118 novels.

The middle class was now buying the *Rubaiyat*, which that suave apologist, Elbert Hubbard, had published in soft leather — a convenient gift — and was to continue in vogue for some decades. The gutters of sentimental piffle were also clogged by *A Cigarette Maker's Romance*, another of the heavily-scented plots which F. Marion Crawford periodically shipped back to muddied home waters from the crystalline fonts of his Florentine villa.

More sinewy stuff came from the pen of one roving American: *A Connecticut Yankee in King Arthur's Court*. Most readers put into its shrewd humor all their own blatant provincial feelings of American superiority and quite failed to penetrate Mark Twain's satire. Emily Dickinson's poems, first printed that year, were not appreciated until nearly forty years later.

The public was greatly stirred by Salvation Army Generalissimo Maud B. Booth's *Beneath Two Flags*, chiefly because of its arraignment of London slums. This pampered the strong anti-British feeling of that day. "What a picture is that which General Booth has drawn of 'Darkest England,' " wrote the *Weekly Tulare Register* of California (February 20, 1891). "More homeless, destitute, unemployed people in those little islands than there are inhabitants of the Pacific Coast from Alaska to the Mexican border. And can England's aristocracy and affluence sleep and feel secure with every tenth person in the kingdom brawling about like ravening beasts of prey capable of anything?" Pots have usually called the kettle black.

Frank Norris matriculated at the University of California but would soon be ejected. Syracuse University showed its hospitality for budding genius by bouncing Stephen Crane because he doubted St. Paul's theory of sin and had shocked a Professor's wife by calling Miss Willard "a fool."

In August, Richard Harding Davis, the fifth-rate fake Kipling, published "A Walk up the Avenue" in *Scribner's* and thereafter

[140]

mounted gracefully into celebrity. Bret Harte brought out *A Waif of the Plains*, a sentimental frontier stereotype, Eugene Fields published a little volume of western verse, and Whitcomb Riley produced his *Rhymes of Childhood Days*. Oliver Wendel Holmes made his gentle, but not toothless, bow with *Over the Teacups*.

With his *Youma*, a novel of weird Caribbean background, Lafcadio Hearn in his lovely sensitive style tried to cash in on the general interest in the exotic, ever-strong in a people addicted to barbaric sideshows. He knew soon he could never be appreciated in America and took his mutilated body off to Japan, where he found love and peace and wrote a great masterpiece.

The big sensation of 1890 along exotic lines was Henry M. Stanley's *In Darkest Africa*. Stanley was received everywhere with a goggle-eyed acclaim, probably never again equaled till the 1898 inland tour of Hobson of the "Merrymack" and the "Merrysmack." Stanley cleaned up on lectures. The day after Christmas, 1890, he talked in Des Moines, Iowa, a state which two years later provided the bellwether of Populist revolt, General James B. Weaver, perennial leader of lost causes.

One book, to repeat, which received scant attention from Eastern pundits was Ignatius Donnelly's fantastic best seller *Caesar's Column*. Soon read by millions, it had tremendous influence on the impending political breakup.

Various "pungent replies" to Bellamy's *Looking Backward* now appeared and were more lavishly praised than the historic volume which called them forth. However, *Looking Backward* kept on flooding the country. It was being distributed to subscribers, numbering 4,000,000, to the *National Economist*. Bellamy's scientific wonders and his society of perfect justice presented a rainbow picture of felicity and beauty in sharp contrast to the actual Middle Border and the gutted furrows of the broken South. A web of Bellamy Nationalist Clubs spread quickly over the country.

And so Crawford lit up the sweaty dreams of the vulgar; Stanley satisfied the escapists, Bellamy, the hopes of the oppressed and the idealists; while Donnelly, the florid Minnesotan, mirrored the general sense of universal disaster that hung over the land fleeing the first harsh impact of the closing of the frontier and the unemployment and unrest due to the rapid amassing of wealth, the rise of monopolies, and the narrowing circle of individual opportunities.

But the literary realist of the Middle Border was Hamlin Garland, the single taxer, who created harsh but sensitive and true pictures of western farm life and joined the Alliance and Populist crusades. He was the Middle West's greatest contemporary chronicler. In the midst of more passionate denunciations, of demagogic rantings, of the boisterous upsurge of the more prosperous cities, and of the measuring of all things by the crude dollarmark, he had considerable difficulty in being heard. His quiet honesty was not in tune with either gingerbread or imitative classic architecture. It was not in tune with the strong servility to all cultural things European. It was not in tune with the flamboyant, over-sentimental taste of the times. It had an earnest Puritan flavor, but breathed a moral and spiritual tolerance that was bigger than the narrow concepts of much of the Middle Border, where he was born and with which he increasingly identified himself. His words still glow with a small steady flame.

When Hamlin's father came back from the Civil War in 1865 to the little cottage in Green's Coulee among the wooded hills of Wisconsin, the small boy had forgotten his existence and did not know who he was.

Long before that, the older Garland, a six-footer with flashing, eagle-gray eyes, had come as a young man with his sister Susan and his parents from Massachusetts to the forest lands of Wisconsin, where he worked as a lumberman and logger on the river, then farmed — until he went off to war and came back with the peculiar measured stride of Sherman's veterans.

Young Hamlin read the Bible, an occasional page from *Harper's Weekly,* and the *Farmer's Annual,* with its gaudy pictures of cherries and plums, fat sheep, pigs and cows, its sentimental old-fashioned poems. Later he got hold of *Aladdin and His Wonderful Lamp.* In later years, Garland remembered the joy of riding the Magic Carpet, attending the building of towered cities and the spread of gorgeous feasts. In his hand was the shell from which cool water gushed, on his feet were winged boots, and on his head the Cap of Invisibility. In reality, he was a captive in poverty in a little snowbound cabin.

His father became dissatisfied with Green's Coulee. Bumps and ridges blocked his plow. The clearing of most of the quarter section had not been accomplished. Ditches had to be dug in the marsh and oaks uprooted. He harped on the easy plains where fields stretched level; and his complaints of the tilted fields of Wisconsin sank so deeply into the minds of his sons "that for years thereafter, they were unable to look upon any rise in the ground as an object to be admired." At other times the father talked of the splendors of Boston, where he had worked as a boy. The dream of young Hamlin was formed then and there — to get to Boston and become a part of its superior cultural life, to escape the Middle Border, not then realizing that all his life would be inspired by it.

His father, however, looked west, ever west. He was part of the open frontier, one of the unconscious empire builders. For him, Iowa became the pot of gold at the foot of the rainbow. His mother, averse to the new move, took for the theme the then popular ballad:

We'll stay on the farm and we'll suffer no loss
For the stone that keeps rolling will gather no moss.

But it was the frontier song of the Alleghenies that held his father:

Cheer up brothers, as we go
Over the mountains, westward ho . . .
Then over the hills in legions, boys,

Fair freedom's star
Points to the sunset regions, boys,
Ha, ha, ha, ha!

There they'd "reign like kings in fairy land, Lords of the soil."
The homestead was sold, and in February they moved out
over the snow in sleds, heaped high with family effects, to La
Crosse, standing by a frozen river. They crossed over toward the
western hills and started to ascend into the snows, on to Caledonia
in the white prairie until they came to the farm they had bought.
Once more the land was cleared, with the aid of Norwegians, one
of whom gave their "housemaid" the smallpox.

Soon there were other moves. Finally land was purchased in
Mitchell County, just south of the Minnesota border. This time
they traveled in August. Each mile took them further into the empty
prairie. By the second day they came to a meadow "so wide that
the western rim touched the sky without revealing a sign of man's
habitation." The grass was tall as ripe wheat; there were pounding
herds of wild horses.

When ten years old, while his father walled up the house for com-
coming winter, Hamlin herded the cattle and did the plowing, no
easy job, for the sod was deep "nigger wool," and the wet stubble,
matted with wild buckwheat, rolled up and threw the plow from
the furrows. Otherwise the steel ran smoothly, not a root or a stone
as big as a walnut, but it was tough work, and savage flies made
every minute a torture. It was hard blistering toil, day after day,
deep into November. The boy's heart grew bitter and rebellious.

When the frost hardened the ground, he had the joy of a respite
and read *The Female Spy*, a Civil War story, and presently went
to school in Osage. The only diversions were dances — "first lady
lead to the right, deedle, deedle, dum dum, gent foller after" —
the yearly circus, and revival meetings, night after night of them
whenever an itinerant preacher came through to shout and gasp
in holy hysteria.

[144]

Hamlin ransacked all the neighbors' houses for miles about for books: Porter's *Scottish Chiefs*, Scott's *Ivanhoe*, Codey's *Ladies' Book*, and *Peterson's Magazine*. From his father, reader of the *Toledo Blade* and the *New York Tribune*, he came to have a very corporeal conception of Horace Greeley and Petroleum V. Nasby, the much-derided reformer. Franklin's *Autobiography* was a wellspring of joy.

He came upon a poem, "Kit Carson's Ride," by Joaquin Miller, a work of "tumultuous rhythms" that told the story of a race for life on the Texas plains before a prairie fire and aroused his admiration; he recited it "with great success" at the Burr Oak schoolhouse one winter night. Later in manhood he climbed up to Miller's quaint place high in the Oakland hills, with its queer little pyramids and stone piles, and listened to the poet tell how he learned from the Indians how to make rain by chants.

Farm tragedies came soon enough. One day, just as the sown wheat was tingeing the brown earth with a tender green, a great wind came up and ripped up the soil, forming a cloud hundreds of feet high that drove everybody to shelter in a day turned night. All morning this "blizzard of loam" raged, filling the house with dust, almost smothering the cattle in the stable.

The small amount of new wheat not blown away was left with exposed roots and soon shriveled up. "As the day wore on, father fell into dumb, despairing rage" that terrified his sons and wife. They had cultivated the fields so well, breaking up the clods into fine loam, whereas the rough poorly tilled fields of their lazy neighbor had scarcely suffered.

At best, life seemed coarse to the boy as he read his magical books. Vicious flies, the army worms, the plagues of mosquitoes, the currying, the milling, were hard never-ending tasks. Endlessly they shoveled and hauled away animal manure. Some farmers found it easier to move the barn, but Hamlin's father was "an idealist." At other times drouth came. Sometimes stacks burned and hundreds of dollars went up in smoke.

The country settled up, and the "Lyceum" appeared. As agriculture grew more diversified, the county fair came along, and in spite
of the harsh toil, Hamlin found those years on the prairie, from '71
to '78, full of much that was alluring and splendid. It was a democratic world. Nobody looked down on anybody else. All were
striving shoulder to shoulder within the new frontier.

The Grange came along, and a cooperative was started. Hamlin's
father, an enthusiastic supporter, was put in charge of the new
grain elevator and made official buyer for the county.

It provided a new community outlet, a new spirit of joy and
friendliness. In winter there were oyster suppers, with debates,
songs, and essays at the Burr Oak schoolhouse, and a Grange picnic
each spring in a grove somewhere along the Big Cedars, "almost as
well attended as the circus." To it came lodges from far and wide
in great processions of horseback riders, wagons, and buggies,
people carrying banners, bands playing. Galloping marshals in red
sashes kept order. Finally all merged into one mighty column
It was grateful relief from the sordid loneliness of the farm. Even
more glorious and crowded was the annual three-day county fair.

Grange ideas influenced Hamlin strongly. Also, about this time,
he stumbled on essays by Robert Ingersoll that moved him deeply.
John Burroughs' words filled him with delight; later he met him
personally. Then one day Hamlin read Hawthorne, and his spell
was laid on him "everlastingly." It was his first "literary passion,"
and he was "dazzled by the glory of it."

Hamlin had hardly graduated from school when once more his
father was on the move, this time to Orway, in Brown County,
South Dakota, where the soil was thick and dark and unused, but
where once more they would all have to work their fingers to the
bone to get a fresh start.

Hamlin, now old enough to escape, left for the East. After two
days' travel, he reached the town of Hastings. He did not know that
three miles from here in the abandoned town of Nininger lived a
man with whom in a few years he would find intellectual and

political companionship in the same cause — the famous novelist-politician Ignatius Donnelly, who more than twenty years before had failed dismally and had gone on to better things.

Hamlin took a boat to the town of Redwing, thirty miles south. Though it was a commonplace little settlement, he was thrilled — as youth is always thrilled by the new — and his excited imagination transformed the place into something "very distinctive and far-off and shining." He was soon dead broke, and from then on began a weary and heart rending search for work.

Once he walked twenty miles, without food and through mud, to apply for a job teaching school, and twenty miles back in the dark through cold rain. Finally he landed in Chicago. He was dismayed by its great banners of black smoke.

Presently, with his brother he ventured east to Boston, which meant to him Whittier and Hawthorne, Wendell Phillips and Daniel Webster. They rushed about the Commons, to Faneuil Hall, Bunker Hill, Kings Chapel, Longfellow's house, the Washington elm, the Navy Yard. Concord enchanted them; Hawthorne's home, Sleepy Hollow, the grave of Emerson.

After two years, by then very homesick, he turned his face west again. In Iowa, he encountered train after train swarming with immigrants. A new land rush was on — Norwegians, Swedes, Danes, Scotchmen, Englishmen, Russians, a flood of land seekers "rolling toward the sundown plain, where a fat-soiled valley had been set aside by good Uncle Sam for the enrichment of every man." The streets swarmed with boomers. Hamlin, too, was caught up in the restless enthusiasm and with a friend set out to find a preemption claim out on the level plains, dotted with the bones of bison, and mark it with "straddle bugs" — three boards in a tripod to indicate occupancy.

His father, too, was taking up new land here. Hamlin tended a store his father put up, but put more time in on Chambers' *Encyclopaedia of English Literature* and Greene's *History of England* than in work behind the counter.

Hopes began to dwindle when the hot summer brought no rain and the crops "baked on the stem . . . inflammable as hay." Eyes ached with light, and their hearts sickened with loneliness. In May, the claim had been beautiful green sod; by August it was "hot and hard as a brick pavement;" by winter, the bitter loneliness of arctic desolation came sweeping in with the furious blizzards. The temperature sometimes reached forty below. Against these terrors, they had only a thin pine board shanty, only buffalo bones for fuel. After that winter, Garland never again sang of "Sunset Regions" with such spirit.

From his little cabin, he turned his face toward settlement, eager once more to escape "the terror and loneliness of the treeless sod." He thought bitterly, this was a poor recompense for his people, particularly his mother, who after a lifetime on the frontier, still had to toil, to freeze, and in summer cook for travelers.

He was then twenty-three — it was 1884, another year of foreclosures for the Middle Border. That winter he read George's *Progress and Poverty*. It altered his life. For the first time he began to sense what was the matter with the land systems of the West, and he caught a glimpse "of the radiant plenty of George's ideal Commonwealth." "The trumpet call" of the closing pages filled him with a "desire to battle for the right." Here was an "opportunity for the most devoted evangel."

All summer he brooded over things, then mortgaged his claim for $200 and went east again to Boston. Everybody was going west; he was reversing the current, going against the current, going east to brave the difficulties from which other young men were trying to escape.

He tried to live on a few dollars a week. His shoes and clothes gave out. He stifled his body-hunger, when not watching the antics of cockroaches in his room, by reading in the public library; the works of Darwin, Henry George, Herbert Spencer, the great classics. Spencer, after Garland's usual five-cent breakfast, brought the universe into order and harmony.

[148]

Whitman's *Leaves of Grass* changed the universe for him, told him "the true meaning of democracy." Later he made a pilgrimage to visit Whitman in his mean quarters in Camden, New Jersey, where the "good gray poet" was living, ill, neglected, starved, and half-paralyzed. So had America rewarded his genius.

From a thirty-cent balcony seat, he saw Booth play much of Shakespeare and was so deeply moved, he used to walk in the rain and snow past the actor's home. For twenty-five cents, he could get standing room to hear the Boston Symphony. For six years he read steadily in Boston's public library: Taine, Ibsen, Björnson, Darwin, Turgenev, Tolstoy, Zola. His reading made him free.

He loved Boston and the East, but it did not inspire him to write. It was "a song already sung." Homesickness overwhelmed him. More pungently then, he smelled the fresh-turned furrows out on the plains. Still, he did try his hand at writing. He wrote a piece about an Iowa corn-husking scene, and he sold a few poems to the *New American Magazine*. Finally *Harper's* paid him $15.00 for a poem about the prairie. He spent most of it for a new silk dress for his mother, the first she had ever had. In 1888, he sold several pieces to *McClure's*.

He listened to Ingersoll's pungent oratory and absorbed some of his ideas as a freethinker. He met Howells and admired him. He read and admired Tolstoy. He reread Tocqueville. He studied Taine and Ibsen.

But he was getting hungrier and hungrier. When his clothes were almost in rags, he was given an opportunity to teach a class, and after a time was making $12.00 a week. A wealthy woman asked him to give four lectures in her home, and he made $90.00. He was beginning to emerge from the cesspool.

From Veron's *Aesthetics* and Max Nordau's *Conventional Lies* he determined to carry on a fight for *Veritism* — his word — in American fiction. It became the war cry of a small group of writers, tired of time-serving and false literary gentility, who were starting to annoy the more complacent. Painfully making his way, Hamlin

[149]

began writing stories with western settings, a genre not much in demand. Magazines preferred eastern or European settings with romantic feudal trappings. The essence of his literary creed was set forth in articles, gathered into a book in 1894.

All the time he was putting away small sums to be able to revisit the West. Finally was able to make it. At once he felt the difference between the two worlds. Boston had filled him with a false picturesqueness. It was a place of warmed-over intellectual food. Here in the West, everything was significant rather than beautiful, familiar rather than picturesque. "This was my country. These were my people." Even so, the lack of color, of charm, in the lives of the people anguished him. He was struck anew and more forcefully by the purposelessness of life on the plains, and wondered bitterly what all his vast westward reality meant. Concealed by a beard, he watched the people, the types; old acquaintances did not recognize him. He saw the father of one of his boyhood chums, a little more bent, thinner, grayer, and he asked himself what it brought a man to toil for sixty years with no increase of leisure and no chance for mental growth or grace. Wistfully the man was saying, as of old, that times were hard, the crop would not amount to much. Even young men looked worn and weather-beaten, silent and sad, crude of dress, misshapen in form, were without laughter. Nothing concealed the futility of their existence. These folk were "like flies in a pool of tar."

When he made himself known, hard, crooked fingers lay in his hand, and he thought, with a trace of fastidiousness: "Is it not time that the human hand ceased to be primarily a bludgeon for hammering a bare living out of the earth?" He thought of William Morris and Henry George. Nature was not to blame, only the laws of man.

The free days of the border were over. There was no longer joy at home or even good food. Every house he visited had its individual message of sordid struggle and despair. "Bess had taken upon her girlish shoulders the burdens of wifehood and motherhood

[150]

almost before her girlhood had reached its first period of bloom."
She was cook and scrubwoman, mother and nurse. He looked upon
her shabby furniture, old chairs, faded rag carpets, and spavined
sofas, and the empty walls of her pitiful small house seemed a
prison. He remembered her as she was in her radiant girlhood,
and his throat filled with "rebellious pain."

All the false romance of farm life vanished, leaving only "hard
and bitter reality." Nature was as beautiful as it had ever been, but
"no splendor of cloud, no grace of sunset" could hide the poverty
and degradation. It merely accentuated the sordid drudgery of daily
toil. Youth grew quickly old and bent. Girlish loveliness soon
shriveled to thin worn age void of hope. His own mother had
trod this path of slavery, never one day of leisure, only the routine
of thankless toil from before dawn until late at night. Society was
hardening into tragedy and hopelessness. This was not the true
destiny of man. Hamlin left the town of Osage in "a tumult of
revolt."

As he went farther west, the land and people became lonelier.
There was no more free land on west; those who had failed to
come in the first rush now had to pay speculators' prices. It meant
they could never win the game as farmers. It was a wasteful
method of pioneering, lonely, desolate, tragic. These settlers, their
wives and daughters, he wrote, had been pushed out into this lonely
circle by the grasp of landlordism in more settled areas. He saw
that the westward movement had really been started in the old
world by people with no share in the feudal landholding of their
native lands. Similarly, in the east of the United States speculation
in land had prevented them from making a living even by leasing
a plot of ground. The free songs of moving west had in reality
been "the hymn of fugitives!"

Why, he demanded, should every free hour be filled with a
harsh effort merely to feed and clothe the family? What was wrong
with society if unremitting toil brought only poverty?

He neared home, the town of Ordway in South Dakota. Its only

[151]

outstanding temple in that level treeless plain was the tall grain elevator. Otherwise it was a meager collection of weather-beaten wooden houses, no shade, no trees, no grass, just desolate and drab.

Once more he went to work in the harvest field, hating the dirt. Each night after a slosh at the well and supper he tumbled utterly exhausted into bed in a hot little room.

But he had found the permanent theme for his future literary labors, for the pamphlets and articles he would write for Populism, the speeches he would make in future campaigns for candidates other than himself.

He used the money he earned as boss stoker to return east. There, as the years rolled on, he described the bitter harsh reality just as he had seen it.

The whole West was reaching a more articulate stage, and Garland was part of its speech. He had fled from the frontier West back to the East, driven by hatred of unrewarding toil devoid of music, art, literature, or beauty. Out of the contrast of those two worlds, he was to find his role and his message, much as Henry James, in an entirely different and more superficial way, was finding his voice in the contrast of Europe and America. But Garland's strong moral sense did not permit him to become a genteel disillusioned escapist. James hankered after a bloodless cultural world dying under the impact of the new machine age. He was caught between two worlds.

Garland was also caught in a dilemma. But he sought to glean the best from both worlds, and he looked with more hope to the future. He was embittered by eastern indifference to western problems and to the greatness of the American continent and its culture, by all the sterile aping of European fads and distaste for any realistic interpretation. He was also greatly upset by the narrow over-moralistic attitude on the plains, the ignorance, the provincialism, the scorning of cultural attainments. He found the uncouth rural hatred of urban life well-nigh unbearable. To the farmer the city symbolized only the Shylock banker, the grasping middlemen, it was an enemy of religious faith, the harbor of sin and drunkenness. This, Garland now felt, was only a distortion, ignorant at best. "Sodom and Gomorrah" staggered through all the cruder western speeches and writing, but Garland saw clearly that the hornyhanded West greatly needed the culture, the art, the quickened intellectual life of the eastern city. To berate the city and not see the pigpen drudgery and privation near at hand was fatal blindness. He loved beauty and hated injustice, so he saw no reason to make a fetish of yokel hatred of beauty and art. He wished to share his own successes and wider horizons with the folk he left behind.

There was little hope for this as long as the farmer remained a bankrupt drudge. In literature Garland might let the East know what was going on in this great America. But for the westerner, the only immediate road was to crusade for the farmers' candidates.

His only literary market was in the East, but western tales had to be sentimental drivel or absurd frontier adventure. The West was always pictured either as a romantic paradise or a place of desperados — of brave virtuous maidens or cancan whores turned virtuous. His starker pieces came back, occasionally with personal notes protesting against his false picture of life on the plains. Gilder, of *Century*, told him to keep his fiction pure and clean, that people were trying to bring up their children with refinement.

Neither East nor West liked his portrayal. The West was even more outraged by the truth. The farmers did not wish to see themselves depicted as they really were. They, too, much preferred romantic drivel and sentimentalized trappings. And western boosters wanted only glowing Dolphin Island accounts. Reread today, Garland's tales scarcely seem startling, almost too mild and genteel, in spite of their bitterness in a decaying world. He wrote nothing as bleak and bitter as Harold Frederic's novels, yet he was harshly accused of crudeness and of disloyalty to his own land and folk.

But he kept on undaunted and included "heat and cold and dirt and drudgery" in what he considered "proper proportions." Other writers told only of pleasant weather; their heroes "tossed fragrant

[153]

clover," wore jaunty broadbrimmed hats, girls lounged in dainty white under shady trees, at frequent intervals, singing "The Old Oaken Bucket." He "included the mud and manure as well as the wild roses and the clover."

To work all day in the dust at the tail of a strawstacker was no joke. "To husk corn for ten hours on a mile-square field in a savage November wind, with your boots laden with icy slush and your fingers chapped and bleeding, does not make for song (yodelers leaning on pitchforks). Even haying meant steaming sweat and aching arms."

He was right, of couse, but perhaps too earnest. Romanticism also has its place. Hamlin must be turning over in his grave at the pretty falsities of *Oklahoma,* but one would not like to lose its superb lyrics, the dances, the fanciful allegories, the joyous humor just because Oklahoma isn't really like that and never was.

Soon the parting of the ways came for him. Should he merely write or also try to improve conditions? This has been the eternal dilemma of the honest writer in every clime and age, although it weighs down the souls of American writers more than those of most nationalities. Americans are apt to make of it an iron-clad "either-or" proposition, a spiritual torment, an artificial duality.

"To refuse the call," wrote Hamlin solemnly "was to go selfishly and comfortably along the lines of literary activity I had chosen. To accept was to enter the arena where problems of economic justice were being sternly fought out. I understood already something of the disadvantage which attached to being called a reformer, but my sense of duty and the influence of Herbert Spencer and Walt Whitman rose above my doubts. I decided to do my part."

He did find one good wise patron, the editor of the *Arena,* who asked him to write a serial novel based on the Farmers' Alliance, "a prodigious uprising among the farmers, then at its height . . . as picturesque . . . as the *Vendee.* . . . Go to Kansas and study Alliance leaders, also to Georgia. We will provide transportation."

[154]

And so the spring of '91 marked the end of his quiet life as a teacher in Boston. The *Arena* put him "on wheels." McClure commissioned him to interview Eugene Field and James Whitcomb Riley.

He went to Washington and wrote of "the Alliance Wedge in Congress." He met such personalities as "Sockless" Jerry Simpson, the congressman, and became friends with the leaders of the farm movement that swept into office on the tide of revolt in 1890. There he met "Milkman" Benjamin Clover, sodhouse-dweller William A. McKeeghan, "Calamity howler" Omer Kem, fiery Tom Watson of Georgia, and Senator William Peffer of Kansas, with his great Mosaic beard.

He went South and visited Negro churches and cotton plantations: "I began to know my country." He felt the new pulse of the farmer movement. Not until then could he begin to suggest in the novel he was writing "the nation's widespread stir of protest." His book, *A Spoil of Art,* was about a radical congressman and a suffragette wife, and his work "degenerated into a partisan plea for a stentorious People's Party." It became a tract for the 1892 Populist campaign.

He went on west and met the stormy personalities of Kansas and elsewhere. He came particularly to know and admire tall handsome Mary Ellen Lease. He liked the busy "petite brunette" Prohibitionist and Alliancer, tiny Miss Annie L. Diggs. Miss Sarah Emery, author of the *Seven Financial Conspiracies,* was a large attractive woman, with a daring boyish bob, who had campaigned ever since the Greenback uprising. He met Coin Harvey, the famous money pamphleteer, and General Weaver of Iowa, who was to head the Populist movement.

He attended the nominating convention at Omaha, on July 4, where his own father was coming as a delegate. Garland met him at the train, took him to the Murray Hotel, introduced him to General Weaver, and paid his bills.

That Sunday, Garland was the cardinal attraction at a single-tax

[155]

gathering on Farnham Street. He had already published a single-tax novel, *Jason Edwards: an Average Man.* He read his story *Under the Lion's Paw* with a smooth, musical, though not very strong, voice, "but with such effect," according to the *Omaha Bee,* "the audience was frequently in tears," and at the close "the applause was tremendous."

Mary Lease shared the platform, declaring that "the prairies of Kansas" were "dotted with the graves of women" who had "died of mortgage on the farm." Mary Lease certainly had not died, but her husband, a misfit druggist trying to be a farmer, almost did. Garland and Lease were to campaign together from platforms, cracker barrels, and courthouse steps. The old-time newspapers frequently sneered at him in a patronizing way. Mary was the one who really got the ugly sneers and brickbats, for she was feared. Mile-long parades became five miles long when she was scheduled to speak — with gayer floats, more bands, mightier singing. She spoke at the Wellington Opera house, and the local paper called her a miserable caricature of womanhood, hideously ugly and foul of tongue. The editor, to be sure, had been singled out by her scorching tongue. He was at a loss, he said, to know why the old hag had attacked him, but apparently the people's party needed a female blackguard to spout foul-mouthed vulgarity at $10.00 a night. Doubtless the petticoated smut-mill earned her money; but her venomous tongue was the only thing marketable about the old harpy. Fortunately, in another month the lantern-jawed goggle-eyed nightmare would be out of a job.

Garland had none of the reverberating satire, the down-to-earth pungency of Mary Lease. Beer tells how in 1891 Crane called on Helen Trent, the contralto singer. Had he seen Hamlin Garland, the new writer from the West, while he lectured at Avon?

"Oh," Crane said, "like a nice Jesus Christ."

Presently disillusionment overtook Hamlin. Basically he was an artist, unsuited for the rough-and-tumble of practical politics, unable to trim and tack and mouth platitudinous rhetoric. His hopes were "turning to ashes in his mouth."

At the same time, he felt more than ever out of place in the rarefied literary atmosphere of Boston with its decaying culture. The city "had begun to dwindle, to recede. The warm broad unkempt and tumultuous west, with its clamorous movement, its freedom from tradition, its vitality of thought, reasserted its power over me." For all his personal fastidiousness, he had never taken root in Massachusetts. He decided to try New York, "the new literary and financial capital of the nation." But there he felt still more lost, with "no feeling of being at home" in the "tumult," so he decided that his real roots, like his writing, were in the West, that there, at the scene, he should live and work.

But on his return his reactions were equally dismal. Once more he was appalled at the deterioration. In Columbia, the hotel stood empty, its windows broken. In Ordway, his old parents were giving up the battle, thinking of homesteading farther west. It was too great a struggle at their age, he told them, and took over their support. First he made them travel out to California, then to Chicago to see the World's Fair. Its stupendous splendor was almost too much for their tired eyes and toilworn bodies, and he gathered them quietly into a house in West Salem in the Dakotas and suddenly had a great feeling of peace and happiness, a feeling that he had found his haven, the place where he really belonged, here forever part of the Middle Border.

He would go on writing about it for many years — he won the Pulitzer prize for biography in 1922 — but he slipped more and more into mere propaganda or escapism — not art for art's sake, a credo he never accepted, but his heroes became romanticized battlers for the good of humanity. Beauty was hitched to service and dedication. Humor was never his strong point. The upsurge of the nineties which coincided with clamorous farmer revolt and the feeling of new freedom and Utopian achievement was his best time. Afterwards, the failure of western freedom cast a shadow on both his hope and fine clarity. All the indecisions of his youth came back to plague him. From the start he had been torn between the desire to become an escapist and the wish to integrate himself with

[157]

his environment. An emotional and intellectual paradox, he could not endure Middle Border reality, yet he wrote of that reality. He had fled to the East, and though its culture was infinitely superior, he could not take root there.

He was a bit like W. H. Hudson and his Argentina. When Hudson was in Argentina, he wanted to be in England. When he was in England, he wanted to be in Argentina. Out of that conflict came beautiful writing, and who will say that it would have been better had he been able to make a decisive lifelong choice?

Garland, though few writers in America have been so identified with regional nuances, was never completely happy with his final choice. But when disillusionment came with the decline of Populism and the rise of imperialism, he had no place to turn. He visited Mexico for his life of Grant, went to the Yukon soon after. He then fled further away from Boston or Yucatán. He took refuge in psychic research. He became a spiritualist, as did many other Populist leaders.

But before that intellectual and moral deterioration set in, even in Boston he was part of the Middle Border as it was being torn by the dust and battle of hot political revolt. That revolt was something unique in American life, the men who led it were unique, often picturesque, and Garland was moved to become its best and most sincere spokesman on the intellectual literary level.

He is not one of America's great writers, but he occupies a special and significant niche. He can never be overlooked in the story of the long struggle for the preservation of homely American virtues, of the struggle for human freedom and decent human relationships. He wrote the history of a generation, of a great movement, the struggle and defeat of the Middle Border, and this, however much ignored, is one of the greatest sagas of America.

VIII
SOCKLESS SOCRATES

In south central Kansas in the "big seventh," the largest congressional district in the United States, the ex-Canadian Populist Jerry Simpson ran against Colonel James R. Hallowell, Republican, to win "the famous roundtrip to Washington." That was in 1890.

The Republicans had ruled Kansas unchallenged since before the war, but now the plucked chickens of land and railroad speculation had come home to roost. Taxes soared as the railroad bonds of town, county, and state came due, but land and property values were falling. Crop prices were down to bedrock. Corn, which cost more to ship than it was worth, was being burned for fuel. Drouth, locusts, blizzards had swept the land. The seven plagues were a reality. Many a Moses was at hand, however, and as farms went under the hammer, the tide of popular resentment, which had risen steadily since the Civil War, was ready to break its banks and seek new political channels. The ruling party politicians felt the earthquake under their feet and were frightened by the amazing overnight change in the public temper. Bitterness and mud-slinging became worse than usual.

Colonel Hallowell, a smooth college-bred corporation lawyer, a polished orator and fastidious dresser, was well supplied with railroad funds and favoritism. Simpson was a yokel. The *Cresset* (Republican) reminded its Barber County readers that when Jerry was nominated, he was "a busted community. He could afford only a $14 suit, of ready-made clothes, had borrowed money for it, and had to depend on his followers . . . for his hotel expenses." During the campaign, he was called a clown, ignoramus, boob, ragamuffin; he was charged with being an infidel, heretic, and anarchist.

He made the most of these charges. He was one of the people, "no upstage railroad lawyer." An ex-sailor, Jerry would lurch to the platform — there in landlocked Kansas in the heart of the dry continent — with the rolling sea gait that never left him, to tell his hilarious listeners how "Prince Hal" was carried to Dodge City in a palace car by the railroad corporation. "Already they've got a mortgage on him."

And so "the Prince of royal blood travels in his special car, his dainty person gorgeously bedizened; his soft white hands are pretty things to look at; his tender feet are encased in fine silk hosiery, what does he know of the life and toil of such plow-handlers as we are? I can't represent you in Congress with silk stockings — I can't afford to wear 'em." And so, Simpson became "Sockless Jerry," "the sockless Cicero of the Sunflower State."

As per custom, the two candidates debated around the "gaslight circuit" on outdoor platforms. The Larned *Eagle-Optic* told of one occasion when Jerry met Hallowell in debate "with the courage of Abraham of old, determined to offer up the sacrifice even as the lamb upon the altar. No one even dared to hope that the common farmer, reared without opportunities for securing more than a limited common school education, inured to toil, compelled to earn his bread by the sweat of his brow, unused to public debate, unskilled in political warfare, branded as an ignoramus, could stand for a moment unscathed before the fiery impetuous eloquence of the full-armored well-equipped prince. It was like David going out from the tents of the Israelites to meet Goliath, the giant of the Philistines, and the result proved just about as disastrous to the modern braggart."

The audience "had come to see Hal strip off the epidermis of the hay-seed clodhopper . . . but the hayseed clodhopper proceeded to scrape the hair off the spine of the gentlemanly prince . . . until . . . his false position on public questions . . . was punctured as full of holes as a fish net."

Campaign reunions were lively those days. The glee club sang. Many speakers talked, and people, without movies, radios, or social contacts, listened on till all hours with undimmed interest. Practical frontier jokes often enlivened the proceedings.

Following Jerry's speech at a very late meeting in Deerfield, Chairman Scott, the famous Kansas Alliance organizer, asked the crowd to remain seated, saying "Prince Hal' had arrived in town unexpectedly and would appear on the platform. Presently, a Mr. Funk came forward, outfitted like the other candidate, partly buried in a tall, silk hat. He made his bow, while three "chorus singers" on the stage, dressed to represent the people, sang, "Good-bye, Prince Hally, Good-bye."

Simpson himself described one meeting. "I arrived at Scott City on the night of the eleventh and the next morning when I went out on the street the wind was carrying the dust in clouds to the South; in fact we were having a regular norther, and I thought our meeting would be a failure. But, in spite of the wind, the dust, and the cold, about ten o'clock there began to arrive farmers' wagons, loaded with people, carrying banners and mottoes. 'Down with Wall Street.' 'Give us $50 per capita currency.' 'Give the farmers as fair a chance as you give the bankers.'"

Floats, laden with pretty girls knitting socks for Jerry, passed along the town streets. Before the campaign was over, he received more than 300 pairs. Dinner was spread out on the picnic grounds, after which came the speech-making.

He was an inveterate storyteller. Many of his tales had an anti-Semitic flair. The "Eastern Jewish Shylocks" was not an infrequent Populist phrase. A Jew and an Irishman were in a boat. The Irishman tried to make the "descendant of Abraham" acknowledge the divinity of the Child and the Virgin Mary. The Jew refused, so the Irishman threw him overboard and held him under till he gave up his "dombed heathenism." "Oi'm glad to hear that," said the Irishman, "but Oi'm 'av the opinion that if ever yez got to land ye dombed sheeney yez will take it back so Oi'm goin' to drown yez now and save yure immortal soul." So the Republican party should be killed while in a repentant state of mind so as to save its soul.

In the fiery farmer press, Hallowell became "the Bogus Butter Prince," a "speckled bird," "a plutocratic hireling," "a railroad razoop." Men were free with words those days, and audiences demanded strong vituperation. The *Atchison Champion* wrote that Prince Hal was "a political shyster of the vilest type, a ranting demagogue, whose howling for prohibition with his hide throughly soaked with whiskey, stamps him as an arrant political knave, a trading, trafficking political vagabond, a conspicuous party bolter, an ex-United States District Attorney who [sic] President Harrison absolutely refused to appoint to a responsible position in the Department of Interior for reasons which Hallowell . . . well knew. . . . a brawling, bloviating, hypocritical pretentious political tramp, who is a Republican for revenue only; such a creature, if he had as much sense as he had gall, and as much regard for decency as he has for notoriety would keep his mouth respectfully closed."

But a sarcastic anonymous verse, "The Kansas Bandit," said that Jerry was an "agriculturist," not a "farmer:"

> The farmer works the soil
> The agriculturist works the farmer. . . .

Prince Hal's dilemma arose not from the arguments of Jerry but from

> Lack of moisture in the atmosphere. He
> Was the victim of climatic scarcity.

His district expected him

> . . . to produce territorial
> Humidity, and divide the rain-belt with
> The sea-board states. . .

Once asked why he had settled in Kansas, Jerry replied: "The magic of a kernel, the witchcraft in a seed; the desire to put something into the ground and see it grow and reproduce its kind. That's why I went to Kansas."

His answer was more poetry than truth. Jerry, never much of a farmer, had not been successful. He went out to Kansas with $10,000 capital, his life savings, which he proceeded to lose. His failure, shared with so many of the Middle Border, carried him into the lists of reform. He was more successful as an unpublished poet, a speaker of flashing homespun wit, a politician.

When he honeymooned with his bride from Indiana, Jane Cape, whom he married October 12, 1870, more than once she heard him declaim his favorite passage of poetry: "To thine own self be true . . ." Above all, he loved to read and quote Shelley and prose-poet Tom Paine, rebels both. From them he got his simple, lifelong article of faith: "Life is good; Church creeds are a misfit; love thy fellow man."

A descendant of Scotch dignitaries, Jerry was born March 31, 1842, in Westmorland, New Brunswick. This was the year of Dorr's insurrection in Rhode Island, which was a popular revolt for political rights against the landholders. The motto of Jerry's father, a sawmill owner, was Integrity, Industry and Independence, characteristics he passed on to young Jerry.

According to the biographical sketch in Jerry's hometown Alliance paper, the *Barber County Index,* the future Sockless took his parents to Oneida, New York, at the age of six. That was in 1848, one year before Ignatius Donnelly was graduated from a Philadelphia high school.

[163]

But Jerry, the future congressman and Medicine Lodge apostle, obtained no such schooling. In his early teens he worked for a New York neighbor for $6.00 a month, then at fourteen ran off to be a cook on a lake steamer.

That was in 1856, the year Donnelly took his bride to lonesome Minnesota. Probably, on his occasional trips to Duluth, the latter may have seen, without knowing him, his future associate in politics, either on some vessel docked there or out in the lumber camps, where Jerry worked during the icebound season when navigation was closed.

Whether young Simpson worked on any of the vessels of the rising firm of Hanna, Garretson and Company, is not recorded. The Hannas were already eminent men, known throughout the Lakes basin, and a few years later Marcus Alonzo, future boss of victorious McKinley Republicanism, everything that Jerry detested, was to be seen rustling boxes and barrels in the family warehouses. As a purser on various vessels, he may even have handed out Jerry's stipend.

Jerry voted for Abe Lincoln, as did Marcus Alonzo. Jerry had marched off to war with the Twelfth Illinois Infantry; Marcus Alonzo stayed home, carefully tending to the double entry-books of the firm. That was the year young Henry George, with a single coin in his pocket, eloped with Annie Corsina Fox, then spent the war years in odd printing jobs, fighting to make a living.

On enlisting, Jerry said, "Handcuffs and auction blocks for fellows who work don't heave to alongside of justice." But his war service was brief and inglorious. Discharged August 31, 1861, because of chronic diarrhea, he hurried back to the Lakes. At the age of twenty-two he was given first-mate's papers. He plied those inland waters until he was thirty-seven and had risen to barge captain.

"Out on the solemn waters, under the more solemn skies," writes one of his biographers, that bubbling little Kansas mushkettle, Annie Diggs, "young Simpson queried much of life and destiny." He loved to read and was rarely without a book at his elbow. He was particularly fond of Dickens, because of the novelist's warm humor and sympathy for the poor. Other favorite authors were Carlyle, Scott, Burns, Shakespeare, Hugo, Emerson, and George. He was an omnivorous reader of the Bible.

But though Jerry eventually acquired a better education than many contemporaries, he never learned to spell. Once in Congress he spelled his home town "Medison Lodge," to the merriment of a constituent leaning over his shoulder.

Jerry retorted: "I wouldn't give a cent for a man who couldn't spell a word more than one way. Why should I learn to spell when I can hire a fifteen dollar clerk to spell for me? Could that clerk get elected to Congress?"

Jerry's bad spelling became famous. Years later, his hometown opposition paper, the *Cresset*, punned that Jerry held audiences "spellbound — a great speller, to say the least." But if Jerry never learned to spell, when he chose he could swing as elegant prose diction as any Harvard Lodge or Yale Dwight.

Furthermore, his inability to spell had brought him a pretty devoted wife, Jane Cape. When Jerry was twenty-seven, he stepped off the boat to attend a party in Jackson Center, Indiana. He was a magnificently tall powerful fellow, who could hold his own in any physical combat, yet studious-looking with his glasses and shrubby moustache. (Later, in Washington, one well-to-do woman claimed with surprise that he looked far more like a quiet clergyman than the wild ass of the West he was reputed to be.)

At the lake-gathering he wore a neat suit and a bow tie that did not conceal his big Adam's apple, and he walked with his seaman's lurch. Doubtless he was "smarted up" like the other young fellows, grease on his boots, sweet scented oil on his hair — as Miss Diggs claimed — although later, out on the hustings, if not in Washington, Jerry always affected a Lincolnesque disorder in his dark locks and zealously cultivated the sockless legend.

The girls at the lake party were also "smarted up" in their Sunday best, perhaps a new ribbon or two. In those early days, the highlight of a party was the spelling bee. The gawky seaman went down the first round, Jane Cape took first prize.

According to gurgling Miss Diggs, Jane Cape, "a round rosy slip," was "the merriest, sauciest, darlingest of all that jolly company" and, with her big blue eyes, imperious too. Later, after years of facing the whipping winds and blizzards of the open prairies, Jane was described as being of swarthy complexion and after she achieved the status of a congressman's wife was said to have become snobbish and desirous of entering select social circles.

When in Washington, she was supposed to send back items of interest to the Populist *Barber County Index*. Often her letters were gush and twaddle about pretty social events, the gowns and hairdos of the capital, and the editor of the *Index*, Leon Eli Beals, sometimes tossed them into the wastebasket with a disgusted snort. Probably he misjudged the interest of the lonely farm wives of the plains, who, however ardent for Populist reform, were eager to compensate for their own faded calicos and roughened complexions by reading of pearls and diamonds and silk furbelows of the wives of the plutocratic cabinet ministers who so ably represented them in the social shindigs of democratic Washington. If Jane went into rhapsodic ecstasies over the glitter and costliness of the elaborate gowns of the democratic great, she always appended as a moral the sad contrast of the homely sunbonnets of the Kansas plains. Pointedly she declared that Washington society, with its ostentatious Harrison and Elkins dynasties had forsaken the democratic-republican simplicity of Jeffersonian days and was in marked contrast to the short and simple annals of the poor.

In the early days of Jerry's courtship, life beyond the Alleghenies was simple and homely, and Miss Diggs — conveniently forgetting for the moment the frequent murderous frays of the frontier, the wild scenes of shooting and drinking, the gaudy west-end Chicagos, the red-light tenderloins of Cheyenne and other western towns, the land-grabbing, the Wallingford schemings, and the rise of the great Robber Barons of the railways, the mines, and the cattle range — describes it movingly:

"In the late 'sixties' the people of the western states were for the most part poor of pocket but rich in the ways of industry and of small possessions . . . The ugly words graft and boodler had not been spawned . . ." (Shades of Credit Mobilier and the spoilsmen of the Grant regime!)

"These be memories of such clean days," she perorates, "that sometimes clutch the heartstrings of millionaires stifling amidst their heavy scented luxury. The call of husking bee, of spelling match, of singing school harks back to simple days before big money came to the glare and blare of life, and trade their feverish falsities for wholesome homely ways.

"Those were the days when men believed in public men . . . days when the Fourth of July meant inspiration . . . good days for ingraining character: good days to shuttle through the loom of time and make the warp of life."

In those simple days, she declaims, it was enough for a swain if the "marriage dower of his beloved were but a cow, a feather bed, and some homespun things."

Just what good the cow would do the young seaman, or whether Jane had such an animal, Miss Annie Le Porte Diggs did not state.

All that the bride of those days expected of her man, she relates, was a strong right arm or that he be skillful at some handicraft. Jerry certainly had the strong right arm and had proved his seamanship.

They were married in October, 1870, not a happy year for many folk. Black Friday of 1869 — when Gould and Fisk, in "cahoots" with the Grant administration, had tried to corner the gold of the country — still weighed heavy, and the country was creeping along half-wounded by national graft and the piratical forays of the Robber Barons toward the terrible panic of '73. But Jerry had a good berth, and bad times didn't singe him.

For long periods young Jane was left alone in the Indiana farmhouse, jointly owned with the sailor's brother. Neither liked the long separations; they were in love, and the anxiety when fierce storms swept the lake were nerve-racking for her.

In a storm off Point Betsey, his barge, the "J.H. Ruter," carrying 65,000 bushels of corn and rye, was torn away from its tow-steamer and was driven ashore off Luddington, where the crew was saved by the nearby life-station. According to Miss Diggs, Jerry was praised for his conduct and his salary was raised, but others said he was to blame for the near-disaster. Soon after, he was left jobless, unable to get a berth.

Memories of childhood days in New Brunswick came back to Jerry — the old instincts of the soil. And so, in the winter of 1878, he sold his half-interest in the house and took Jane and Hallie, their year-old son, to Jackson County, Kansas, where he built a new home and a sawmill. He was merely one of millions, rushing west at the end of the long depression.

Bad crops had followed the 1873 panic — for six years the country languished. But the '79 crop disasters in Europe, bumper yields on the prairies, high prices, sudden revival of trade, a new railroad boom, and new manufacturing, produced a fresh clamor for free lands. On the tide of rising prices, literally millions of folk resumed the epic march. The drums of prosperity, of bonanza, of economic freedom boomed again. Jerry had hit the crest of boom times.

But in 1884, little Hallie, only seven, was killed by a log. Embittered, Jerry sold out and moved to Barber County in the south central part of the state, where he bought a section of land 4 miles east of Medicine Lodge, took up a 160-acre government claim adjoining — "The government bets you fifteen dollars you can't stick it out" — and raised cattle, or tried to.

It was a pretty good bet—for the government. The terrible winter of '85-'86 wiped Jerry's herd off the face of the earth. His cows died faster than he could skin them, and spring found him nearly broke, $10,000 gone up in smoke. In 1888 and 1889, drouth and crop failures almost depopulated western Kansas and badly seared Barber County. By then Jerry was worse than down to the socks, the article he was later reputed never to wear.

He turned to hog-raising. Corn was dirt-cheap, so this promised to be a better, if less agreeable, venture. Once, leaning over his hog pen, he remarked, "The more I see of human beings, the more I admire hogs. When a hog gets his belly full he goes off and lies down to sleep. But a man then tries to take possession of the whole trough." Jerry must have had unusually well-mannered hogs.

His physical prowess was bruited far and wide. One day he got into an argument with Lee Carson, Medicine Lodge blacksmith, reputed to be the strongest man in the whole county. Lee slapped Jerry's face. Jerry slapped him down three times, and when two constables laid hands simultaneously on his shoulders, with a single shrug he tumbled both into a ditch.

To complicate his life, Jane, suffering from old ailments due to childbirth troubles, became an invalid, and his new son, Lester, was weak and sickly.

Later, as a small boy, Lester was often run off the floor in Congress for peddling Henry George's *Progress and Poverty* and the notorious campaign book of Tom Watson of Georgia. He died in early youth — from wild dissipation, according to unfriendly neighbors.

Busted as a lumberman, cattleman, farmer, and hog-raiser, Jerry auctioned off his stock and moved into town, where he took a job as marshal, which consisted mostly of digging sewer ditches—"going down for diamonds," he told kibitzers.

Having found the struggle with Nature severe, hampered by mortgage and high freight rates, not liking ditch-digging, Jerry became more and more convinced that political and economic remedies were necessary. His own plight was mild compared to those of many neighbors. All had faced blizzards, grasshoppers, and drouths for years, fighting on, hungry, toiling from before dawn till after dark, hoping against hope, and finally choked by mortgage, high freight rates, middlemen and speculators, had given up the unequal struggle and moved away, leaving their lands and personal belongings in the hands of banks or land sharks. Some committed suicide.

Jerry read Henry George's *Progress and Poverty* carefully from "kiver to kiver" and came to the conclusion that the "greatest obligation of government is to secure freedom of land to all the people." He read George's book on the tariff and became an ardent free-trader.

He had been mildly interested in the Patrons of Husbandry in northern Indiana, and he had founded a Grange in Jackson County, Kansas. Later, he organized a Farmers' Alliance local in Barber County and became a lecturer. "The Grange was full of poetry but the Alliance was full of politics." Jerry headed toward the hustings.

The Greenbackers and the Union Labor party held his interest. He was a Greenback candidate for the state legislature in 1886 and a Union Labor candidate in 1888.

Of the first election, his opponent, G.S. McNeal, said, "Jerry had already demonstrated some ability as speaker in county lyceums. . . . I happened to have the honor of running against him, and while I defeated him, it was no victory to blow about." Jerry soon became "a good talker . . . possessed of ready wit, and with an instinctive and correct appraisal of the value of publicity."

"Two years later," McNeal tells us, "Jerry was again candidate and as that happened to be the year when Kansas rolled up a Republican majority of 82,000 . . . he was buried under the general landslide. There were those who predicted he would never come back again, but they had no vision of the future. 1889 was the great corn year of all Kansas history, but the price soon went down until corn sold at ten cents per bushel or less and was burned for fuel. . . .

"The people of the state had plunged into debt with a recklessness seldom, if ever equalled and now pay day had come and ten cent corn and forty cent wheat to pay with . . . The people saw red and talked of the altar of Mammon and the great red dragon [Wall Street] and the 'crime of '73.' The words of the agitator fell on fertile ground. The Farmers' Alliance spread like a fire on the dry prairie driven by the high wind."

Barber County was in particular a hotbed. There Carry Nation held her Saturday prayer meetings, kneeling in her long black skirts in the dust of Main Street to exhort cattlemen and farmers coming into town for weekend drunks. There flourished strong suffragette and prohibition societies, and speakers of national fame were brought in. There the new farmers' paper, the *Index*, edited by Leon Beals, hammered away at the Republicans and the rival *Cresset*. Not only the Alliance, but the secret Videttes, an inner clique organized by Beals, were strong there. These were groups of super-militant farmers meeting clandestinely in dry creek-bottoms in hidden cottonwood groves, in outlying barns and hot attics — with passwords and ritual and military ranks.

The Republican party, despite its overwhelming landslide in the previous election, became thoroughly alarmed at all the hubbub and got up a platform as radical as anything suggested by the Alliance. It released all candidates from caucus so they could meet all comers with any sort of promises.

Though Jerry was not of the inner Vidette circle, the Alliance chose him for candidate. His droll convention speech and his ready campaign wit won him the election, by an 8,000 majority.

The *Barber County Index*, December 3, 1890, published a poem on the event:

They've come to see their Congressman and take him to the train,
They know the value of a man with hayseed in his locks,
Whose name is Jerry Simpson, and he don't wear socks.

The new congressman "will not hang up his socks tonight," said the *Omaha Bee*, the day before Christmas. "He doesn't wear any."

And so, in the "cyclone of 1890," Jerry rode the Populist storm of revolt to a seat in Congress. He "Jerry-mandered" it in "a bare-footed race" on an "anti-fashion platform."

In Congress, he proved to be one of the keenest, most disconcerting members ever to grace a seat. He hit the national headlines day after day. In him the starving farmers of southern Kansas had

[171]

found a clever leader "who could hold his own with the sharpest railroad attorney." Annie Diggs described his appearance at this time: "his muscular build, his broad shoulders, his lithe supple frame . . . His face . . . a blend . . . of rugged strength and keen intelligence. His clear brown eyes looked men and measures squarely in the face."

About a year later, in the *Index* of January 13, 1892, Mrs. Simpson, in describing the White House New Year's celebration, gave a vivid picture of the social setting into which the hayseeds had tumbled.

On "a most lovely day; more like balmy Indian summer" than "dreary winter," 8,000 people crowded into the White House to shake President Harrison's hand.

"The historic 'East Room' famous ever in song and story, and literally full of traditions, was brilliant with the electric lights that have recently been substituted for the dim yellow gas lights. A new velvet carpet covered the floor, and the furniture . . . if not gaudy, certainly possessed luster. Flowers were in abundance, and the White House florist arranged on one of the mantles in the 'Blue Room' the figures '1892' of bright red carnations on a cushion of white camelias. As the little clock in the Blue Room parlor struck eleven, the strains of 'Hail, the Chief,' burst forth from the musicians of the celebrated Marine band of which Professor, John Philip Sousa was the leader. The President, Vice-President and cabinet members entered.

"The wardrobes of the wives of these officials were elaborate . . . so expensive . . . it would be idle to speculate as to their value."

Mrs. Harrison's gown was "pomegranate-colored satin with brocaded border in different colored flowers. The front of the skirt was yellow satin draped on lace, which was beaded in amber. The bodice was open at the neck. She wore a diamond necklace and eardrops and carried a pointlace fan and a bouquet of orchids."

Mrs. McKee: "white satin brocade in pink rose petals across the hem a deep flounce of pink chiffon. The waist was low and finished with frills of chiffon, and had high puffed sleeves of the latter. A sash of pale blue moire ribbon was worn. Her ornaments were diamonds and pearls."

Mrs. Morton: "superb costume of old-rose satin, brocaded in waved lines. It had a plain skirt and high-necked waist. It was richly trimmed with passementerie and a beaded fringe of the same color."

Mrs. Foster: "light yellow satin very richly trimmed with yellow passementerie and lace . . . slightly open at the neck and had elbow sleeves. Her jewels were pearls."

Mrs. Miller: "heliotrope velvet combined with mauve brocade. The long train . . . heliotrope silk. Real lace trimmed the border."

Mrs. Wilmerding: "still wearing mourning, had on a plain white eau de spoe. The bodice . . . slightly opened at the neck and prettily finished with chiffon frills."

Mrs. Wanamaker: "French toilet of deep heliotrope satin brocaded in white wave lines . . . panels of ecru lace, down each side of the train. The bodice was open at the neck, trimmed with ecru lace."

Mrs. Noble: "Trained gown of yellow brocade, high necked and handsomely trimmed with real lace and jet pendants."

Young Mrs. Elkins, wife of the new Secretary of War, "seemed most attractive and charming."

Jane went on the describe the diplomatic corps, the Supreme Court members, the congressmen and their wives, the numerous army officers, General Schofield and Lieutenants Bliss and Schofield of his staff, the naval officers, the District militia, the departmental officials. Her mouth waters with the display, but she philosophizes about "these evanescent demonstrations that appear largely a mock formality and a hollow seeming of delight on the part of many participants." The eagerness to be "in the swim of American imperialism which apes the methods that obtain at the thrones of the most oppressive and prescriptive monarchs' and potentates upon this beautiful planet."

Apparently there was quite a transformation in Jerry also. Someone taught him to smoke Havana cigars — he had once been against tobacco — as he and wealthy reform Congressman Johnson of Ohio rode their bicycles along the capital boulevards, often accompanied by Hamlin Garland and others. Although Jane was never able to teach him to spell, she did teach him to dress, and the "sockless" hayseed actually became the best-dressed man in Washington politics. The Republican *Cresset* told its readers: "Jerry Simpson's new spring outfit makes the Washington dudes green with envy. He came out last Sunday with gloves, a dazzling necktie, striped trousers, and a very pretty walking stick." Later, when he attended a formal banquet in Ohio as Johnson's guest, his attire made more ironic news for the rural hometown paper, the *Cresset*. March 11, 1892, it versified:

> My name is Calamity Jerry
> In socks, economical, very,
> I'm a jay in daylight
> But watch me at night
> Disporting with champagne and sherry.

Jerry, a stern prohibitionist, did not drink.

The *Cresset* gleefully quoted Congressman Snodgrass of Tennessee: "When I came here I expected to find an old sturdy sockless fellow, who would not even purchase socks under the protective tariff ... You may imagine the astonishment ... when ... [Mr. Simpson] was pointed out to me wearing diamonds, dressed in satins and cloth, and when I saw him riding down Pennsylvania Avenue on a bicycle with a cigar in his mouth, I say you can imagine the astonishment I felt at that sad spectacle."

"Jerry Simpson is losing his radiance," said the *New York Tribune*. "He no longer draws as he did when he first bulged into Washington in all his weirdness. With his home-made raiment, his cowhide

[174]

brogans, his disheveled hair and his eye in fine frenzy rolling, Jerry was worth the price of admission at all times; in that thrice holy Mecca of cranks he was an infinite delight, a well-spring of joy, a never failing sweetness. But intoxicated by his first installment of salary, he flew upon the wing of the vestibule limited to Great Gotham, put up at the Windsor, had his hair mowed by a clipper, hobnobbed with Henry George, lunched at Delmonico's, bought socks, put on patent leather shoes and, in short, emerged from his picturesque chrysalis a cheap, commonplace, half-groomed imitation dandy. His day is over. He continues to talk to reporters, but nobody cares what he says. . . . Jerry Simpson in ill-fitting slop-shop finery is no longer a drawing card."

"I am ridiculed for dressing like a hayseed," Jerry drawled, "and denounced for putting on respectable attire."

And on March 18, 1892, the hostile *Cresset* smirkingly told its readers: "Kate Field has discovered that Jeremiah Simpson really wears half hose. If Kate speaks from observation, Jeremiah will have something more serious than the bicycle and dress suit stories to explain to western society."

It was a never-ending theme, and for years he received free socks through the mail from amused, admiring, or self-seeking people, and adoring females.

In Congress, Jerry contributed constantly to the liveliness of proceedings. According to the *Barber County Index*, he promptly challenged the Democratic and Republican congressmen to point to a single law in twenty years for the benefit of the producers.

Jerry Simpson: Why spend money on harbors to promote foreign trade, then build a tariff wall to obstruct foreign trade? Why not let the foreigner flounder in the harbor?

Once when a fellow congressman was spreading his wings in behalf of the high Dingley tariff on the theme, "Buy American," Simpson strolled to the other man's seat and peeked inside his silk hat. He asked for the privilege of a question. Why had the speaker bought a *British* hat?

[175]

Amid the roars of the House, the other congressman spluttered angrily that it was an American hat bought in New York; he had merely put in a London label for eclat. More roars.

Jerry said there were 30 reasons the pension bill should be passed. The first was, the old soldiers and their families needed the money; he had forgotten the other 29.

When one congressman made an emotional harangue about the American eagle, Jerry shouted: "The American eagle — take that buzzard away from here, he's picking the bones of the poor farmers."

One congressman derided Jerry for believing in evolution and claiming to be descended from the monkey.

Jerry: "Your family ends where mine began."

Representative Snodgrass of Tennessee, in a ferocious attack on northern veterans, heaped Jerry with personal abuse.

In his famous "monkeys throw nuts" speech, Jerry replied: "Snodgrass charges that I went without socks in days gone by; now, every little red-headed editor out in my part of the country has used that argument against me [laughter]; but I hardly believed that the representative of a portion of the great state of Tennessee would resort to such pettit-fogging tactics as that. . . . It is a long distance from Andrew Jackson to the gentleman who now represents the third district of Tennessee. . . . I am willing to stand along side him and have gentlemen compare our wearing apparel, if they think necessary [laughter]. Look at him now, with his Prince Albert coat and his flaming necktie and diamond ring [laughter]. One thing I will say, Mr. Chairman, I may have been accused of going without socks; I may have been accused lately of being 'the dude of the House;' but no gentleman has accused me of being the fool of the House [laughter]."

June 9, 1892, he took the hide off Joseph Taylor, congressman from Ohio, who said Kansas farmers ought "to work more and talk less." Jerry told how Taylor owned farms in Kansas but was merely a bogus farmer, exploiting the real farmers who did the real work. "On the one side we have these fat, well-fed gentlemen, and on the other, the old farmer, poor, with his ribs sticking out like the hoops of a barrel. While the fat fellows have been living on the fat of the land, on porterhouse steak and the choicest cuts, the other poor fellows haven't had a piece of meat except the dewlap of some superannuated cow for the last ten years, yet the gentleman from Ohio, and the class of farmers that he belongs to, tell the farmers to work a little harder and talk less politics and not complain and they will be all right."

His hometown *Cresset* pictured him as gloating over the assassination of Frick, a Carnegie superintendent, by the anarchist Berkman, and attacked his "red flag" policies. Actually Simpson had merely said that the attack on Frick was a symptom of the people's anger at the abuses of the Robber Barons.

One of Jerry Simpson's stunts was to get Henry George's book on free trade printed in the record. Over a million copies were sent out under free frank at a cost of 5/8 cents a copy. Congressman Johnson sent over 200,000 into Ohio alone. In Indiana, 70,000 were distributed.

Simpson blocked a bill to steal Chippewa Indian timber in Minnesota. He proposed a topographical survey of the country to promote irrigation, stating that people were still allowed to settle where they shouldn't. Nothing came of it.

In December, Jerry went to the annual Farmers' Alliance convention in Ocala in the interior of Florida on the low wooded ridge down the center of the state. Near there the Indian chief, Osceola, had once struck his hunting knife scornfully through an American treaty which drove the Indians from their homes and from the lands that now Alliance members were trying to save for themselves.

With the other delegates he was given a "festal boar barbecue," taken through the orange groves, and sailed down the St. John's. In St. Augustine, they were the guests of Senator Mallory in the luxurious Ponce de Leon Hotel where they ate better fare than some

[177]

of them had ever known. That was when Jerry Simpson compared it to the slim farmer diet in Kansas and said humorously he was going to sell his farm so he could have enough to put up at the hotel for a day. A new People's party would soon change such things; he had come here to get the Alliance to create such a new party.

But the Alliance could not be pushed into endorsing a new-party movement. At the moment, southern Alliancers were rapidly capturing the machinery of the Democratic party and feared they would lose these political gains if they left to form a new party. Jerry, fearing delay, knowing how hot the iron was in the Middle-Border states, assembled the professional third-partyites in a special separate conference in Tallahassee.

It was decided that an 1891 convention should be held to organize a new party. Jerry hurried back to Kansas to push the matter. By 1892, the new Populist party was fully launched at the July 4 Omaha convention.

In Kansas, the most exciting campaign was again in the Big Seventh, where Jerry Simpson was up for reelection. He was heartily endorsed in a convention in the towering red brick courthouse of hometown Medicine Lodge for having stood so bravely the assaults of plutocracy. "He has not bowed down to the golden image and has come out of the fiery furnace with no smell of fire upon his garments."

Into the fiery furnace he must go again. He was opposed by another "sleek" young railroad lawyer, Chester I. Long. According to the *Barber County Index,* the latter was originally Ichabod C. Long, but for political and sentimental reasons had transposed his initials so they would be the same as those of a girl with whom he was once infatuated.

Soon the voters were agog over Jerry's sensational accusation that an attempt had been made in Georgia to assassinate him. The rival *Cresset* scoffed: just a cheap stunt to get publicity, to make the hair of the public "stand on end like quills on the fretful porcupine." The public "will not believe that Jerry's death is longed for enough to lead to the spending of much money in hiring of desperados. . . . The martyr business is overdone in Kansas, and if he persists in searching for a halo he will get a horselaugh. . . . The transformation of Mr. Simpson from head clown to the wan-eyed persecuted hero is too sudden a transition for the people to stand and maintain their dignity." Besides, it was an insult to the home town. Medicine Lodge has as an intelligent and law-abiding a population as any town in Kansas. Will the assassination stunt bring investments or credit?

But the *Index* said, "Otis was mobbed at Princeton. . . . Weaver met with howling mobs in Georgia, Tom Watson faced mob after mob, . . . Jerry was threatened at Meade, . . . rotten-egged in Tennessee, thus the forces of plutocracy are gathering for the fray. Free speech, personal liberties, the rights of majorities are being assaulted on every hand. It is time for every American citizen to stop and ask, 'Where am I at?'"

The *Cresset* retorted, "Jerry's intemperate language got him into trouble. Ladies had to leave the audience." It spoke of his "indiscreet mouth and his perambulating pen." He ought to "go home to Canada." And what did the "Jim Crow crew of Third Partyites" expect down in Georgia anyway?

On the eve of the election, the Republican *Cresset* declared sensationally that the Assistant Secretary of the People's party, the chairman of the party, and a member of the Democrat State Committee had cooked up the "cheap" assassination plot merely to create sympathy for Jerry. The plan was to have Simpson waylaid, beaten and bruised. Jerry objected to being beaten up but finally agreed, if it were only a little beating. Lies, lies, replied the Populists.

The *Ashland Journal* remarked sourly: "Jerry Simpson struck politics in the dark of the moon." The *Index* retorted: "Yes, and he hit your old party so hard that you saw a million stars and had no use for a moon. You have been afflicted with strabismus ever since."

The *Cresset* charged that the Populists were utilizing the secret oath-bound Band of Gideon (a southern version of the secret Northern Order of Videttes) to undermine the ruling system. In Medicine Lodge, the Videttes were holding clandestine meetings in the attic of the mill. The paper charged that a former Populist candidate for governor was organizing an out-and-out dangerous military annex of the People's party, a secret military body to bolster armed revolution.

With such violent interchanges, Jerry's campaign meetings grew in size. Camp meetings, barbecues, and schoolhouse reunions were jammed. The folks sang "The Farmer's Wife," "Shylock," "The Blue and the Gray," and "My Boy, Keep to the Middle of the Road:"

> Alliance men, stand firmly for the right
>   Keep in the middle of the road
> Turn aside neither to the right nor the left,
>   Just keep to the middle of the road.
>
> When the big Krupp guns of the old party press
>   Shoot falsehoods, load after load,
> Just walk right along and never mind a bit,
>   Keeping in the middle of the road.

On Tuesday, September 10, Jerry campaigned at a barbecue, 7 miles northwest of Sun City. Some families came 50 miles in covered wagons. He asked all intending to vote the Populist ticket to stand up. The entire crowd, with only one exception, jumped to their feet with a cheer, and the ladies threw up their bonnets and declared they also wanted a chance to vote the Alliance ticket.

At a picnic and barbecue on September 12, although the morning was stormy and the mercury dropped 30° in 30 minutes, nearly 1,000 enthusiasts turned out with wild flowers and banners. Reverend Pinkston offered prayer. A big dinner was eaten to the sound

[180]

of music by the trained choir of Deerhead Alliance and Monument Alliance. During the recesses from the speaking, young people danced to "soul-stirring music" by veteran violinists John Dollar, his son Arthur, and other local artists, who played tirelessly all day long, — "a feast of reason and a flow of soul."

And so Jerry was sent right back into the fiery furnace with a whopping majority. Wrote one of his local supporters, "We rounded up cattle with him in days gone by when he had no socks, but we 'socked' him through Congress two years ago, and on this election night he was again with us all night."

He lost to Long in 1894, and by 1896 the great people's revolt had been sucked into the narrow sluices of Bryan's silver campaign — to pour on through and be lost. But in spite of that surrender, Jerry was up to his old form. Debating Long in Wichita, he jibed at the Republicans for resorting to the old bloody-shirt style of sectional hate campaigning — now, 35 years after the war. Millionaire Russel Alger, the lumber king, had put his private railroad car at the disposal of a whole load of doddering veterans, who were constantly losing their wooden legs or glass eyes.

"I was down at the Santa Fe depot yesterday," said Jerry, "listening to the generals making their speeches from the rear of millionaire Alger's car. One speaker, General Sickles, said that Adam was the first Populist [voice: 'Hurrah for Adam.']. God created Adam and said he was good and gave him domination over all the beasts of the field — and I suppose that included the elephant. Now, Adam *was* a good Populist. He didn't believe as we believe now in any special privileges, for he says if there is any fruit tree growing in this garden that has any good fruit on it, I want some of it, too [applause]. And so he plucked the tree of knowledge, and has been educating his child ever since."

Apparently Adam was not the best of teachers, or the education was faulty. This was Jerry's last important fling, for though fusion with the Democrats, led by Bryan on the fake silver issue in 1896, enabled Jerry to stage his brief comeback in a local Kansas election,

[181]

fusion blunted his lance and his spirit. Under the master guidance of Mark Hanna of the Great Lakes shipping family, the United States embarked on its long era of imperialism. The new era was not shaped for the sons of Adam in the Middle Border but for the Algers, the last of the great Robber Barons, combining politics and profits, war and contracts, glory and personal privilege. In the new clamor of national might and international revivalism, the voice of the free spokesmen of the plains could no longer be heard.

For a short time — about a year — he published *Simpson's Bayonet* in Kansas City, then his health failed, and the sailor of so many land-battles lurched away to a lonely lair in the Southwest, there to take up spiritualism; there to die five years later, all but forgotten. But for a while he had stood out as one of the most original, picturesque, and forceful champions of human freedom ever to sit in Congress, a star among those few truly democratic representatives, who, down the long years of the Republic, have stood their ground, firmly and faithfully, in the battle of the people for economic democracy.

[182]

IX

GREENBACK

MOSES

The turmoil of third-party politics, mirror of western discontent and farmer unrest, had been rising. Donnelly's Anti-Monopoly party and Davis' Labor Reform party had been straws in the wind. The 1872 Greeley revolt against the dull round of military office-grabbing made no great dent, but by 1876 disgust due to the Grant scandals promised closer political contests, though candidates were mostly old-style.

For President, the Republicans put up Rutherford B. Hayes of Ohio. Samuel J. Tilden, the Governor of New York who had prosecuted the thieving "Canal Ring," led the Democrats. Independent reform elements hoped that revival of suffrage in the South would weaken the Republicans and that popular hatred of federal corruption would break down old party lines. May 17, the Independent National Greenback party met in Indianapolis. Donnelly, acting as temporary chairman, called for a party "in whose judgement and whose heart the poorest man who toils in the mines of Pennsylvania or the mills of New England will outweigh . . . Jay Gould or Cornelius Vanderbilt."

The Republican party of the people against the slavocracy had died in 1866, he declared. The citadels of the dominant party were now in the cities of the East. Western farm states, for all their wartime cooperation, had received slight consideration. High war tariffs were benefiting a few privileged interests and industrialists at the expense of most of the population.

As a debtor community, the whole Middle Border was feeling acutely the pinch of deflation. "Them steers," said Solomon Chase, "while they grew well, shrank in value as fast as they grew." Low crop returns plus heavier mortgage burdens crushed the farmers. Deflation broke them. Mortgages were tripled. Add to this interest rates of 12 percent and more in the West, higher rates in the South. Backs grew bowed and faces furrowed. Only financiers and mortgage holders grazed in rich clover. The bankers, complained the farmers, collected interest on the non-taxed bonds they deposited with the government and still greater interest on the notes they then put in circulation. On this deflation issue, remarks Parrington, the Middle Border "came finally to fight its great battle, pitting its homespun experience against the authority of bankers and the teaching of the schools."

The bankers claimed that the gold standard (most of the gold was in their hands) represented stability. The anti-bullionists claimed that gold merely permitted private manipulation and thus wild price fluctuations and steady depreciation of all other values, i.e., *instability*. The Greenbackers, accepting the quantity theory of money, considered the only reliable currency to be government currency based on the national wealth, flexible in volume, steady in value, and administered in the interests of the people as a whole — in other words, a managed non-metallic currency similar to that now in existence in most of the world. It has not produced the ideal price stability demanded by westerners. But in the seventies and eighties, managed currency — in government — was heresy. Only the longhairs and the crackpots advocated it.

Long before the rise of this new currency party, pamphleteers, among them wealthy Peter Cooper, had been busy. For 35 years Banker Eleazer Lord of New York, watching the bungling and crookedness of Civil War financing and subsequent deflation, demanded a sound national currency as opposed to a wildcat gold-speculative currency. "Automatic adjustment" coin, he maintained, i.e., a currency based on monopolized gold, was a simon-pure myth. Gold should be treated like any other labor-produced price-fluctuating commodity. America had "slavishly" accepted the English standard of currency, their aristocratic definition of wealth, and their fake distinction between capital and credit — "with disastrous results."

It was much the same issue as that after the Revolutionary War. Only Rhode Island acted in behalf of the people, and it was almost excluded from the newly formed government. It was a factor in Shays's rebellion. By the time of the Greenbackers, the question again had become one of life and death. The major controversy was whether the control of currency issues, with the corresponding power of inflation and deflation, should rest in the hands of a few predatory private citizens or in those of the elected representatives of the people; whether currency should be "a hangman's noose in the hands of men who precipitated Black Friday" or whether it should "benefit the whole nation" — "class currency versus true national currency." The whole issue was promptly obscured by demagogic cries of "stability," "inflation," "dishonest repudiation," and by panaceas little connected with the vital problem involved.

The cardinal aim of the Greenback party was to have issued federal greenbacks, not private bank notes, thus depriving private banks of multiple profit-making on the nation's own money. Put a sufficient quantity of people's money into circulation, the party insisted, and prices would increase, debts would be reduced to normal. They wanted no further issue of gold bonds, making them "hewers of wood and drawers of water" to foreign interests. Nor were more government bonds to be sold for the purchase of gold, cried the Greenbackers. United States notes, bearing interest

[185]

not exceeding one cent per $100, should replace gold bonds and become part of the circulating medium. Thomas Jefferson was quoted: "bank paper must be suppressed, and the circulation restored to the nation, to whom it belongs."

The most ardent spokesman for the "British gold idea" was David A. Wells, Commissioner of the Revenue Bureau, an able reactionary economist. Wells largely suppled the ammunition for Edwin Lawrence Godkin of the *Nation* and for Charles A. Dana of the *New York Sun*, who had become "a cynical and star spokesman for the venal habits of the Gilded Age."

Outstanding currency "expansionists" were the brilliant economist, Henry C. Carey, Wendell Phillips, ironmonger Thaddeus Stevens, and the slippery demagogue, General Ben Butler. Vernon L. Parrington in his *Main Currents in American Thought* finds the best of the argument on the side of the currency reformers. Wells's neat logic of a laissez-faire gold standard and private issue of bank notes, was "out of date on the day . . . penned. . . . The needs of business had outgrown the bullion theory . . . credit was taking the place of metallic currency," and, he added prophetically, "the fiction of a gold standard would be adhered to till another seismic dislocation proved its utter inadequacy to a world in confusion, and it would be unofficially abandoned" — what happened under Roosevelt II. In the meantime, the "selfish and narrow policy" of a right gold theory of false laissez-faire, buttressed by private banker monopoly, prevailed in America all through post-Civil War days, bringing distress to the country and hardship to the Middle Border.

The self-appointed delegates to the Indianapolis Greenback convention nominated for President the aged millionaire philanthropist and currency reformer, Peter Cooper, founder of Cooper Union, "the patriarch of Broadway." Cooper was at the opposite pole from Gould, though both were wealthy. Gould was a financial pirate; Cooper, a thoroughgoing humanitarian, a cultured man, a fine thinker, and a creative spirit. At his own expense, he circulated "more than a million of documents," and in his ninety-second year, in his *Ideas for a Science of Good Government*, he could still write, "I have always been, am and ever shall be with the poor toilers and producers. Therefore, I desire Congress to legislate for the poor as well as for the rich who can take care of themselves."

Aged Peter Cooper conducted no effective speaking campaign, and his name made little dent in the bitter, unimportant controversies of the Tilden-Hayes campaign, with its ensuing scandals over bribery, election frauds, and the buying up of entire states by both major parties. In such a nasty dust storm, only grit got into the honest flour of sturdy Peter Cooper. He received few votes.

The next few years were an uphill struggle for the new party. One Greenbacker complained: "There is no money to pay the ordinary and necessary expenses of a campaign. There is no press to advocate organization, to lead public opinion; and the whole army of anti-monopolists . . . is . . . at sea" — and apparently not knowing where to head in for a landing and a fight.

But conditions in the country were bad, and many a local grievance channeled into the new party. In Montgomery, Alabama, a Greenback convention denounced the use of convict labor in private enterprise. The Austin, Texas, convention, with forty delegates, eight or ten of whom were Negroes, put out a platform like that of the early Grange and the later Populist Party, denouncing the old parties for ignoring the principle of the rights of all, "irrespective of state, riches, poverty, race, color or creed." The old parties "encouraged sectionalism, favored monopoly, and carried on a financial system so radically wrong as to pauperize the masses to support a chosen few in idleness and luxury." Besides a "national greenback," the new party wanted property to be taxed equally, a graduated income tax, more efficient criminal procedure, and honesty and economy in the administration of public affairs. Universal manhood suffrage without property restrictions was called for. Better public schools were demanded. There was to be no more squandering of the public domain upon private corporations, and the contract system of Oriental labor, in competition with honest labor, was to be abolished. These principles, which have become the law of a good part of the land, brought down upon the heads of the reformers an avalanche of abuse.

An Iowa party, first organized in the low-yield corn year of 1876, showed strength in frontier drouth counties. In 1878, when the price of corn was only eight cents, the state platform declared that the "public lands are the common property of the whole people and should not be sold to speculators nor granted to railroads or other corporations but should be donated to actual settlers."

In the seventies and eighties, said Cyrenus Cole in his *People of Iowa*, barbed wire "worked a revolution in farming." Previously, grain-growing and cattle-raising were the dominant activities. But soon cattle had to be kept in pastures and fattened on corn in feed lots. Prairies "that had simmered under the summer suns and had glistened in coats of snow began to be dotted with homesteads and with groves." But it brought little prosperity.

Grain-growing soon got another setback — the chinch bug. "The farmer thought it was one of the plagues of ancient Egypt, but it was more likely a warning that they had cropped their soil to the point of exhaustion. . . . The result was soil so weak in Nitrogen that the plants no longer had strength to resist the ravages of these insects." Production fell from sixty bushels an acre to twenty. "Prosperous fields of green would in a few days look as if they had been scorched by an invisible fire. When there was no wheat to devour, the insects attacked green corn, and they invaded even the homes of the people. What had been the land of hope became the land of despair."

The answer was political revolt. "There was groaning enough those years." Cole relates, "something was wrong in the world . . . politicians came forward with platforms and promises and nostrums. . . . The millenium was in their mouths. There was anti-railroad and anti-monopoly talk, but the men who believed in greenbacks were the most profuse in their promises. Make more money and there will be more prosperity."

[188]

In the nation at large, the off-year elections rolled up a million Greenback votes. Though in Iowa they received only 43,439 votes, a mere 15 percent of the total, they elected 2 state senators, 5 assemblymen, and a number of congressmen. Among the congressmen elected was General James Baird Weaver—"Jumping Jim," sent "to enact the millenium." Edison H. Gillette, another Greenback revolter, they called "Heifer Calf," because he had wept before an audience while telling the tale of a calf that was worth no more than a few farthings. Another of the prophets they stoned with the opprobrious name of "Calamity," although his real name was L.H. Weller.

Amid the rising tide of protest, the Republicans in 1880 nominated for President James A. Garfield of Ohio; the Democrats, Winfield S. Hancock of Pennsylvania. In Cleveland, Ohio, a wealthy gentleman, Mark Hanna, promptly organized the Business Men's Marching Club to parade for Garfield — with silk hats. The idea took hold all over the country. It was quite a sight, in smaller communities, to see the local nabobs, who never before had dared face ridicule with such headgear, marching down the streets in high silk hats to the racket of bands and popping anvils. It was class alignment with a vengeance, but it tickled yokel folklore instincts.

That year Jay Gould, siphoning income out of branch lines, milked the Union Pacific of a cool $10,000,000. But over 33 percent of North Carolina farmers had become tenants, and it was to rise to 60 percent.

In June, the Greenback party again celebrated its national convention in Indianapolis. The active support of James R. Sovereign, Grand Master of the now powerful Knights of Labor, was obtained. Labor should be protected by law, given a legal eight-hour day, be paid not in company script but in cash, and be safe-guarded by proper sanitary conditions and factory inspection. No convict or child labor should be allowed. A national bureau of statistics should be established. The Burlingame Treaty admitting Chinese should be abrogated. Railroad land grants should be forfeited for non-

[189]

fulfillment of terms and the acreage restored to the public domain. Interstate commerce should be regulated. Taking a stand against "gigantic corporations and monopolies," the party condemned cruel class legislation that favored money lenders above those who risked their lives. The party opposed any increase in the standing army in time of peace and denounced "the insidious scheme to establish an enormous military power under the guise of military laws." No more sectional strife, no war on class, only against institutions. Government of, by, for, the people instead of government of, by, for the bondholder.

For its Presidential candidate, the delegates chose the Greenback congressman from Iowa, James Baird Weaver, Civil War veteran, and for Vice-President, B.J. Chambers, a prominent Granger and author from Texas.

The congressman was an erect soldierly man, with a parted heavy white moustache (at times he wore a Mosaic beard) wholly covering his mouth. He had the stern look of a commander. Matthew Josephson, in *The Politicos,* calls him "an ardent Abolitionist, a Radical Republican, a war hero. Though he might safely have climbed the ladder of the great war party, his earnest nature had disposed him first to independence, then to desertion of the Republican 'church' and the embrace of an agrarian radicalism that brought down the fiercest condemnation on his head. He was no violent Jacobin and of course no 'anarchist' as the Eastern press insisted, but rather a rigid Middle Western Puritan" given to florid oratory.

He was born on the frontier, at Dayton, Ohio, on June 12, 1833 the fifth of thirteen children. His English-German father was a skilled mechanic, millwright, and farmer. His Scotch mother was the daughter of Captain Joseph Imlay of the Revolutionary Army. Among Weaver's ancestors was Betsy Ross of flag fame. A grandfather had commanded a fort in Ohio and fought Indians.

When James was only two, the family moved to a Michigan forest farm, 9 miles from Cassopolis. In 1842, when he was nine, they moved to the territory of Iowa, reaching the Keosaqua River in October. They wintered in an unfurnished frame house opposite Ely's Ford on the east side of the Des Moines River.

A treaty with the Sac and Fox Indians barred white settlers west of Van Buren County prior to May 1, 1843, but as a hunter James's father went on in and selected a location to be proved up as soon as lawfully possible.

And so, at 3:00 P.M. on May 1, Abram Weaver — his entire family and household goods perched on a wagon drawn by two horses, chicken coops fastened to the rear, cow behind, trusty rifle in hand, and a watch dog to sound the alarm at night — set out to take up a quarter section of virgin soil on Chequest Creek, four miles north of where Bloomfield, the county seat of Davis County, now stands and near the present village of Belknap.

They lived in a bark shanty on the creek bank until a log cabin could be built. The roof clapboards were riven with an old-fashioned adze; the floor was of green logs, split, smoothly hewn, and brought to a straight edge — a "puncheon" floor.

Ground was at once broken for seed corn, potatoes, and vegetables. The nearby Sacs, Fox, and Pottawattamie Indians were "very friendly and. . . . visited our home more or less every day until the spring of 1844 when they mostly disappeared, vamoosing toward the west." Weaver played with the fleet-footed Indian boys. called "skinaways." They could climb "like squirrels and skip like fawns" and were expert with bow and arrow.

Two years later, a log schoolhouse was put up on nearby White Oak Ridge. There, on the homely benches beside a wide fireplace, beneath a greased paper window, James learned to spell from a book a Bloomfield merchant had given him in exchange for a coonskin. Frequently, as James passed over the Indian trail to school, he encounted wolves, so "neither red haws, ripe plums, hickory, hazel or walnuts could tempt children to loiter. The wolf should have due credit for his contribution to pioneer scholarship."

His mother wove jeans; his father purchased leather to make

boots and shoes; their mittens were knitted from homespun yarns. As Weaver described it: "Mother's loom and father's handicraft had been busy preparing for the approaching winter." Nature's storehouse was still full and free. Deer, wild pigeons, prairie chickens, and wild turkeys abounded. It was a busy life, demanding foresight, but every necessity of life was piled right at their doors. The south side of the cabin was always covered in winter with coon skins, wolf and deer hides, tacked up to dry — these were legal tender at the store.

At night, snug in their cabin, snow piled up outside, James's father played the flute. When the pioneer preacher was about, he joined in vocally. "How those early saddle-bag preachers could sing!" exclaimed Weaver — "charming days, when we were all close to Nature's throbbing heart."

In fall and winter, his father built houses for neighbors, made furniture, cut hoop-poles, and made staves and barrels. He was elected district court clerk, and the family moved to town. He secured the mail contract between Bloomfield and Fairfield, and young James, then fourteen, was yanked out of school and put to toting the mail on horseback. Often he had to swim icy swollen streams, frequently had to fight other boys. When winter blizzards arrived, his route was difficult and dangerous. He kept on studying as best he could by himself at night, often so weary he could hardly keep his eyes open.

There were numerous Texas War veterans in the district, and their stories excited young James and made him fret to go adventuring. In '48, news of the gold discovery at Sutter's Mill in California thrilled everybody. James caught the fever, but his parents dissuaded him from joining the rush. Disgusted, he kept on carrying the mail, considered it "too prosaic." After 1851, when he was eighteen, he attended three terms of school and the following year studied law.

His brother-in-law, Dr. Phelps, returned from California by sea to New York, with a snug quantity of gold. Phelps invested in cattle and prepared to drive them overland to California, along with fifty steers tamed to the yoke. James gave up his law study and hired out as helper.

They left in March, 1853, following bad roads and crossing swollen streams, reaching the Missouri by the middle of April. They plunged into the wilderness, where they killed antelope for food, shot wolves and cougars. A sandstorm that lasted two hours and forty minutes gave them trouble. In the Green River country of Utah, hostile Indians alarmed them. But on August 15, after six months of such travail, they arrived safely in Sacramento, California.

After the cattle had been sold, Weaver mined a bit and shortly embarked for New York via Panama on the "John L. Stevens," with $2,500 belted around him in $50.00 octagon gold slugs. His party fought off bandits in the Panama jungles.

On his return he clerked at Bonaparte, Iowa, then, in 1855, entered the Cincinnati Law School, where he studied under Bellamy Storer. His diploma was signed by Rutherford B. Hayes.

He married Miss Clara Vinson of St. Mary's, Ohio, a teacher at Keosaqua, whom he had met while clerking and had courted by crossing on the ice over the Des Moines River. Borrowing $100 at 33 1/3 percent interest, Weaver set himself up to practice law at Bloomfield.

Exciting times were at hand. The repeal of the Missouri Compromise had aroused all Iowa. The southern half was pro-slavery, but Free Soil candidate, James W. Grimes, won the gubernatorial election. Weaver, then a Democrat, debated in schoolhouses, arguing that if slavery were interfered with the Union would be endangered. But the arguments of his opponents, plus his reading of the *New York Tribune* and *Uncle Tom's Cabin,* converted Weaver to the anti-slavery cause, and in the next election he stumped for anti-slavery candidates. He was forceful and eloquent. When he spoke in the old courthouse at Keosaqua, a circuit court judge was so "tickled" he went home and "kicked a solid walnut table to pieces" out of pure joy.

During one debate, said Weaver, "the crowd broke into a frenzy that resembled the sweep of a cyclone through a forest. Men grew pale and clenched each other in frenzy . . . The moral sense of the multitude had been reached."

In 1860, Weaver was elected to the Republican state convention at Des Moines and went on with the Iowa delegation to Chicago, where he helped nominate Abe Lincoln.

In the ensuing campaign, Weaver enlisted Preacher McKinney to tour with him. McKinney had been lashed in Texas for addressing the Negroes and had returned with his shirt torn to shreds. "I recounted the outrage on McKinney," said Weaver, describing his own platform tricks, "and waved . . . [the ragged shirt] before the crowds and bellowed, 'Under this bloody shirt we propose to march to victory.' I was a very young man in those days."

Weaver claimed he had invented this stock Republican campaign trick of waving a bloody shirt before the crowds to discredit the pro-slavery Democrats, a trick used to befuddle northern voters up to the time of the Spanish-American War. In many a later campaign, Weaver writhed at the misuse of this demagogy.

When the Civil War came, Weaver enlisted and became a lieutenant. The farmers hauled the warriors to the nearest railroad station, 35 miles from Bloomfield. In St. Louis, sickness hit so badly only 400 men out of the entire regiment were fit for duty. Set to guard McDowell College, the outfit fell into disgrace for looting the museum. But they played a brave part in the capture of Fort Donnelson, Tennessee, an engagement that elevated Weaver to major. After the battle of Corinth, the regiment went into winter quarters at Pulaski, where the Ku Klux Klan was later born. Weaver, a colonel, was commanding officer.

A stern disciplinarian, he punished any improper deed of his men against the civilians, but superior orders obliged him to levy $2,000 on the wealthier citizens for the support of southern refugees. Later, when running for office, although he produced affidavits from Pulaski citizens attesting to his excellent conduct there, he was repeatedly accused of looting and worse atrocities. The southern Democrats had their own "bloody shirt" for campaigns.

Colonel Weaver's last war campaign was Sherman's march to the Sea; he entered Savannah in triumph. He was mustered out on March 27, 1864, and a year later received a commission as brigadier general. Along the Iowa frontier, lawless copperheads (those opposed to the war), draft evaders, and deserters had formed the Knights of the Golden Circle. Weaver headed an expedition against them that restored order in the state.

In 1866, at the age of thirty-three, he was almost nominated for the lieutenant governorship and, the following year, was elected district attorney for six counties. But instead, he accepted an appointment by President Johnson as internal revenue assessor, a post he held for six years.

Weaver had become a very earnest man, a devout Methodist churchgoer, and a fanatical prohibitionist. The Methodists were up to the hilt in politics and were powerful, but their influence was also fiercely fought, and this opposition cost Weaver the Republican nomination for Congress in 1874. The saloon element and their henchmen controlled the convention. He then bid for the Republican nomination for governor on an anti-saloon platform, plus public control of railroads. Repeatedly he declared, there is "one thing I intend to live and die by — I am a prohibitionist."

The *Bloomfield Democrat* announced he had stated that "the time has come for American civilization to assert itself against European dictatorship" — which implied that the saloon elements were backed by foreign immigrants. "This means that a foreign-born citizen has no right to drink a glass of beer against the protests of a native American cold-waterite. The General may yet have to regret this enunciation of Know-Nothing sentiments."

But he had a majority of the delegates at the Des Moines opera house in his pocket. However, at the last moment railroad henchmen, the saloon elements, and the party ring pulled the unwilling ex-Governor Samuel J. Kirkwood, a pro-liquor and corporation man,

[195]

out of his bed and rushed him before the convention and stampeded it.

Weaver was consoled by being given a nomination for the state senate, but he was knifed by "the Ring" in his own party and was the only candidate on the ticket not elected.

Dissatisfied with the whole Republican outlook, particularly on the currency issue, he denounced the new Resumption of Specie Payments Act as causing fearful and rapid contraction of currency already barely adequate for business — "a crime against Providence and the common sense of the age . . . [a scheme] of the eastern gold jobbers of both parties, to bring the West to their feet as suppliants when the crash shall come." It came.

In 1877, he became a candidate on a fusion Greenback-Democratic ticket and was sent to Congress, along with "Heifer Calf" Gillette and "Calamity" Weller.

He was a big man, with a broad forehead, large calm eyes, and huge flowing beard. The new Moses spoke to Congress soon after his arrival in Washington, and throughout the sessions his sonorous and powerful voice rolled repeatedly against the marble columns.

On May 29, 1879, speaking against "worthless money, depreciated money," he declared that the people should have "cheap money and dear property. . . . Property is held by the many and money by the few. Money today is master and king in America and property goes begging" — a conspiracy of the moneyed interests against the people. The private banks could "bear" or "bull" the market as they desired and thus control the value of every day's labor and of every product in the country. The Treasury itself speculated with gold to enrich the banker clique. In 1875, the Treasury "sold at public auction over forty million dollars of gold, then . . . immediately turned around and under the Resumption Act sold bonds to buy gold back again [laughter and applause]." In all it had sold $433,000,000 worth of gold in this scheme to increase the bonded debt.

"Our people out West," he charged, "do not like . . . the contrast that exists between the inflation mortgages on their farms and the resumption hogs they are forced to sell . . . let us act as representatives of the whole people, and not as politicians, nor for the rings and cliques of the country."

He came out against further Republican bayonet elections in the South and introduced the Weaver Soldier Bill to correct the injustice of the soldiers being paid "in depreciated currency while bondholders were being paid in gold." He poked fun at an angry colleague from New York who, he said, shook "his little fist in my innocent face . . . The gentleman goes into hysterics every time he mentions the soldiers' bill." It failed, of course.

In 1880, he sought to introduce two currency resolutions, but the Speaker refused to recognize him. Every day for thirteen long weeks Weaver doggedly sought recognition. The newspapers railed at his "aggravating persistence," and on March 6, *Harper's Weekly* cartooned him "as a donkey, braying to the utter consternation of the House." The members have their hands over their ears or are crawling under their desks. The mace is blown violently from the hands of the sergeant at arms. Weaver called the attention of the House to the cartoon.

Mr. Garfield: "Which figure represents the Congressman from Iowa?"

Weaver: "The large figure with the long ears, of course, represents me. You know the ass in the Bible saw the angel before Balaam, the rider, saw him [laughter]."

Not until April did the Speaker finally recognize Weaver, who declared that during the Civil War, gold, silver, and the Shylocks of the country had failed the government in the hour of trial, making legal tender paper necessary. "It was the fiat of the government to save the national life; and that same fiat is doubly necessary today to save the liberties of the people. . . . The issue is between the corporations and the people." The corporations had become "legal Goliaths," and the people must "put hooks into the jaws of these Leviathans and control them." The tendency toward the concentration of wealth must be struck down.

On May 10, he spoke on the public debt, "not a plant of American

[197]

growth, but . . . borrowed from the effete aristocracies and monarchies of the Old World." To pay it off he proposed to use the silver in the Treasury, operate the mints to full capacity coining silver, and put an income tax on bank notes.

Wrathfully, he read into the *Congressional Record* an article by "a man who claims to be a Christian," a man in control of one of "the great periodicals [*Scribner's*]."

It said: "We cannot do what the French government once did under similar circumstances, banish fifty thousand of them [tramps] to colonial or penal servitude: and it is a great pity we cannot . . . The tramp . . . has no more rights than a sow that wallowed in the gutter or the lost dogs that hover around city squares. He is no more to be consulted in his wishes or his will what is to be done with him, than the bullock in the corral. . . ." Weaver bitterly condemned the men and conditions that had brought about the forced poverty.

At the June 5, 1880, national Greenback convention in Chicago, he was nominated for the Presidency with three cheers and a tiger. Eight hundred and thirty delegates, 44 of them from the Socialist Labor party, were present from 36 states. In his acceptance speech, delivered in Bloomfield, July 3, Weaver recalled once more that the bond-holders had been and were being paid in gold, the soldier in greenbacks. The soldiers were now taxed to pay bonds, while bond-holders were tax-exempt. He proposed an adequate circulating medium and rapid payment of the national debt. The producer and consumer should be brought together. He promised to regulate interstate commerce and transportation. An area of public domain larger than the territory occupied by the great German empire had been wantonly donated to wealthy corporations. He proposed its recovery.

He hoped to banish sectionalism and unite the people. Only issues, not parties or men, interested him. It required "ten or fifteen years to develop the leaders of a great party, and fully as long to shake them loose again. . . . [and never except] by a movement from without that crushes the organization over which they dominate. . . . The Lord is raising up that party now. The workmen are all at work in the quarries, and every block in the temple shall be at peace. . . ."

In Congress and during the campaign, he attacked the hard-money men of both parties. The hard-money Republican Moses of 1880 would "die on Mount Nebo." The new Democratic Moses, "if he represents sectional strife and the financial views which are now starving the people of this country, will perish also without realizing his exalted hope; but not because he struck the rock from which the water was to issue, but because he and his friends have joined hands across this aisle with the hard-money men on the Republican side of the House to dry up the fountains of prosperity of the people."

If such injustice continued, the people would thirst for the wine of violence. The danger was not from the defeated Confederacy but from the uneasy masses out of employment, without food, and destitute of raiment. "Sir, I want it distinctly understood that cotton is no longer king in this country, nor is gold, but the laboring man; the industrial classes are sovereign and their behests must be obeyed and be obeyed speedily."

Charged with accepting money from the Republicans, he admitted accepting contributions from Republican silver advocates and $800 from Democratic Senator John P. Jones, but he had paid all his own personal campaign expenses — $1,695 — out of his own pocket. This was no fusion campaign, he insisted, but an out-and-out fight "against the Democratic and Republican wings of the Money Power." He spoke to 1,000,000 people in 16 states, but the party vote was smaller than 2 years before, and in his home state of Iowa he received only 32,701 votes.

But he did not let up. In June, 1881, he went on a speaking tour of New England. In July and August, he delivered 26 speeches in Kansas — "in the midst of drouth and hot winds, with the mercury from 104 to 110 degrees in the shade." But he was greeted by audiences of from 3,000 to 5,000.

In 1882, he was defeated for reelection to Congress, but in 1884, a new fusion arrangement sent him back.

His program, all through the Cleveland administration, remained the same. On December 21, 1885, he introduced his bill to create a Department of Labor. In 1886, a strike tied up 6,000 miles of railroads in the Southwest, mostly the Gould system. Weaver defended the strikes: "If this Congress will not protect labor, it must protect itself."

Since 1881, he had been proposing direct election of United States senators and, in December, 1885, introduced a resolution to that end. It was deemed a dangerous revolution. In Woodrow Wilson's day it was still "revolutionary."

In February, 1886, he delivered his longest speech: "The Conspiracy and the Reaction." "The Conspiracy" was that which gave control of the currency to private national banks.

1) *1867.* Congress prevented the repayment of the debt in the "currency of contract" and substituted gold payments for greenback payment on bonds obtained with greenbacks.

2) *1873.* Silver was demonetized — by stealth. "The Crime of '73."

3) *1875.* Specie payment was resumed, thus "non-interest bearing currency" was converted into "interest bearing debt." This had filled the country with "wrecked fortunes, suicides, helpless poverty, broken hearts, and big fortunes."

4) *1876.* The first sign of protest by a group of patriotic men, led by the venerable Peter Cooper.

5) *1878.* The Bland Act, allowing for the purchase of a limited amount of silver, was the "first blood for the people," but another law led to the further destruction of the greenbacks as currency.

6) *1884.* "The people took hold of Uncle Sam's wagon,

[200]

lifted it out of its old ruts and out of the mire, unhitched the old team, hooked on a fresh one and changed drivers. Why return to the miserable old ruts from which with great difficulty we have been extricated?"

On January 18, 1887, he spoke in behalf of the Reagan Interstate Commerce Act. It was "weak and hazy, but so were the Ten Commandments."

He attacked the project to build a federal fort in Chicago on land donated by wealthy citizens who feared the labor movement. "If . . . the gentlemen donating the land have more than they need, then let them build homes upon it and donate it to the poor around the streets of Chicago . . . [and they] will have less use for military encampments there." In the name of the laboring men of this country, do not pass legislation for "overawing the people by military establishments." Let Congress undo the legislation which had brought about discontent. It was the greed of the rich, not the dissension of the poor, that Congress should dread.

He supported the Mills Bill to lower the tariff. To claim that labor was benefiting from protection, he declared, was "a fraud and a pretense . . . our tariff laws pour a golden stream into the pockets of the manufacturers, but it never returns to bless and enrich the children of toil." Hotly, he attacked the lumber and barbed wire trusts.

E.H. Funston of Kansas shouted back at him: "He came down into my district last fall and made a canvass there. The people of Kansas have learned by experience that whenever there is a drought, in the Rocky Mountains we get grasshoppers, and whenever there is a failure of crops in Iowa, we get cranks."

But Weaver continued to hammer away. He repeatedly denounced the big railroad grants. The Free Soil (Republican) party had had a land program, but after it became the party in power, it had turned around and granted the public domain to the corpora-

[201]

tions and private speculators. He mentioned the rape of the coal lands and the denial of public access to water. Constantly, he pointed out that two-thirds of America's farms were already mortgaged.

In 1888, Weaver orated grandiosely in favor of building the Nicaragua canal; it would destroy railroad monopoly. The bill, which favored privileged speculators, was finally approved February 20, 1889.

Weaver also persistently sought the opening up of the Indian territory to white settlers. In the Cherokee strip, six million acres were leased by the Indians to whites, who then subleased it at a net profit of nearly half a million dollars. The land was not used by the Indians but was already in the hands of speculating cattle companies. He named them. It was a question not of protecting the Indians, but of honest homeseekers versus rich cattlemen. Not to open that beautiful region to settlement was "to perpetuate a mongrel race far removed from the influence of civilized people — a refuge for outlaws and indolent whites, blacks, and Mexicans."

Like most land reformers of his day, he thought it improper for railroads and cattlemen to steal the public domain, but it was quite all right for the settlers to steal lands from the Indians or Mexicans and eject them from their homes! By solemn treaty, signed in Medicine Lodge, Kansas, a few years earlier, the Indian Territory had been ceded as a perpetual home for the Indians, provided they would abandon Kansas. Weaver helped tear up that treaty.

There had been schemes to take forcible possession. David L. Payne, leader of "the boomers," had repeatedly entered the Territory with various armed groups and as many times had been arrested and expelled. With every lawless expedition, the number of his followers increased. After Payne's death in 1884, the raids were continued by W.L. Couch and other lieutenants. President Cleveland removed such intruders several times a year until 1887. But powerful land-grabbers and congressmen were behind these filibusters, and the suits against Couch and others were dropped.

Weaver was closely linked with them. Repeatedly, he was

accused of being their paid attorney, but he always insisted he had never received a penny of remuneration.

In 1889, he led the House filibuster that forced the passage of the Oklahoma Settlers Bill, and, by Presidential proclamation, the lands were opened April 22, 1889 — the "First Run." Many speculators tried to beat the gun, and several weeks before the important day, troops of the Fifth United States Cavalry arrived at Oklahoma City to make it hot for unlawful boomers. "Beating the brush and scouring the woods, they gathered quite a body and drove them before them to the Kansas line, burning huts, tearing down tents and dugouts," the *Barber County Index* recounted.

At Kiowa, in Barber County, Kansas, and at other border points, a vast crowd of adventurers, boomers, and homesteaders congregated. Fifty thousand claimants strained at the leash to make a grab for only 5,000, or less, worthwhile claims; hundreds of Congressmen, federal officials, favorites, railroad men, and others were on the scene well ahead of time. Also, the better-heeled could come in quickly by train, as some 6,000 or 7,000 did, a number larger than all the available sites of any value. These deluxe travelers were able to seize nearly all the best homesteads and townsites before the border racers could get near. The poorer overland wagon "boomers" were so incensed that only the proximity of troops prevented them from burning the railroad trestles.

It would not have been a fair race even if all had been aboveboard. Only the fleet, the strong, and the violent criminals, not the best farmers or most worthy citizens, would have won. But the cunning and the political favorites had already beaten even the strong and the fleet. Thus, the great opening represented the gullible trait of Americans to gamble recklessly on games wholly fixed beforehand by surefire cheaters. There was nothing just or orderly or scientific in the procedure.

But despite such marked cards, the gullible were on hand in swarms. Portable houses were mounted on wheels; picturesque covered wagons stretched for miles in unbroken line; buggies, springboards, gigs, every type of two- and four-wheeled contraption was straining at the leash. Men on horseback impatiently wheeled their horses to be ready at the precise moment. At a blast of an army bugle, precisely at noon on a beautiful spring day, the rush began.

General Weaver, for a long time closely associated with Couch, was well ahead of the rush. Enjoying official privilege, it was charged, he came down to the Oklahoma station long before the opening day to warn interlopers to get out. Then, on the Friday preceding the opening day (according to the not-always truthful *Medicine Lodge Cresset*), he returned "with a crowd of favorites," whom he had had deputized as United States marshals, to keep people from the town sites until the proper moment. But, exploded the *Cresset*, these supposed marshals were really boomers who had previously violated the law and used this expedient to get in on the ground floor to grab the best sites. Among those who came in ahead of time, with Weaver's assistance, was the indefatigable Couch.

A few weeks before the opening, some stragglers, according to the *Cresset*, discovered a shingle on a site adjoining future Oklahoma City:

> J.B. Weaver of Creston, Iowa, wishes
> to claim this quarter section whenever
> he may lawfully do so.

Many disorders resulted. Claim jumpers either were killed or themselves killed. The unsuccessful had to crowd into the new settlements, where vice, violence, and crime flourished. In 90 days Guthrie grew from a jack-rabbit hole to a city of 10,000 inhabitants, where prayer meetings and gambling houses, churches, dancehalls, and whorehouses worked overtime.

At Oklahoma City, the first comers held a meeting on the open prairie, with a large drygoods box for a platform, to organize the city administration and deal with encroachments. The meeting had no legal status, for no provision had as yet been made for governing the new territory. Weaver served as vigilante chairman. Captain Couch, who had so often defied the government, was named mayor, and a federal officer administered the illegal oath. Thus, order was imposed by the swift, the cunning, the greedy, the demagogues, and by the super-idealistic Weaver.

Weaver had been able to spend only two weeks on his 1888 reelection campaign — again on a fusion ticket with the Democrats. Shortly before the election day, British Minister Sackville-West sent out a stupid letter advising all naturalized Englishmen to vote Democratic. This produced a nationwide storm of protest and hurt the Democrats badly.

Weaver debated his Republican opponent, Major John T. Lacy, from an open-air portico. In front of him birds playfully fluttered against each other. General Weaver threw his arms heavenward. "The very birds in the air bring happy omens of our victory."

Lacy cried out, "Beware of them, General! They are English sparrows."

The bird story convulsed the whole state, and though Weaver called Lacy "the dapper little corporation attorney," the latter walked away with the election.

The bickering Greenback party disintegrated. Weaver himself was read out of the quarrelsome clan because of his insistence on prohibition and on Democratic fusion. Fusion, cried a delegate to the final party convention in Iowa, would make our "rag baby" a political orphan. Actually, it was already a corpse. Weaver was one orphan with no political heaven.

The Farmers' Alliance was arousing Iowa. A branch of the Northern Alliance, organized as early as 1880, had spread over the state. Although it remained strictly nonpartisan, it had come under the control of the richer Republican farmers in the eastern corn, hog, and dairy counties. The Southern Alliance, more militant for reform, reached the grass roots, and it was preparing to resort to political action. Weaver and J.R. Sovereign, Grand Master of the Knights of Labor, spent most of 1891 in introducing the rival southern organization into Iowa.

The greatest farmer discontent was in the western drouth section of the state, still devoted chiefly to wheat, rather than to the new dairying and intensive crops, and there the Alliance began electing candidates.

Weaver rallied 74 farm and labor leaders to a "people's independent convention" at Des Moines on June 3. From 60 counties, 425 delegates showed up and adopted the name, the People's Party of the State of Iowa.

With the aroused farmers at his back, Weaver proposed to create a powerful third party with a militant program. In November, 1891, he spoke at the national Indianapolis convention of the Southern Farmers' Alliance and was present at the famous Reform Conference in Chicago in January, 1892, which, according to Frances E. Willard, the Prohibitionist, proposed to form a union of all the reform elements of the country. It sent delegates to the famous "Populist" St. Louis convention of February 22, 1892.

However, there Weaver counseled delay in launching a new national third party until more states were organized and all independent forces of the country were ready to combine. But enthusiasm mounted, and a Kansas cabal, controlled by the mystrious Videttes, stampeded the assemblage. The Peoples' Party of America was born. A nominating convention was called for Omaha, Nebraska, July 4, 1892.

Here converged all the discontent of three decades into a great third-party uprising — all the varied movements that had sprung into being due to carpetbaggery, Gilded Age corruption, land steals, the ruthlessness of the Robber Barons, the grasshopper plagues, the drouths, the loss of farms, the railroad abuses, the currency juggling. Here converged Greenbackers, Anti-Monopolists, Union Laborites, the Knights of Labor, Prohibitionists, suffragettes, Bellamy Nationalists, single taxers, Socialist Laborites, Grangers, silverites, bimetallists, Alliancers — dozens of groups. There, in the great flag-draped Coliseum with its 9,000 seats, 1,776 delegates — a symbolic number — came cheering with banners.

There came the picturesque politician and author, Ignatius Donnelly of Minnesota, who brought forth delirious cheers every time he appeared on the platform; Hamlin Garland, writer and single taxer; Terrence Powderly, America's outstanding labor leader, a scholarly looking man with a pince-nez; Cyclone Davis of Texas, America's greatest orator; A.J. Streeter, former Alliance head and Union Labor candidate for President; Mrs. Clara B. Colby, Vice-President of the Women's National Press Association; tall, willowy Fanny Vickery of Kansas; Anna L. Diggs, the indefatigable Prohibitionist and reformer of Colorado and Kansas; Van Wyck of Nebraska, who, as Republican congressman and senator, had uncovered Civil War corruption and the Grant whiskey steals; Young Milo Reno of Iowa, slim and dark and all his life addicted to fist-fights, fiddling, and dancing, who had stumped for the Granges at the age of ten and was still denouncing the villains of high finance during the post-World War I deflation and plight of the farmers and was to become editor of Henry Agard Wallace's paper, *Wallace's Farmer;* Dr. C. W. Macune, President of the Farmers' Alliance, author of the famous Sub-Treasury Plan for crop storage and government loans; Mary Ellen Lease, the great Kansas female orator; pretty Eva Valesh of Minnesota; Senator Steward of Nevada, a silverite; Betty Gray, who owned a large Texas plantation; Mr. Jaxon, a halfbreed, French-Canadian, who had helped lead the armed Riel land rebellion; Dr. Hauser of Indiana, author of *Is Marriage a Failure?*

It was a blistering hot day, men sat in shirt-sleeves, women in summer dresses. They raised the roof singing: "Good-bye, old party, good-bye;" "Taught to bow to money rule, it made of me a doggone fool." Exactly at 3:00 P.M., Chairman Henry Loucks of South Dakota emerged painfully from the wings on one leg and a crutch and called the gathering to order.

[207]

The opening speech was delivered by Tom Crator of California, a big man with a ringing voice. "We meet in the midst of a nation brought to the verge of moral, political and material ruin." Newspapers were largely subsidized or muzzled, business was prostrate, homes covered with mortgages, labor impoverished, land concentrated in a few hands. "A vast conspiracy against mankind has sacrificed our homes, lives and children on the altar of Mammon."

The rafters shook with a roar of applause from 10,000 people, and the delegates really went wild over the platform, largely written by Ignatius Donnelly, which boiled down to the idea that wealth belonged to the people who produced it. In the shouting melee, with straw hats sailing in the air, snow-haired, 6-foot Captain Lloyd led the swirling contingent playing Yankee Doodle on his flute. He was hugged by Fanny Vickery and hoisted on stalwart shoulders. A fife and drum corps struck up "Dixie," and a band played "America." On top of a human pyramid, an old Negro wept with clasped hands. A girl danced on the platform, women danced and whirled in the aisles, some fell on their knees and prayed, and a great bellow of song and laughter came when the crowd burst into "Good-bye, old party, good-bye."

Among these varied and strong personalities, Weaver loomed large. Only Donnelly of Minnesota equaled him in political experience. But Donnelly came from a Catholic family. Weaver was a fervent Protestant. Also, Weaver had been in the national Congress more recently. Already he had campaigned the country as a Presidential candidate, and when Walter Q. Gresham, a leading silver Democrat and ex-federal judge, declined to accept the Populist nomination, the tide turned in favor of Weaver, thanks in good part to the efforts of Mary Lease.

His running mate became General James Graves Field of Culpepper County, Virginia, head of the Baptist church in his state. This was playing the war veteran and Protestant racket with a vengeance. Field was a recent convert, far from being a farm reformer; Weaver himself was more concerned about currency than farmers' needs, but the two men were a romantic symbol of reconciliation between the sections and of the welfare of the farmers. The People's party — "the nimble rainbow chasers" — girded for battle with a platform, demanding land and labor reforms, a subtreasury plan of rural credits, direct election of senators, public control or ownership of the railroads, currency reform, an income tax, the initiative and referendum, etc. In an eloquent acceptance speech, Weaver promised to save the government from the monopolies and restore it to the people.

Weaver, then fifty-nine, still with physical stamina to make an incessant campaign, at once set forth on his tour, accompanied by his wife, by Mary Lease, the Kansas orator, and others. His first major stop was Denver, Colorado, hard hit by the depression and the official silver policy and seething with revolt. Party lines had already been demolished.

On the Pacific Coast he drew record-breaking crowds. Already the state had at least three Populist newspapers. He swung back through the Northwest.

In the South, despite big crowds, he had tough sledding. The South was not prepared to permit a northern general to barnstorm in search of votes, even if his running mate might be a Confederate officer. Carpetbag dictatorship had been succeeded by race-hating one-party dictatorship. The Democratic party ruled in a period of lush pickings, enormous graft, and political debauchery, and the bosses, worse than the carpetbaggers, did not want the free spirit of man, let alone the Negroes, encouraged. Weaver's meetings were repeatedly attacked by gangs of young southern gentry. In Pulaski, Tennessee, he was spit at by old women and had to leave town in a hurry. Georgia was the worst. His meetings became riots. He and Mrs. Weaver were rotten-egged and grossly insulted. Local Populist congressional candidate Tom Watson had to fight for Weaver's right to speak, gun in hand, and Weaver had to flee from that great democratic state for his life. Tom Watson kept on fighting. Forty riflemen guarded the platforms when he spoke.

Once he led two thousand armed wool-hatted red-hill followers and surrounded the county courthouse for two days and nights to deter would-be lynchers of a Populist Negro candidate.

When the returns were in, Weaver received a total of over 1,000,000 out of 12,000,000 and had chalked up 22 votes in the electoral college as compared with 227 for Grover Cleveland and 145 for Benjamin Harrison. Populist governors were elected in Kansas (L.D. Lewelling), North Dakota (Eli Showbridge), and Colorado (Davis H. Waite). Besides numerous local officials, 8 Populist congressmen, and many others pledged to the party program as a result of fusion deals, were elected. William Jennings Bryan could not have won in Nebraska without Populist support. But the campaign, with its bitter partisanship, pretty much wrecked both the Northern and Southern Farmers' Alliance.

This election was Weaver's greatest day. Thereafter his stature diminished. Little by little he abandoned the broad program of his party and reverted to his old-time currency crusade as a cure-all for every evil.

He had always been close to William Jennings Bryan. Their congressional districts were near one another, and during the forthcoming years the two men were to stump the country in behalf of free silver for the Bimetallic League, an organization subsidized by the wealthy western silver interests. Whether Weaver, like Bryan, was paid to propagandize for the powerful silver companies, there is no direct evidence. In any case, Weaver's currency ideas narrowed down to a mere symbol — that of free silver.

By 1896, Weaver was ready to stampede the Populist party upon the Bryan silver bandwagon. He did not see that this was rank betrayal of the farmers and their broad "middle-of-the-road" Populist program. By tricky means at the national Populist convention, he and Senator William V. Allen of Nebraska downed the midroaders, who were in overwhelming majority, and swing the emphasis to silver. The convention was steamrollered in the same highly boss-ruled manner that characterized both old-party conventions. The endorsement of silver was made 'he major plank, and William J. Bryan, standard-bearer of the Democratic party, wa. nominated.

Bryan never so much as acknowledged the Populist nomination, though in the campaign he did use Weaver in predominantly Populist states, ignoring him elsewhere. He turned his back completely on the Populist Vice-Presidential candidate, Tom Watson of Georgia.

After that uproarious campaign, which saw the eastern "goldbugs" victorious with McKinley, Weaver's day was done forever. The great Farmers' Alliance was forever broken. The People's party was broken. It had gone "to that bourne, the Democratic Party, from which no third party ever returns." All its subsequent efforts were feeble.

Weaver, having successfully destroyed his own organized backing, went into the Democratic party and stayed there. A few years later, he is found in the humiliating role of opposing candidate Tom Watson, 1908 Populist candidate for President, and stumping for a corporation nonentity, Alton B. Parker, the type of man he had so long fought, and for a platform contrary to everything he had ever espoused. Watson received only 28,000 votes. Socialist candidate Eugene V. Debs, put in jail during World War I, polled 421,000. Taft became President.

Presently Weaver settled in Jasper County, Iowa, just east of Des Moines. There he served as mayor, and produced a two-volume glossy-paper history of the county. It was a quiet ending for a stormy career. But he belonged in Iowa, and Iowa took him back to her breast.

Whatever the record of his later years, Weaver was one of America's great progressives. Nearly all of the ideas he sponsored, and often originated, as head of various third-party movements and as member of Congress, are today part of the law of the land. Perhaps more than any one else, he is the real father of the Interstate Commerce Commission. He led the vanguard of his day, and was reviled even after more opportunistic men later took the credit for carrying out what earlier he had advocated. His book, the now-forgotten *Call to Action*, the campaign document of '92, sold over 1,000,000 copies. To this day it remains a significant contribution to American political thought and practice. It is probably the most statesmanlike campaign document ever issued by any candidate for the Presidency of the United States. He was America's first modern "progressive" of national proportions.

The country has mostly forgotten him, as it has so many of its prophets, but unwittingly the country has put its legal stamp of approval upon most of the ideas and principles expressed by him in his long uphill fight.

X
MEN OF
POPULISM

The People's movement of the nineties, which canalized into "The Great Third Party" and reshaped the programs of the two older parties, was more than a battle of farmers versus trusts. Religion also was woven into the woof. Ignatius Donnelly, Minnesota reformer, in his best-selling novel, *Caesar's Column*, made God the first ruler of his Populist Utopia in Uganda. The new crusaders constantly identified their movement with Christianity; Jesus Christ, sometimes Adam, was confidently called the first Populist.

The farmers, when they formed themselves into the Alliance, or into "Unions" and "Wheels," as in Louisiana and Arkansas, often met in the local church, and frequently the pastor gave them guidance; often, as with Granges of the seventies, he was made an honorary member. Each group had an elected chaplain, and meetings invariably opened and closed with prayer. At the great St. Louis convention in December, 1899, the Alliance amended its constitutional preamble to begin, "We believe there is a God . . ."

"Stump" Ashby initiated the 1894 Texas Populist convention by leading the delegates in singing, "Jesus, Lover of my Soul."

The battle songs of the farmer movement were often parodies of old hymns or were sung to religious tunes. Thus, "Pull for the Shore, Sailor" became "Pull for the Shore, Farmer," which kept the "Glory, Glory, Hallelujah" chorus of the original. "Send Alliance News," in the key of B-flat, kept some of the lines of "Let the Lower Lights be Burning."

The rank and file Populists were in good part "Anglo-Saxon" Methodists and Baptists, and they carried all the techniques of the camp meeting revival over into their political rallies. "To the Populists as to the Second Adventists," remarked the *St. Louis Republic* in June, 1894, "ascension robes and a few hymns are part and parcel of the faith."

It was a standing pleasantry in Texas that the People's party was composed of "one-gallus" farmers and ex-Campbellite preachers. Among the most prominent of the latter were Reverend V.M. Browder of Gainesville, a caustic orator, and Reverend J.W. Baird, who, before he became a reform politician, had rounded up the cowboys on the plains and, with no roof over his head but the blue of heaven, preached sinners to repentance. He had "snatched many a brand from the burning" and had seen his head "grow gray in the cause of the Master." But when he took to the Populist stump, his gray locks did not save him from many a shower of rotten eggs from the open-minded citizenry.

The *Dallas Morning News* carried an article on "Protestant Preachers" in the new movement. "It is a popular belief that more than two-thirds of the Populist orators have at some time or other been connected with the ministry . . . Brother Ashby, head of the Populist State Executive Committee, rode for many, many years an old roan pony to the various outposts of Christianity in Navarro, Limestone and Firestone Counties. He was a circuit rider in the early days before there were any big towns." Later, he told the farmers he had left the ministry to preach "the gospel of universal emancipation. Now I preach politics during the week and religion on Sunday."

Populist Senator James H. Kyle of South Dakota was a pillar-to-post frontier preacher before an impromptu Fourth of July speech on monopolies cast him high up on the shore of independent political leadership. Brother S.O. Daws, early president and lecturer of the Farmers' Alliance in Texas, had been a "side-issue" Baptist preacher. The brilliant and jovial E.L. Wood, Washington lobbyist and orator, had been another Methodist circuit rider. Mary Lease of Kansas was said to have been ordained, and General James Field, Populist candidate for the Vice-Presidency in the national campaign of 1892, was actually head of the Baptist church in Virginia.

In many ways, Populism was a worldly offshoot of the Protestant religion. Texas Catholic counties (largely Mexican) and Louisiana Catholic parishes returned few People's party votes. It was even charged freely (and for the most part falsely) that the People's party was an anti-Catholic party, closely associated with the American Protective Association, A.P.A., the great secret anti-Catholic and pro-American society (descended from the old Know-Nothing party) that spread so widely throughout the country those years. The fact was, in the middle years of the party, Dr. C.W. Macune, head of the Farmers' Alliance, angrily left its ranks because it refused to take an open "anti-Romish" stand. Yet Ignatius Donnelly of Minnesota, the great Populist orator, if not very religious, was a Catholic.

Populism tied in with the revivalism of the Bible Belt. The Plains' religions had been part of the age-old equalitarian movement. The Populists were therefore products of an earlier church revolt that had told every man he could read the Bible to discover right and wrong for himself. Holy justice supported the opinions of the individual common man. All opinions, regardless of the education of the possessor, at once had divine origin and authority. Religion and ignorance could thus march blissfully arm-in-arm. This automatically endowed each Populist with holy sanction and put

[215]

the seal of eternal virtue on his opinions. Such a note of divine approbation was struck again and again in nearly all Populist literature. Dunning, the historian of the Farmers' Alliance, repeatedly gives thanks to God for the movement and its ideas. "Without God's support, no such grandiose cause could have emerged."

For most Populists, the Bible, as with later Jehovah's Witnesses, was ultimate authority on all moot points. W.S. Morgan, in his *History of the Wheel and Alliance*, published in 1891, says bluntly, "Had it been intended that 'In the sweat of they brother's face thou shalt not eat bread,' it would have been so ordained." The Agricultural Wheel, one of the major farmers' organizations of the time, took its name from Chapter 10 of Ezekiel. Coin Harvey, currency propagandist, in his novelized tract, *The Tale of Two Cities*, cites the Bible to uphold his views on money-lending. In his handbook of Populism distributed by tens of thousands in the Longhorn State, Cyclone Davis remarked, "Our platform on the land problem is in harmony with Divine law," and proceeded to prove by the Scriptures that the land had been given by God as a general patrimony to all men.

If all public speakers of the day copiously quoted the Holy Writ to support their views, the Populist speakers went the furthest. They discovered that usury was forbidden by the Good Book 163 times — more often than any other sin or crime. Favorite quotations were Neh. 5: 3, 10, 11; Prov. 22: 22-23; Luke. 11: 46. Reverend W. A. Dumas, a Presbyterian of Montague, in northern Texas, traced every Populist principle, even the famous Sub-Treasury Plan for federal crop credits, as well as the Populist money doctrines and the prohibition of alien land-holding, directly to the Scriptures. His stock speech was entitled, "Bible Indorsement of Populism."

General James Baird Weaver, Populist Presidential candidate in 1892, when writing to a friend about the currency issue, clinched the argument by solemnly referring him, chapter and verse, to the Bible.

The *Southern Mercury* declared, "Populism is a practical religion.

To vote according to our best convictions of right is a duty we owe to the Creator as well as to our fellowmen. For a Populist to fail to vote is to be derelict to a sacred duty."

As one later student remarked, "The People's Party thus became a tabernacle under which gathered all those bent on the divine laws of justice against those who put worldy affairs first. . . . It became, in short, a semi-religious order, its members zealots for the cause of justice."

One and all, the Populist ex-preachers, reported the *Dallas Morning News*, say that their leaving the ministry was "based on a desire to do good to the greatest number. They all hold that true Christianity is a beautiful thing in theory, but that there is a real world of practical demands. They all say they can accomplish more for the moral welfare of the people by going to the people in their conventions and primaries on week days than by waiting for the people to come to them on Sundays. They claim that the Populist Party is the greatest moral organization on earth and made so largely through the influence of the preachers."

The People's movement in the nineties made the decade even grimmer by its moral crusade. Kansas House Bill 898, introduced in the Populist legislature in 1897, sought to enact the Ten Commandments into a statute, as had been done in New Haven more than two centuries earlier, with penalties attached. Skating rinks and billiard halls in that state were tabu, and the attorney general warred relentlessly on "jointists," "boot-leggers," the "small jug business," drug stores that were "running a little loose," and "venders of hard cider." When, in 1889, a new federal law permitted the sale in dry states of liquor in original packages, many Kansas communities rang the church bells to call the citizens together "to repel the invasion" and stage a new kind of Boston tea party. The farmers' revolt gave no quarter to "sin."

Out of the choppy waves of that tumultuous decade sprang again (full-bodied and fully clothed) the earlier New England puritanism. Among the righteous Nordics who turned Populist, new Cotton

[217]

Mathers sprouted like sunflowers from the sunbaked plains. The Populist movement found little support among drink-and-food-loving Germans, Scandinavians, Bohemians, Italians, Mexicans, and other low foreign breeds not dyed with puritanism, especially as the well-meaning reformers had a fierce provincial anti-foreign attitude. The *Southern Mercury* called Bohemians no better than Chinese and refused to retract.

As early as 1873, German political conventions in Texas had opposed, and kept on doing so through the nineties, all *Sonntags und Temperanz-Gesetze*. In Nebraska, in 1889, 50,000 Germans paraded in solid phalanx, demanding the return of legalized beer. In all quarters, the German political groups fought blue laws, Sunday closing, prohibition, and the invasion of the rights of personal pleasure. They were not cordial to Populist puritans.

The earlier Puritanism that colonized America had been a dual revolt against High Church and the upper classes controlling that institution. Hence it had struck out against laxity, luxury, entertainments, and all artistic pleasure — largely aristocratic monopolies. Sin was identified with all upper-class culture.

The Populist revolt of the West, beholding the vulgarity and corruption of new wealth and its lackeys in politics, repeated much of the older religious pattern.

Before their very eyes were the unsavory private lives, the ostentation and arrogance of the Robber Barons. The country had been regaled with plenty of spicy stories. Fisk had died from a bullet shot by the man whom the buccaneer had stripped of both his fortune and his mistress. The *Barber County Index* (January 30, 1889) told the story of "The Richest Woman, The Daily Life of the Widow of Vanderbilt," and summarized it with the adjective "shameless." During the late nineties, Senator Sharon, that mighty wolf of Comstock Lode, was for years involved in a messy scandalous suit brought by the southern belle, Sarah Althea Hill, whom he had done wrong. The exploits of such gentry gained far more attention than the milk-drinking, dime-contributing piety of a

Rockefeller. And so a moral crusade merged with economic unrest. When, in April, Moses Hanson, editor of an idealistic free-love paper, *Lucifer, The Light Beacon,* of Valley Falls, Kansas, was found guilty of sending obscene literature through the mails, the local farmer press applauded mightily. The western rebels also applauded Anthony Comstock, agent of the Society for the Prevention of Vice, when he walked into the Broadway art shop of Frenchman Eugene Caret to threaten him for displaying a photograph of a nude statue by Rodin. The frightened fellow sold out, lock, stock, and barrel, and hurried back to Europe, where, for twenty odd centuries, art had scarcely ever been judged, except by a few of the popes, according to the amount of clothes that hid the human figure. One early plank of the Texas Farmers' Alliance demanded that indecent matter be barred not only from the post office but all public carriers. The peculiarly narrow ideas, the hobnails of those days, of what constituted indecency, trampled down the flowers along with the weeds.

In July, 1890, Miss Frances Willard, that lachrymose busybody who was always given a warm hearing at Populist conventions, jumped down editor Watson Gilder's throat for allowing the word "rape" to sully the fair pages of *Century* — rather amusing, since Gilder, one of the prize prudes of American journalism, emasculated the leading writers of the time and set up all-out purity, which he confused with middle-class gentility, as his stern standard. Beer tells us that five of Frances' sisters badgered New York editors because Carmencita, wholly clad in red and yellow, was allowed to dance in New York. One editor uncouthly suggested that the ladies hie themselves right back to Chicago and clean up that sizzle spot known as the Slide, which put on exhibitions for the male clientele of the World's Fair, though today such tame shows would not raise an eyebrow of the most prudish. The good ladies were astounded, unwilling to believe that such vice existed west of the Alleghenies.

For the rebellious Populists, political corruption and economic

[219]

oppression, liquor and vice, were hydra heads of the same monster. In his *Memoir* (published many decades later), James Harvey Cyclone Davis, the bearded Populist orator of Texas, declared, "During all these years I have faced the fury of a frenzied and ferocious money power combined with a bacchanalian liquor power." To a Colorado convention, Mary Lease shouted that against the seven Kansas Populists sent to Congress, "Wall Street, the Liquor Power or the Gates of Hell" could not prevail. But a group of Washington ladies almost hissed her from the platform for her vulgar use of the Anglo-Saxon word for the hot place.

Visible to the western Populists was the spectacle of universal corruption and bribery, in which politicians and office-holders were everywhere bought outright or controlled by corporations, or by the liquor and vice interests or both. The scandal of the Grant whiskey frauds, but one of a vast assortment of corrupt thievery, had never fully subsided. It had not been so long since Boss Tweed had been sent to prision, leaving behind him a stench of collusion with liquor interests and financial pirates. Most Populists were against liquor, first, last, and all the time, and although the Texas movement produced good tipplers (Ashby and Kearby), many early Alliance and People's party victories in California, Kansas, Iowa, Nebraska, North Dakota, and elsewhere were achieved by fusion with the Prohibitionist party. In Texas, the Populists absorbed the old Prohibitionists .Alliance organizers, to be commissioned, had to be certified as "non-users of alcohol."

The *Young Populist* of that state carried a cartoon of a People's party Temperance Lady wielding a sword, ready to cut the cord of a weight, labeled "People's Party Vote," that it might smash the "Old Parties" getting booze out of both ends of a barrel, labeled "Whiskey Trust."

The *Southern Mercury*, official Alliance and Populist organ, for a time ran a serial poem, illustrated by lurid cuts, and entitled "The Drunkard's Progress," by Professor W.A. Boles. Part IV was titled "The Rum Hole." It carried a crude drawing of a man in a top hat and cloak (queer raiment for a farmer) drinking grog in a tavern beside a spider-pipe stove, and read, in part:

> Now wine and whiskey, port and rum
> Have banished quite the love of home;
> No more he cares for wife and child,
> The Rum Hole has his soul beguiled.

John H. McDowell, boss of Tennessee Populism, editor of the Knoxville *Weekly Toiler*, always turned his heaviest guns on liquor and gambling. John H. Powers, long-time Granger and Alliancer of Nebraska, spent many years prior to 1890 in a prohibitionist crusade. Governor "Bloody Bridles" Waite of Colorado was a sworn enemy of booze. Since his teens, James Weaver had taken a strong stand against drink, and the liquor interests of Iowa are said to have forced him forever from the Republican party. He always strove to secure a prohibition plank in the Populist platform and, in the Iowa state convention at Des Moines, September, 1893, succeeded, despite the political inexpediency of the move.

Bright little Annie Le Porte Diggs, the faithful Boswell of Populism, got her start in a long public career after she discovered that the university students of Lawrence, Kansas, were being ruined by drink and set out to do something about it. Hard liquor never crossed the lips of soft-spoken, saintly Thomas Nugent, Populist oracle of Texas; Cyclone Davis was a lifelong enemy of the "Bacchanalian bewilderment of booze bibblers." Ignatius Donnelly, in *Caesar's Column*, has one of his characters say, "Our poor ignorant ancestors drank alcohol but now it is prohibited."

Harry Tracy of Texas, Alliance organizer in Mississippi in 1889, wrote to the *Washington National Economist*, the main organ of the movement, "I have visited over three-fourth of the countries in the state and have lectured to over 40,000 people. Up to this good hour, among all my audiences, I have seen but one intoxicated person. Just think of it! . . . What a mighty reformation! What a glorious reformation! Every patriot's heart will leap with joy at this glorious news! Every woman in the land must see herein woman's emancipation!"

Mrs. Frances Willard, the outstanding champion of purity, prohibition, and women's suffrage, was usually a delegate to Populist conventions. At the St. Louis gathering in '92, she eloquently supported her platform minority report in behalf of prohibition and suffrage: "Brothers of the Industrial Conference, I feel as if I had been struck by lightning. This is an electoral convention, sure enough. I was so happy as to be a farmer's daughter and that this hand and brain have earned my board and keep since I was eighteen years old."

She mentioned a cartoon in one of the opposition dailies which depicted a huge boulder, labeled "Women's Suffrage," blocking the path of the people's party: "I would macadamize with that stone the solid highway to the places of power."

The cartoon also showed a huge "prohibition" tree felled across the new party's path. Better, she said, that the voter against Prohibition should be depicted "as sitting on a limb and sawing it off between himself and the tree. . . .

"If you enlist the hearts of women along with your farm hands you will have in this movement the ballots that are God's dynamite under the people's wrongs, and we will make the two old parties grievously unhappy before we go from here."

In June, 1894, the *St. Louis Republic* described one notable occasion:

"When the Kansas State convention of Populists arose and sang the doxology, while Reverend Anna Shaw and Miss Susan B. Anthony wept and shouted and the sisters on the platform cried and waved their handkerchiefs, all because a women's suffrage plan had been forced into the resolutions of that body, the acme of hysterical Populism was reached.

"Populism at best is sentimental. It presupposes a condition where all men and women will be cared for by the governmental interposition and then sings and shouts itself onward toward the rainbow of paternalism . . . an imaginary haven of rest and freedom from responsibilities. . . . But it is a curious and seemingly inexplicable condition which places together in political turmoil the songs and hysteria of women with the ambitions and plottings of men."

All this fuzzy mixture of economic demands with personal conduct and women's rights was scarcely productive of strength or harmony in a political and economic movement. One railroad magnate and politician of Kansas once said cynically, "For years we used to bring up the liquor question to consume the time of the legislature so they would not have a chance to look into our affairs or pass regulatory laws, only to wake up one fair day and discover to our chagrin that Kansas had gone bone dry."

A better sense of proportion might have caused the long-faced western farmers to have realized that their way of life and prosperity would be more drastically altered by the discovery that year by Professor Petermann of Grembleau, Belgium, of the relation of atmospheric nitrogen to plant growth than by the evils of wine, women, and song.

XI
BLOODY KANSAS

"The history of Kansas from the pen of a second Macaulay, who may perhaps be born in the twentieth century, will be among the classics of the future." So wrote W. H. Kent, editor of the Populist *Topeka Daily Press,* in 1893, a time of threatened civil war.

Lorenzo D. Lewelling, a former coal miner, had just been elected Governor by the embattled Populist farmers, and the atmosphere had become so bitter, armed violence seemed inevitable. Everywhere in the nation respectable folk were shocked and frightened by the farmer victory. The Republicans fought tooth and nail to prevent elected Populists from taking their seats in the Kansas legislature. The Populists fought back. Mobs gathered. Disorders broke out. Farmers came swooping in like hornets. Armed railroad deputies went to work. The militia clanked down the streets of the capital.

Kansas had more reason for farm revolt than most states. For 2 decades the political backwater from the closing frontier had been rising, flooding agriculture with ruin and drowning old-time opportunity. Political protest steadily rose as the "hungry seventies" and the "dreary eighties" gave way to the "stormy nineties." By 1894, the value of Kansas agricultural products was only $113,000,000, as compared to $147,000,000 10 years before, and the railroad bonds of the sixties and seventies were now coming due. Men could not see the handwriting on the wall — the peak had already been reached in corn and wheat production. Between 1881 and 1887, the wheat acreage of Kansas dropped from 2,000,000 to 1,250,000 acres; corn from 1,000,000 to 406,000 acres. Also, for season after season there were no crops. Drouth had lasted years.

June 24, 1892, an angry reader, "Aztec," denounced the *Medicine Lodge Cresset* for saying that ripening wheat fields stretched solid for five miles on both sides of the Medicine River. "I will now give you until the Fourth of July to retract . . . There is only one wheat field, and drouth and grasshoppers have destroyed that. Say, rather, that John V. Uperman shot five jack-rabbits to keep from starving."

At the same time, price declines probably cost the Kansas farmers over $235,000,000 in the 1884-1894 decade. By 1885, corn had dropped to the low price of thirty-two cents; by 1889, to ten cents. The cost to raise corn those years, said the Bureau of Labor and Industry, according to Raymond C. Miller, in the *Mississippi Historical Review*, was $75,000,000 more than the price received. Corn was burned for fuel, hogs were shot and left to rot, even though men were hungry in the cities and farmers could not carry their overhead, let alone buy machinery or clothing. That 1887 winter, collapse came as blizzards killed the cattle. Drouth thereafter wiped out crops. People actually began starving.

Mary Ellen Lease, in the 1890 campaign, scarcely needed to remind the farmers of eight-cent corn, ten-cent oats, two-cent beef, "and no price at all for butter and eggs." The people, she said, were "at bay," and "the bloodhounds of money could beware."

All this would have brought farm bankruptcy even were there no great load of public and private debt. By 1887, the per capita

Kansas public debt was three times what it had been in 1880, and private debt was four times that of the nation as a whole. The Auditors' Report for 1890 stated that Kansas property was assessed at $348,459,943, whereas the total public and private indebtedness of the state was $706,181,627, more than double. Kansas had made rapid progress backwards.

In 1888, in Kansas, there was 1 mile of railroad for every 9⅓ square miles, and 5½ miles of track for every 1,000 persons. For this, the people had paid in debt and taxes, yet private holders kept the completed lines, which had cost them little or nothing. The roads were built by land grants, state and federal, guaranteed by public mortgages, boosted along by gifts and bonuses, national, state, city, township, and village, even by individuals and farmers' clubs. Bonded indebtedness rose dizzily. By 1890, railroad bonds guaranteed by all local political units totaled $50,000,000; by the state $75,000,000, far more, according to Populist Sentator William Peffer, than the roads were worth to build. Much of this was for railroad subsidy bonds now falling due.

"The crushing burden of mortgage debt at ten or even fifteen percent [an understatement] then borne by southern and western agriculture with high renewal charges, was nothing less than a national outrage," says Allan Nevins in his *Grover Cleveland.*

Foreclosures and collapses darkened all Kansas. Mortgages had been contracted when corn was over forty cents. "The farmer who had paid half his mortgage found the other half now equalled the total value of his farm." He now had to put up grain to an amount that previously would have paid off the whole mortgage several times over. Even if he had no mortgage, mountains of taxes, due to the public railroad debt and declining population, made a relentless demand for cash.

W. Scott Morgan, in his *History of the Wheel and Alliance,* quoted a Kansas farmer that it would take "sixty acres of grain and twenty-five acres of oats" to pay his interest on $1,000, and two-thirds of his remaining acres to carry the other one-third to market.

[227]

Sockless Jerry Simpson said sarcastically, "Loans on mortgages to farmers in Kansas would be paid — but not in gold of which there was not enough to fill the old rotten teeth of the people." But most could not be paid in any medium. Loan companies foreclosed and became possessors of large tracts of land. Farm leader Sam Wood declared that by 1890, 90 percent of all the land in southwest Kansas was in possession of loan companies. Things finally got so bad that "even the speculators fled."

Thousands of landowners abandoned their farms. Whole counties were left practically deserted. Between 1888 and 1892, half the people of western Kansas trailed eastward in covered wagons drawn by gaunt ponies. Simply to escape being "reduced to serfdom," says Elizabeth Blair, "they sought relief by a general exodus from their native land."

As previously noted, Donnelly in his *Golden Bottle* put the matter into terms of contemporary bathos, the fate of a Kansas farmer's daughter, Sophie:

"One bright morning a pitiful cortege of grim, visaged men and weeping women went forth from that little paradise of fields and woods and prolific greenery, and took their sad way to the great city of Omaha, to struggle with thousands of hungry ones for daily food. It is the old story, grasshoppers, poor crops, 'pools,' 'trusts,' 'rings,' high prices for what we bought; low prices for what we sold."

The Republican boomers now became victims of their own propaganda. Farmers, long beguiled by Aladdin tales of limitless beauty and wealth, refused to believe that Nature had gone back on them. The unexpected bumper crop of 1889 merely worsened their condition. They began seeking some other scapegoat besides God.

The western farmer could do nothing much about drouth and nature, fires and plague and sickness, but optimistically he thought he could do something about transportation, land monopoly, high costs of farm machinery, something about currency contraction, price instability, and deflation.

Part of the answer was the Alliance movement, which took God in as an active partner.

The Alliancer went into the fray, singing "Where will the Farmer Be?"

Chorus:
>Drowned by the combine and
>Drowned by the trust,
>Sank by his interest or usury unjust
>Held down by taxes on more than his head —
>Where, oh, where, will the farmer be? . . .

Or "Hard Times:"

>The times are hard, I do declare,
>I'm moneyless and flat;
>I feel indeed the worse for wear,
>So does my dear old hat;
>My coat is thin and so am I.
>I do not care for that
>While we are marching to victory.

He read his own papers and pondered. He read Harry Tracy in the *National Economist*, March, 1889: "The citizen who has watched or is familiar with the drift of events in the United States since 1850 cannot fail to see that our government has been . . . steadily changing from a Republic to a moneyed oligarchy. . . . The government is practically already in the hands of our moneyed autocrats. . . ."

In the same organ, they read A. J. Streeter, ex-president of the Northern Alliance: "We the farmers produce more wealth than any other like number of people in the earth . . .

"We work more hours in a day than any other class of people on earth . . .

"We pay more taxes."

And yet, he continued, "We are growing poorer year by year. . . . Every cotton crop is produced at a loss . . . every corn crop in Illinois since 1881 . . . at a loss." Nearly all farms were now mortgaged. The causes were: "too high rates for transportation, too high rates for interest on money; too little money in circulation . . ."

In January, 1890, a Medicine Lodge farmer, Eli Benedict, wrote to the *Wichita Eagle* "We are only farmers but . . . we have stood all we can. We have tried to support our families. We have looked ahead with hope for a big crop, to have better times . . . that crop of 1889 was all we could ask, but the prices we got for our stock and this crop is [sic] in the tide of lost hope. . . . We will have better times as soon as we elect one of our number to help make laws for our own protection, which we are going to do by our votes at the next election, and don't you forget it. . . . All we earn goes to make a few richer. It must stop, and stop in 1890 and 1891 . . ."

The first point of attack was the railroads. "Kansas," Mary E. Lease told her listeners, "suffers from two great robbers, the Santa Fe railroad and the loan companies."

As Elizabeth Barr put it in her *The Populist Uprising*, "The transporation corporations . . . made discriminating freight rates in such a way that they had complete control of the distribution of products and had the industries of the people at their mercy." This ruined "hundreds of independent salt producers in Kansas, as well as producers of oil and minerals." It "took the natural resources of the state from the hands of the people and gave them over to the trusts and combines. . . . It was the ruin of the cattle men, as the large packing houses were given such heavy rebates that the independent shipper stood no chance in the market. . . .

"Not content with extortion from the people," the transportation companies "oppressed the laborers beyond endurance. According to the Kansas Bureau of Labor . . . [in 1886] the railroad did not pay a living wage on which a family could subsist comfortably while employment lasted, to say nothing of saving for a period of enforced idleness."

And so the people now conveniently forgot that they themselves were in good part responsible for their condition. They, too, had been reckless boomers; they were the very ones who had created the public debt which so weighed on the necks of the farmer in taxes and high freight rates.

They forgot that their own elected leaders, though often corporation-controlled, had warned them, long before they themselves awoke to the danger; they forgot that they themselves had rarely supported anyone who told them the truth.

In 1883, Governor Glick had stated, "Millions of acres of land and millions of dollars of money have been donated to aid in the construction of the various railroads of the state. . . . [The] generous people of Kansas . . . expected generous or at least fair treatment in return. . . ." But by "pooling their earnings, stifling competition and other high-handed outrageous things," the railroads did "serious wrongs to the people." State policies were manipulated the burden of taxation shifted to the farmer. "Never in the history of the world have any people been subjected to greater abuse than have the people of Kansas for the last five years."

Armed railroad deputies now rallied to break the new Populist administration. The Santa Fe offices in Topeka became the headquarters of a post-election revolution.

But before the last-ditch fight in Topeka developed, the new party, flushed with victory, enjoyed a few days of undisputed glory. Thousands of elated farmers poured into Topeka to see the people's government installed and celebrate their triumph.

The ceremonies, January 9, were conducted in Representative Hall, "superbly decorated and never . . . so beautiful. . . . The brightest evergreens, encircled with many a fold," covered the electric lamps of the great central chandelier. "From this emerald midair bower — a miniature hanging garden of Babylon — cables

[231]

of like material extended from the corners of the hall, the strands made firmer by knots of red ribbons. More evergreens, fluttering flags and rich floral ornaments adorned the walls, while the speaker's stand was fairly buried beneath the lavish display of tropical plants . . . crowned by a great basket of the choicest roses. . . ." So went the description in an enthusiastic Populist paper.

Above the main entrance was a portrait of John Brown, anti-slave leader in the pre-Civil War fight in Kansas, hero of the battle of Osawatomie and of Harpers Ferry. On either side of the speaker's desk were portraits of Washington and Lincoln; on the north and south walls, life-size portraits of the ex-governors of Kansas; and, most conspicuous of all, the state's great flag — "a circle of farmlands on solid dark blue, its graceful folds lashed to the gallery pillars with wreaths of evergreen and roses. . . ."

"A few moments before eleven o'clock, the ladies of the Shawnee County Alliance . . . unfolded to the view of the audience a gleaming banner of silk, trimmed with gold buttons and bearing in letters of gold, the favorite motto of the Farmers' Alliance:

'A government of the People, by the People
and for the People shall not Perish.' A. Lincoln."

A great shout went up, then a life-size portrait of Governor Lewelling by a Topeka artist was uncovered.

"Oh, it was a glorious day for those loyal people who had stood up for Kansas in her hour of peril, and at a time when the ruling power had reduced them to the condition almost of serfs, while yet retaining as sovereign citizens of the Republic, a full knowledge of the grievous wrongs to which they had been subjected."

Promptly at twelve o'clock, Governor Lewelling, his wife, and their two daughters, Jessie and Pauline, entered. Breidenthal, the state Populist Chairman, called the assemblage to order. This, he declared, was "the first signal triumph over plutocracy, the knell of corporation rule." Those present would hand down "to their children and their children's children" a legend that would be "cherished as sacredly and rebound as greatly to the chief actors in the bloodless revolution by which Kansas was redeemed, as fell to the lot of the Pilgrim Fathers, the signers of the Declaration of Independence, or the heroes of 1776, who freed this nation from foreign rule."

There was no inaugural ball. "More-hell-less-corn" Mary Lease, one of Lewellings' chief campaigners, had vigorously objected to any "ceremonious squandering of the people's money" and was "dead against any low-necked and swallow-tail affair."

One could easily understand this, sneered *Harper's Weekly*. Mrs. Lease, a sparse lady, "didn't want to appear in décolleté." For the Populists, anyone who put on feathers was "a malignant Republican office-holder soon to be shaved by the people's guillotine." Also, Governor-elect Lewelling preferred to wear his trousers tucked in his bootlegs "to keep his silver dollars from falling through the holes in his pocket."

"The swollen aristocrats," sarcastically commented another hostile paper, "may not presume to teach the plain people how to inaugurate their government. . . . What Mrs. Lease says 'goes' in Kansas, and if anybody is disposed to doubt it, let him consult Mr. Mary E. Lease."

The campaign that had put Lewelling into office had gotten off to a tumultuous start, with a shattering of old party lines, frayed nerves, and angry namecalling. The Republican press denounced the Populist state convention at Wichita on June 15, 1892, as being "thoroughly under the control of the fixers," meaning the secret Videttes; "pandemonium was unrivalled . . . the convention was a howling mob beyond the control of any reasoning power."

In the *Topeka Daily Press*, W. H. Kent said such reporting was a sign of Republican perfidy. "Actually," he declaimed, "the Populist convention was the most harmonious ever assembled. The platform was so broad, so comprehensive, so just to all classes that the

Republican convention a little later, with a flourish of virtue and fairness, practically endorsed it by adopting nearly every plank with a very weak attempt to conceal the theft." According to Kent, it was the Republican party convention that had "fought, raved and howled like maniacs."

"The once proud Republican party," he declared, "is no longer the Republican party save in name but has discarded the principles of Lincoln . . . to bend the knee to corporations, and lend willing obedience to the edicts of the money kings issued from the palaces in Wall Street." As "pliant tools of the corporations," the Republican office-holders had sunk "deeper into the mire of corruption and degradation."

For the Republicans, both Democrats and Populists were perfidious villains. The Democratic convention "went hay wire" and endorsed the Populist candidates by a vote of 390 to 39. A "handful of erstwhile Democratic wheelhorses" left the hall to organize the so-called Stalwart Democratic party.

As "assistant Republicans," reported Kent, they exerted "every effort to retain the corporation party in power . . . Their pretended convention at the Grand Opera House in Topeka on October 7, was . . . made up of railroad attorneys and corporation hirelings who came to the capital city on passes issued by the hundreds, to demonstrate the extent of their vassalage to the brass-colored monopolists."

The whole electoral machinery of the state was "in the hands of as corrupt a gang of Republican partisans as ever existed . . . legislators were brazenly overwhelmed by false counts, but Populist Governor Lewelling's majority was far too large for him to be made to lose the election.

The Populists had clearly gained full control of the Senate — 25 Populists to 15 Republicans. But it was touch and go for control of the House. Each side was set to use any and all methods to cement a majority.

The Republican State Canvassing Board met in Topeka,

November 28, to uphold corrupt county canvassing boards that had "counted out Populist representatives" and overlooked "clerical errors (?) that would elect Republican members." The board threw out 6,000 votes of colored Populist E. B. Cabbell, because on many ballots his name had been spelled "Campbell." Only after great hue and cry did the board declare Cabbell elected. In another instance, a county clerk calmly transposed the Democratic majority to the Republican candidate — a stratagem accepted by the Canvassing Board with "callous calm." In another case, an exact Populist-Republican tie had resulted from fraudulent Republican tampering with the returns. According to law, lots had to be drawn in the presence of both interested parties, but the Board, in secret session, "alleged" that the slip drawn had read "Republican." When the northern district of Horton County returned a Populist majority, the clerk arbitrarily threw in the Republican vote of a town outside the county to give a Republican candidate the election.

Lewelling, in a later 1895 message, summarized the matter: "The conduct of the Canvassing Board was so extraordinary, it was publicly and severely rebuked, even by leading Republican newspapers. . . . The majorities claimed for several of the persons to whom certificates there thus issued ranged from fifty to twenty-four votes; and in at least four instances the ballots themselves showed that even these majorities had been obtained by means of false precinct returns. Ballots entirely blank . . . had been counted for Republican candidates, as had also ballots bearing the names of the candidates of the People's Party." He recited the various electoral frauds in detail.

In all, the Populists were contesting eighteen legislative seats, the Republicans seven. Six seats were being contested because the candidates had been holding federal jobs at the time elected, which was prohibited by the state constitution.

These matters had been taken to the Supreme Court, also controlled by the Republicans. That august body declared it could not alter any findings, whatever the injustice, because the Canvassing Board, having disbanded, was "dead."

The Populists insisted that the Populists counted out had a right to a seat in the legislature straight off, that the legislature alone had a right to review the elections and seat permanently the true incumbent. The Republicans insisted that the decision of the Canvassing Board was final.

The controversy aroused the whole state. The Populists charged that for weeks "the agents of the corporations had spread broadcast the report of a possible armed clash," that armed hirelings had been set to roaming the streets to overawe the authorities. The Republicans charged that the Populist clans had been called to the inauguration in order to overawe the legislature and threaten it with violence. This charge, Kent declared, was merely to give the Republicans and railroad guards "an excuse" for their own violence, "an excuse for striking another blow at the liberty of the people."

The day following the governor's inauguration, the House convened in Representative Hall, still decorated. Populist Secretary of State Osborn appeared with a duly certified membership role and proceeded, as per precedent, to act as presiding officer, pending temporary organization. A Republican objected and an uproar was precipitated. It became so violent that Secretary of State Osborn vanished with his list, and a Republican representative seized the chair. The Populists immediately rushed up J. H. Dunsmore of Neosho to take it away from him. More bedlam. In the midst of wild pandemonium, two separate bodies were organized side by side under the same roof. The Populists seated ten of its contested candidates but got their first setback when three Democrats, elected on fusion tickets with the Populists, remained neutral.

Jerry Simpson shouted at Chairman Jones of the Democratic State Committee, "treachery. . . . We want nothing more to do with your crowd!"

"We are ready to quit you," shouted Jones.

But there were tears in the eyes of both men, declared Republican Joseph Kennedy Hudson, editor of the "railroad paper," the Republican *Topeka Daily Capital.*

With the two houses under the same roof, both simultaneously carrying on business, both talking at once, the Biblical legend of Babel was repeated. Neither faction understood the language of the other; they spoke for different purposes; their constituents where wholly different. One represented the established Republican machine, the railroads, and the financial interests of the state. The insurgent groups depended on the aroused farmers. But despite the grimness, some good humor prevailed. Both bodies sent off messengers to inform the governor that the House had been organized.

The two rival houses stayed in session all night. Friends brought in sandwiches, pies, and coffee. By mutual agreement, the rival Speakers lay down together behind the stand — close together, for it was a freezing night and there was no heat — their respective gavels gripped in their fists.

The following day, a joint conference committee tried to reach a working compromise. The Republicans would cede nothing. The Populists, convinced that the people's representatives were being cheated out of their rights, would cede nothing. After a 26-hour session, both sides agreed to recess until 9:00 A.M., Thursday, January 12.

The Topeka Republican newspaper charged that if the Populists gained control, they intended to impeach two Republican Supreme Court judges, that Jerry Simpson, hoping to be chosen senator, had said that, if necessary, every able-bodied Populist in Kansas would be called out "to take forcible possession of the House."

On Thursday, the galleries were packed to suffocation. The 3 Democrats, elected by Populist votes, joined the Republicans, bringing their strength up to 67 members. To have a quorum, the Populists arbitrarily had to certify 13 Republicans as present and participating in their body.

[237]

At 5:20, a message came through from Governor Lewelling, duly recognizing the Populist House. Frenzied cheering broke out on the Populist side.

Editor Hudson now opened his guns on Lewelling in a series of vituperative letters. Once an independent reformer and a Granger, Hudson was now one of the inner circle of the Republican "ring" tied in with Sante Fe Railroad. In addition, he had been promised the eventual job of State Printer. Lewelling, he wrote, should "haul down the Stars and Stripes that float over the capitol and run up the appropriate red flag of anarchy and communism.

"We are facing a most serious condition of affairs, that at any moment may culminate in disgraceful personal struggle and possible loss of life . . . if our state is further disgraced by revolutionary action of the minority of your party in the House, you and your administration will be held responsible."

Lewelling requested the Republicans to appoint a committee to confer with him. They ignored his request. All good humor, after so much sleeplessness and tension and hoarse words, had vanished completely. Passions began to rise. It was rumored that the Populists would forcibly eject the Speaker of the Republican House. Lava-hot words poured from both sides.

That night, Republicans and railroad attorneys, at a great mass meeting at the Opera House, verbally stripped the hide off the Populists. Another mass meeting, addressed by leading Populists, also smelled of brimstone.

On Saturday, the Senate officially recognized the Populist House and duly advised the Governor that both houses were now ready for business.

The Speaker of the Republican House declared sarcastically: "The Almighty has wisely reserved the process of creation to himself alone. All the powers on earth, the Senators and governor included, cannot make sixty-three men out of fifty-eight [cheers]. And in every free representative body in the world the majority governs [renewed cheering]. . . . The constitutional House of

Representatives with sixty-seven lawful members is here and ready for business; and here it will remain, unterrified and unawed."

The Populists proposed that three impartial arbiters be commissioned with final power to decide on all electoral contests. The Republicans rejected this. Each house thereupon busily unseated members of the other house, putting its own candidates in their places.

"Railroad" editor Hudson continued to blast Lewelling: "If you will dismiss your kitchen cabinet long enough to hold your ear to the ground, you will hear from more than a million of your constituents the sincere hope that you, head of the state government, will not disgrace your high office by longer encouraging lawlessness and treason."

He predicted an early doom for an administration "created by Bellamyism, nursed by the principles of Doster and Herr Most, [anarchists] and made ridiculous by Simpson and Willetts [a leading Populist] . . . and cockleburr statesmen." He accused the Populists of being "lawyers, doctors, and money-loaners," not farmers. The Populist House was merely a fiat house. "The massive brains of your leaders have become so tangled up in millions and billions of fiat relief that it is not surprising that even you should have been led into error by them, until you really believe fifty-eight to be larger than sixty-seven." Great mass-meetings all over Kansas, he claimed, were denouncing Lewelling.

"Don't try to be bigger than the people, Governor," continued Hudson. "Political cemeteries are full of alleged statesmen who have tried that experiment." And he demanded sarcastically, "My dear sir, if the army moves upon the Bastile of the plutocrats, will you command in person in the full regalia of a militia Major-General?" He gave caustic ironic advice on how best to storm the statehouse.

Two more tense days dragged by. On the seventeenth of the month, the Governor's message was received in the Senate. Populist Chaplain Todd prayed, thanking God that there was a stalwart

[239]

Spartan band ready to do its duty. He implored the Almighty to give the other side "the breadth of vision and charity that would enable them to see and do the right."

Hudson said Chaplain Todd had put the Lord in the wrong political party.

Governor Lewelling issued a public address giving the Populist side of the issue, and the Senate spent much time airing the fraudulent elections.

The two legislative bodies were now recessing by mutual agreement day by day. In ear-deafening cacophony, both were making appointments, voting laws. To get the three fusion Democrats back into the fold, the Populists were dickering to appoint Democratic Judge John Martin to the United States Senate.

Jerry Simpson didn't like this. Neither did campaigner Mary Lease, who also wanted the job. According to Hudson, the "Jumping Cassandra of Wichita" was preaching her "mournful prophecies of evil to come in case she is not elected to the United States Senatorship, for membership in which plutocratic body she had been working very, very hard." Certainly she fought the "sellout" to the Democrats heatedly. Tirelessly, she told individual legislators that the appointment of any Democrat would be "treachery to the cause."

Hudson's next Sunday blast sarcastically called the Governor's message "as conservative as any Republican measure." No "silk-paper money" was proposed, and the Governor "failed to recommend the building of a single state corn-crib, wheat bin or packing house." The Populists, he jibed, were just "tin-horn reformers," merely "firing to hurt with prejudice, hate and sublimated nonsense." There had been no reduction in salaries as pledged. "Why, I ask, in Senator Jumper's corn-husking tones, are you silent upon these burning questions? . . . Is it possible, Governor, that the close proximity of the Executive office to the Santa Fe building has influenced you to ignore the great objects of your order? . . .

"When I last wrote you, the spirit of war seemed to be rampant in the executive chamber. I have waited, since your proclamation, to see you and your War Secretary [Adjutant A. A. Hertz] . . . appear in the brilliant uniform of the Kansas militia, mounted upon sprightly Norman-Percherons from the stables of the Senator who presides over the Judiciary Committee [a Populist rancher who bred horses]. How like Don Quixote and his faithful Sancho Panzo! As you thundered down Kansas Avenue, your brave hearts palpitating, the observed of all observers, nodding plumes, clanking swords, followed by your bodyguard and the battalions of patriots, you would fire anew the martial spirit of the People's Party that only needs a leader to go forth and regenerate and reorganize society, establish justice, and rag money, and raise hades generally."

The Governor addressed the public through the columns of the *Kansas City Mail*. "The daily press teems with inflamatory utterances containing the basest falsehoods. Mass meetings, managed by men salaried by unscrupulous avarice, have . . . passed resolutions filled with untruthful assertions and vicious insinuations concerning those to whom you have entrusted the responsibilities of administering your state government."

Hudson said this second war-proclamation "would belittle a barroom loafer." It placed Lewelling "in the list of political demagogues . . . riding this calamity wave, regardless of the cost to the state and the people," and he taunted: "If you are going to use the militia, why don't you do it without so much blathering nonsense?"

The war of nerves continued. On Monday, January 25, the Republican House ruled that the unseating of seven Republicans by the Populist body had been groundless. A caucus put up a leading Republican for U.S. Senator and Hudson to be State Printer. But the three seceding Democrats, promised that their party would get the Senate seat, rejoined the Populist House. In a joint meeting of the Senate and the Populist House, only seven members refused to obey the party whip, and Democratic Judge Martin was duly elected. Mary Lease bitterly denounced this as

[241]

"base treason." An effort was made to mollify her by giving her a job on the charities board, but she became so bitter in her criticisms of Lewelling that Republican vituperation of her turned into praise.

On Thursday, the joint Populist House-Senate confirmed other appointments and put in a Populist as State Printer. Hudson's fury increased. He denounced the deal with the Democrats by which a Democratic Senator and a "middle-of-the-road" printer were elected — "all the love-feast, speeches, receptions and falling upon necks in consequence of this little dicker in official boodle . . ." He chuckled at the "daily great act of riding the snorting bronco of Populism and the rejuvinated old cob of Democracy, going in different directions."

The new week started, Monday, January 30, with a spirited speech by the Republican Speaker that heightened ill feeling The Republicans were intent on throwing the controversy into the courts, which they controlled. The Populists were intent upon denying the courts all jurisdiction. The Populist Speaker sent a letter to the Republican House: the legal Populist House, recognized by the Governor and the Senate, could not be "annulled by an other tribunal except by the unconstitutional exercise of power."

Every informed man in Kansas is aware that "the railroads and other corporate managers in the State are behind you; promoting and directing the actions of your party to block the wheels of legislation." They "even go so far . . . as to advance the pay you and other representatives receive through one of its banks of this city, closely connected with certain railroad interests."

Denying all railroad affiliations, the Republican Speaker replied that the Populists could perform no miracles. They were powerless to create "a majority" out of a "minority" or to destroy by "fiat" the "constitutional and lawful body of representatives of the people."

[242]

Both houses continued to carry on business with rival din, and Populist reading clerk, Ben C. Rich, had a booming voice that drowned out Republican speeches. The Populist House discussed legislation to reduce maximum interest rates. The Governor appointed a Populist railroad commission — "to wreck the railroads of Kansas," snorted Hudson. On Thursday, the Republican House passed a resolution to give the Populists ten days to take their seats in the "legal" house or lose them permanently.

For the first time, the Populist House backed water. Foreseeing that the whole question would land in the courts, it unseated its ten "fiat members" until "proper determination of their status" and "doctored up" the original journal of proceedings.

Over the weekend, the Republicans worked to get a court restraining order to hold up all pay warrants of the Populist House and ordered its sergeant at arms to arrest Populist legislator L. C. Gunn of Linn County for refusing to appear before the (Republican) House election committee, and Ben C. Rich, clerk of the Populist House, for interrupting proceedings.

The warrant was served on Rich at the Dutton House, where he was lunching with his wife and a Populist representative. Rich refused to submit to arrest — at least before eating — and the Republican sergeant at arms deputy good-humoredly accepted an invitation to have lunch. According to the choleric Hudson, the deputy was overawed by Rich's fierce buccaneer's moustache.

At 1:15, Mr. and Mrs. Rich were joined by five other Populist leaders and left the hotel on foot. A chilly blast was sweeping down the avenue. Three other Republican deputies bore down on them, but the Populists refused to let them get near. One deputy was knocked down, whereupon all three beat "an inglorious retreat."

Rich was escorted in triumph and a gale of cheers to the Populist side of the House. Guards were put around him to prevent further molestation. A resolution condemned the attempted arrest "by an organized mob, calling themselves the Republican House of Representatives, but which we believe to be in reality the Santa Fe Railroad Company . . . We proclaim to the State of Kansas that the mob was foiled and that our flag is still here."

Both sides swore in scores of special sergeants at arms. Several hundred Republicans gathered at the Copeland Hotel (Republican headquarters) to offer their services to halt forcibly all Populist proceedings. Over fifty were sworn in as deputies by the Republican Sheriff, a "loaned Santa Fe Railroad guard."

Constables appeared with warrants for the Populist representatives who had "broken the peace" in defending Rich. At the conclusion of the House proceedings, they voluntarily appeared before a judge and gave bonds.

After mutual adjournment, the Populists made a coup by seizing the hall and locking the doors, and Rich transferred all his books to the safe in the Populist auditor's office. At daybreak, Rich and his guard went home, leaving six armed men on the stairway.

The Governor and the Populist Speaker called on the sheriff of the county, a Republican, to protect the House and Clerk Ben Rich. He refused, saying that the legitimate house had ample powers to maintain order through its sergeant at arms. He could not take sides, although he intended to maintain peace in city and county. The Governor then sent him an order to stop a lawless body of men who "contemplated a second attempt to arrest said Rich and in other ways to become a menace to the peace and order of the State."

The sheriff ignored this, and, late on the night of February 14, the Governor called out the militia. Angry partisans of both factions swarmed into the city.

In the morning, armed guards refused to let the Republican doorkeeper enter the Hall of Representatives. He went angrily back to the Copeland Hotel, where the Republicans were assembled. They decided to storm the statehouse by force, a maneuver masterminded by George A. Peck, the chief Santa Fe agent and lobbyist.

[244]

Headed by their Speaker Douglass, with special deputies, and about 100 hangers-on, the Republicans marched grimly forward to their rendezvous with destiny. A big mob joined them.

At the foot of the main stairway, the militiamen ordered them not to attempt to pass.

"On whose order?"

"By order of the Adjutant General and the Executive Council."

"As Speaker of the House, I order you to get out of the way."

A scuffle occurred. With wild yells, the mob dashed forward, overcame the guards by sheer force of numbers, and surged up the stairway.

At the top, more militiamen pointed their guns, and ordered them to stop. One of Peck's agents, posing as a reporter, who had slipped in by another route, shouted: "For God's sake, don't shoot! Don't shoot innocent blood!"

The guards hesitated, and the Republicans leapt upon them. With a sledge hammer "secured," according to Kent, "from the Santa Fe railroads yards," the Speaker dramatically smashed in the "flimsy" cloakroom door, and with shouts and waving revolveis the Republicans surged in.

The Republicans now appointed over 600 deputies to keep the Populists out, and supplied them with red badges reading "Assistant Sergeant at Arms." According to Kent, they included bankers, lawyers, physicians, businessmen, mechanics from the Santa Fe shops, college boys, thugs, and Pinkertons.

The Pinkertons, said Lewelling, had been rushed in by the railroads; Washburne College students were enlisted in order to have access to the federal guns at the school.

The staircase landing was blocked with desks, benches, and timbers; so was the Speaker's entrance. Heavy bolts were put on every door, which were further reinforced with heavy timbers, and seats and desks were piled against them. Other barricades were stacked up. Doors leading to other departments were spiked shut. Firearms, clubs, and iron bars were passed around. Later, rifles and ammunition were smuggled in, also baskets of food from the Copeland Hotel. Subsequently, the State had to pay for $1,400 worth of sandwiches and $3.00 a day to the armed deputies.

The arrest of numerous Populist representatives was ordered. Lewelling issued another proclamation, denouncing the attempt to make unlawful arrests and the failure of the sheriff to assist in maintaining law and order. He called for more militia to suppress the Republican "unlawful assemblage."

Oakland Company C, called out the previous night to report, failed to respond on the excuse that their overcoats were locked up in the armory. Two provisional companies were hastily organized, and orders were sent to half a dozen militia companies in other parts of the State to hasten to the capitol. The Republicans confidently predicted a mutiny.

The head of the state militia, Colonel J. W. F. Hughes, ordered by telegram to report at once for duty, leisurely appeared at the Governor's office and pompously inquired if he should don his uniform. He then took two and a half hours to do so. Finally Company C appeared on Capitol Square. Greeted with derisive yells by thousands of assembled Republicans, it bivouacked in the ground floor hall and took charge of all entrances. State officials and judges were given passes.

By 3:00 P.M., the two provisional companies, outfitted at the arsenal, appeared and were similarly jeered. They cleared the crowd away from the doors. The mob closed in on them, grabbing for their guns and hitting them. Populist Chaplain Todd of the Senate engaged in a fist-fight to aid the militia men. The sheriff got the mob to accept a truce.

Company C then marched in formation down the front steps, determinedly cleared everybody away, and posted sentries around the grounds. At 6:45, forty members of Company B marched in.

Behind its upstairs barricades, the Republican House leveled stronger resolutions against Lewelling. The Governor was "coercing" a branch of the legislature. He was "a usurper, attempting

[246]

to place the civil authorities of the state in subjection to the military thereof." Lewelling was showered with anonymous skull and crossbone threats and actually received a valise full of human bones.

At 7:30 P.M., he boldly entered Representative Hall, and was duly escorted to the Speaker's desk. He requested that the hall be vacated so he should not have to eject the Republicans forcibly. The Republicans suggested both sides agree to abandon the hall until a court decision could be reached.

Lewelling repeated firmly, "I ask you gentlemen, that you surrender this hall into my keeping tonight, that you vacate this hall and leave it in my care." He departed.

He was followed on the rostrum by a former Republican governor, heading a citizens' committee, who pleaded for calm surrender when the militia came, so as to avoid a war "more bloody than Kansas had ever known." His advice was received in sullen silence. "Inflammatory speeches were made, and the representatives announced they would surrender only at the point of the bayonet. Republican supporters telegraphed they were on their way with armed forces. Armed Populists were also pouring in from all parts of the state. It looked like a bloody showdown."

Lewelling ordered Colonel Hughes to "proceed quietly" to Representative Hall and "eject all persons not legally there."

At 10:30, Hughes appeared among the besieged Republicans in full uniform. Instead of obeying orders, he announced he had told the Governor to look for some other officer. Frenzied cheering greeted his words. "I am still in command, and I am going to stay here until I am relieved. . . . [hence] you need have no fear tonight. No one will attempt to molest you. If I am relieved my regiment will go with me [deafening applause, and three cheers]."

The balance of the night the Republicans spent singing "John Brown's Body" and taking catnaps.

The Governor and his advisers also sat up all night.

And all that cold night, bivouac fires blazed in Capitol Square.

[247]

The militia members huddled close to keep warm. But guards were advanced to the outer fence, sentries paced around the entire building at a distance of 200 feet, and pickets patrolled the whole square.

But the lines were easily passed by many persons not having the required adjutant general's pass. At 10:00 P.M., two more companies of militia arrived. Topeka presented the appearance of an armed siege. Through the morning mist that enveloped the capitol building could be dimly discerned the last gleams of camp-fires and the blue uniforms of the armed sentries pacing their beats. The tattered remnants of the old flag still floated on the east wing.

Part of the militia turned out for a morning drill, with "all the pomp and circumstance of war." Speakers and newspapers warned that Kansas was on the verge of armed revolution.

"Who were the revolutionists?" demanded Populist Kent.

His answer: the Republicans. "They had committed overt acts hoping to bring about a serious crisis, with the aid of a partisan administration."

"Who were the revolutionists?" asked Republican Hudson.

Answer: the Governor and the Populists, who had attempted to replace law with anarchy.

A few Republican legislators risked going out in small groups to get breakfast. They carried back all the food they could to the others and to the deputies. United States mail carriers appeared with new mail sacks filled with provisions and 10-gallon cans of hot coffee. A throng of federal marshals were on hand to arrest anyone interfering. No one did.

The Governor relieved Colonel Hughes of his command and sent out a call for more militia.

The ousted Populist House now met in his parlors, then in a private building, presently in the capitol basement, which was dubbed "the cave of doom."

The sheriff tartly sent word to the Governor that his use of military power to preserve peace without his consent was "wholly unnecessary," and from Republican headquarters at the Copeland he appealed for volunteers. George A. Peck maintained a suite there and, according to William Allen White, always had $20,000 or $30,000 slush fund and entertained legislators lavishly.

The second man to answer the sheriff's appeal was Reverend W. F. File, pastor of a fashionable Topeka church. By 11:30, nearly 500 deputies had received their blue badges and were rushed to the Santa Fe depot to disarm a provisional militia company coming in from Lawrence, the famous Robinson Rifles. It was one of the oldest military organizations in the state. The new contingent came unarmed, and the deputies hied themselves back to the Copeland.

The adjutant general sent the Robinson Rifles up to the Republican House as unarmed "citizens." They were refused admittance and marched to the arsenal, where they were given rifles.

At 1:00 P.M., the sheriff's force of deputies marched to the G.A.R. hall — another Republican stronghold — and organized into thirteen companies, armed with rifles, shotguns, revolvers, baseball bats, and clubs. He announced that if the militia or any other body attempted to eject the Republican House by force, he would move on the capitol with his whole command and take possession at any cost.

The sheriff's deputies mapped out plans to assault from the east. The Republican House deputies inside would charge simultaneously. Thus the militia, expected to mutiny, would be caught between two fires.

The commander of the Republican deputies in Representative Hall phoned the manager of the Santa Fe railroad to ask him to let the boys in the shops off to join the attack.

Vast crowds gathered about the square. The walls of the Santa Fe yards, just across the street, were "black with curious humanity." The steps of the Baptist church "resembled a ladies' gallery in some public hall." Small boys roamed about armed with clubs and talking "in the tones of a Mississippi fog horn."

The attack was held up. The Governor was dickering with the

[249]

Republican House to try to prevent bloodshed. By nightfall, the militia had been augmented by two more batteries and three companies. Three more units were on the way. Thousands of noncombatants of both sides were swarming into the city. Hourly the situation became more ugly.

At 5:00 P.M., a heavy snowstorm set in and lasted all night. Only the calls of the sentries broke the silence on Capitol Square as the white flakes swirled down. The acting Speaker of the House invited the national guards from Marion to camp for the night in Representative Hall, where it was warm. The invitation was accepted.

All night the Populist House also remained in session, in constant communication with the worried Governor, who was still dickering with a committee from the Republican body. He received many callers, with suggestions or appeals. At midnight, the general solicitor of the Santa Fe Railroad Company pled that he recognize the Republican House. There was a reason for his concern, said Lewelling. "A Populist railroad law more stringent than the Iowa statute" was soon to be put into full force and effect.

But he began to waver. On the morning of the seventeenth, he agreed that the Republicans should retain possession of the hall. The militia would be retired, and the militia en route to the capital would be ordered to return home. On their side, the Republicans promised there would be no arrests or other punitive action. Both sides agreed to abide by the decision of the Supreme Court.

The Populists had consistently refused to admit that the Supreme Court, which had denied all jurisdiction in the electoral contests, could now take jurisdiction to determine the legality of either House. But the Governor now gave the matter over to the Republican court he had already roundly denounced as a tool of the Santa Fe Railroad. His threats had been empty, his display of force had been meaningless. Jubilant, the Republican legislators marched off through 10 inches of new fallen snow for hot breakfast.

By then the snow had smothered the militia campfires. From the smoldering embers, only thin columns of blue smoke rose high into the clear crisp atmosphere. The sun poured a flood of glory over the white expanse. The militia had decamped. The Republican House and sheriff dismissed their hundreds of deputies.

Hudson blasted the Governor with a sneer: "Our people escaped the deplorable disaster of a bloody conflict due more to your vacillation than to your courage."

In a bitter manifesto, Lewelling reported, "the Governor found himself confronted by the sheriff of Shawnee County and a huge horde of drunken, ruffianly deputies," by a legion of "cutthroat scoundrels" from Missouri, "a lawless and treason-infected Republican gang." It was a "vicious and depraved" mob, "filled with ruin," boasting of how it would handle the "Populists." The state militia on whom he had to rely was "cowardly and disloyal" to a man, "stained through and through with treason." The commanding officer was "the first to make known his contempt for his official oath." The Governor had made terms with "a lawless body" only because forced to, "just as the Union men at Fort Sumter" had had to recognize Jeff Davis.

He threatened the Supreme Court with popular vengeance if it knuckled under to the Republicans and outlawed the "legal" Populist House and the laws already passed. The Supreme Court that would declare against the People's House would "have to reverse all respectable precedent and immolate itself to the basest partisan demands. It would face a wave of public indignation unequaled since the days of the notorious Judge Tresillian, who was followed to the scaffold by an outraged people where they beat him with staves to make him ascend, then exulted at his just but shocking execution."

Both houses busily prepared their cases before the Supreme Court. Before the month was out, that body declared the Republican House legal. Populist Judge Allen voiced dissent in a weak minority opinion.

[251]

Populist Senator Leedy, "with windy power," according to
Hudson, proposed the capital be moved from its corrupt proximity
to the corporations out into the prairies, where it would be in
touch with Providence. "I despise the two judges that rendered
such a decision . . . We will get the political hides of those judges,
and when they are hung up to dry we will see them branded on
both sides with the railroad brand. I expect to see this usurper
Horton [Chief Justice], like Jeffreys, hunting the prisons of this
country in which to hide himself from justice."

A few days later, Horton resigned his high office to accept
a more lucrative post with the Santa Fe Railroad.

On Tuesday, February 28, beneath crowded galleries, the Populist
representatives entered the Republican House en masse, bearing
an American flag. This acceptance of the Supreme Court decision
automatically reduced the Populist block.

But the Republicans wisely pursued no Punic revenge. Partisan
bickering out of the way, the House went into high gear to make
up for wasted time. The Republicans could not ignore the Populist
landslide in the state and pushed ahead with legislation remarkably
Populist: a railroad commission law, direct election of senators by
the people, abolition of unjust discrimination in railroad rates, a
mortgage law, reasonable right of redemption of foreclosed
property, and lower foreclosure costs — nearly all the major
Populist demands. Although the Australian secret ballot law lost
by a small margin, a radical bill to prevent electoral corruption
was passed, and a resolution favored "female suffrage."

It was the Populist Senate that now gave Lewelling the knife.
It refused to confirm all but one of the Kansas City police com-
missioners appointed by him, because they were friends of Pete
Kline, the lottery dealer, with whom a backdoor political pre-
election vote-getting deal had been made. Lewelling was there-
after long and furiously criticized, a hue and cry in which Mrs.
Lease joined with the Republicans. A Senate committee, mostly
Populist, investigated charges of political corruption between

the Governor and the underworld. From this time on, Lewelling was under bitterly savage attack from his own followers.

Hudson continually scoffed at the dawn of a new era. The Medicine Lodge *Cresset* accused Lewelling of lowering taxes on first-class Pullman cars and raising it on tourist cars, "the poor man's vehicle." On top of that, Pullman doubled the price of a berth, after Lewelling was given "a free ride in a Pullman Palace train" to the World's Fair. Even so, he had objected to tipping the porter.

Mary Lease warred on the adjutant general so effectively that Lewelling dismissed him. "Second blood for Mrs. Lease," gloated the *Cresset*.

Lewelling was often petty, not as forceful as his bluster, but was far from being incapable. By appealing directly to the voters, time and again he forced the Republican House majority to pass many beneficial laws. In his 1893 message, he pointed out the alarming increase in local indebtedness and the decrease in the amount of money spent for schools. He recommended free textbooks and denounced free railroad passes. He asked for more electoral reforms to safeguard the ballot box both at elections and primaries. Kansas was far behind in this. Individuals or corporations using employment to influence the vote should be severely penalized.

He asked for better protection for debtors. Evasion of the legal interest rate should be made a misdemeanor. For the proper protection of a household, personal property ought to remain unencumbered, lest it be "swept from the grasp of a confiding wife and innocent children." He asked for a proper screening law to protect coal miners and their wages and for the abolition of script and company store credit. A bureau of agriculture should be established.

His message of January 9, 1895, when about to leave office for good, was more outspoken. He condemned fee-grabbing by police and local officials and asked for reform of the criminal pro-

[253]

cedure. He denounced the excessive fire-insurance premiums charged by eastern companies and proposed state government insurance. He came out against excessive stockyard and elevator charges and suggested establishing public elevators and yards. The irrigation monopoly should be broken and convict labor used only on public works. He let out a blast against the coal companies, who had reduced wages to take away all the benefits to the miners of recent laws and during the resultant strike had erected "private forts" garrisoned "with conscienceless mobs." "Private war carried on by armed citizens should not be tolerated as a mode of settling controversies between workingmen and their employers." Systematic murder was not the proper method to test the validity of a legislative act. The corporations had "engaged in an armed revolt against the laws of the state."

He flayed the Cleveland administration, which, during the railroad strikes of '94, permitted the federal courts to raise an army of deputies and turn them loose, armed with Winchester rifles, to overrun the state of Kansas. "These so-called deputy marshals . . . were actually a combination of policemen and soldiery acting under judicial sanction as the mercenary retainers of certain railroad companies. . . . The chief magistrate of the sovereign state of Kansas was treated with no more consideration than were the governments of the Confederate States by the generals of the federal army, coming for the vowed purpose of subjugation in time of war. . . . A protest should be made against these usurpations in language so plain and so emphatic that it shall be understood by Congress."

But the noisy battle of Kansas had had bad results for Lewelling and the People's party. Members considered it a weak knuckling under, and others, a sign of incompetency. Disgraceful third-party disputes after the "War of '93" also greatly disillusioned the voters. Job-hunting and the spoils system were not merely an old party pastime, and the Populists lost heavily in the next local and judicial elections. In 1894, the Republicans made a clean sweep.

The farmers revolt in Kansas was all but over.

[254]

XII
BLOODY
BRIDLES WAITE

Davis H. Waite, the first and only Populist Governor of Colorado, had been a restless man, having engaged in teaching, farming, store-keeping, mercantile pursuits, law, politics, and journalism in half a dozen states before being attracted to Colorado in 1879. There, from August 13, 1891 to August 4, 1892, he published and edited the *Aspen Union Era*, and thereby overnight converted himself from an elderly obscure journalist into the lightning rod of the greatest political upheaval in the history of the state. He ran for Governor on the Populist ticket and was elected.

Born in Jamestown, New York, April 9, 1825, he was sixty-seven when elected Governor of the Rocky Mountain Commonwealth. He had attended public schools and studied law in his father's office. For a time he engaged in "mercantile pursuits" with a relative. In Jamestown, and in Warren, Pennsylvania, he dipped into newspaper work. In 1850, he moved west to Fond du Lac, Wisconsin, then to Princeton, where he opened a store. In 1856, he was elected to the legislature on the Fremont ticket. Three years later, he was in Missouri teaching school, but at the outbreak of the Civil War was run out because of his northern sympathies. Returning east to Jamestown, he practiced law and took charge of the *Chautauqua Democrat*, a Republican paper. He moved west again, practiced law in Larned, Kansas, and in 1878 was elected Republican legislator. A year later, he joined the rush to the new Colorado Leadville mines and hung his shingle out as an attorney.

The railroad reached Leadville in 1880, and workmen for the mines arrived by hundreds. Wages were reduced from $5.00 a day to $2.50. When a strike broke out, the mine-owners put up green pine-log block houses in commanding positions and manned the hills with riflemen. Strikers were arrested and held in a "bullpen" built alongside the jail.

Busy in this strike was Joseph R. Buchanan, a future executive, until he was expelled, of the powerful Knights of Labor. Every afternoon he addressed strike crowds. Usually the meetings were broken up. A strikers' parade was followed by a Citizens' Law and Order parade of leading merchants, "owning mine stocks," and "a variegated mob of half-drunk loafers, gamblers and bums, armed with shotguns and rifles." The town mayor, editor of a paper and a minebroker, "drunker than most," led the procession on horseback, slashing his sword right and left. A young chap was cut across the cheek, and the police had to hurry the reeling mayor away from the fury of the crowd. A "Committee of 100" ordered the editors of the strikers' paper, the *Crisis*, to leave town. Three left, but Buchanan defiantly stayed on. These events moved Waite deeply and aroused his sympathy for labor.

The following year he moved to Aspen, where he became justice of the peace and the first superintendent of schools of Pitkin County. In 1888, he affiliated with the Union Labor party and was local secretary of the Knights of Labor. As a local judge, he was very severe on gambling and vice, which he considered the major cause of poverty.

[256]

He founded the *Aspen Union Era,* which was to become the leading exponent of Populism in the state, also an oracle of prohibition and righteousness. Though tinctured with free thought, Waite was a Presbyterian, holding an important church office, and opened his columns to organized religion and Bible propaganda. He opposed the Catholic hierarchy but praised the papal encyclical for its sympathy with the masses.

Lincoln, he noted, had predicted the enthronement of corporations and an era of corruption in high places as a result of the Civil War. "Monopoly," wrote Waite, "is the great dragon whose breath withers and destroys the fleet of commerce . . . paralyzes the arm of industry . . . and arrays every person against his neighbor." Inevitable conflict would occur between monopoly and the people. Geographically, Colorado was so far from the rest of the country, it was wholly at the mercy of "the transportation monopolists" and their hired attorneys, who stifled all new enterprise they could not control. The Union Pacific, he declaimed, was "nursed as a viper in the bosom of the Republic." The only solution was government ownership.

In Colorado, the richest lands and resources were controlled by corporations, in turn dominated by British capital. The state was merely a colony of the capitalists — another Ireland. "Private ownership in land," he said in the *Aspen Union Era* on January 7, 1892, "is legalized robbery . . . the earth belongs to all the people." Legislation is favor of the debtor class was necessary to save the country.

Although he favored fiat money and was converted to the prosilver position, he feared the silver men would gain control of the new People's party. The real issue was not silver but control of Colorado corporations. Such broadsides soon gave him statewide notoriety.

He helped create the new national third party and was a delegate to both the St. Louis and Omaha conventions. The Omaha platform was a "second Declaration of Independence."

As chairman of the local Populist convention, he pushed through a resolution that landlordism had been "fostered by both the great political parties until whole townships . . . and counties are owned by alien landlords in almost every western and southern state." He attacked the Pitkin County courthouse ring for criminal and wasteful extravagance. The two old parties, wrote Waite, "have only seven principles — two loaves and five small fishes." The Colorado Senate was composed largely of "corporation attorneys in the pay of Wall Street." The new people's organization was "poor but pure."

He stood for uncompromising party integrity and bitterly opposed all attempts of the Silver Democrats, led by brilliant Thomas M. Patterson, editor of the *Rocky Mountain News,* to effect a fusion. He was enthusiastically chosen candidate for Governor.

His personal appearance bespoke his unbending attitude. He was a stiff, stern old man in a straight-up collar with pointed corners sticking into his chin under a big white beard; his mouth was tight-lipped, his eyes imperious behind thick glasses. Every inch of him spelled rectitude and obstinacy.

Bad conditions in Colorado had heightened insurgency. There were more mortgages per capita than in any other state except Kansas. Depression, scarcity of money, low wages, wide unemployment — all these evils were at the door. The price of silver dropped, forcing many mines to close down.

The silver issue broke down all party lines. The angry silverites, belonging to all political groups and all classes, held a big convention, April 26, 1892, and sent delegates to a Washington reunion, where it was decided that all "silver" delegates to old party national conventions should bolt if free silver coinage planks were not put in the platforms or the nominees were not "unquestionably in favor of the full remonitization of silver."

Colorado's Republican boss, Congressman Henry Teller, tried to get a silver plank into the Republican national platform but failed — and bolted. Democratic boss Patterson tried to get a silver plank into the Democratic national platform but failed. The People's party's Omaha convention came out flatfootedly for free coinage of silver.

The big Colorado Silver League called its convention to meet simultaneously with that of the state convention of the People's party. But though both bodies were in agreement on the Silver issue, the naming of candidates and the question of future patronage produced stormy scenes. Patterson wanted the silverites and his own party to endorse Weaver for President but to support the Democratic state ticket. Wild pandemonium broke out — "the most shameful scene in the annals of Colorado politics." Patterson left the hall in high dudgeon. Waite was nominated for Governor.

Patterson next tried to control the Arapahoe [Denver] County Populist convention to secure places on the ticket for his men, but an all-out Populist ticket was named. Because of these dickerings with the Populists, he was ousted from the conservative Democratic executive committee and almost read out of the party. He carried his fight to the floor of the Democratic state convention. There pro-Populists or pro-Weaver Democrats were in great evidence with striking purple badges. The stand-patters, favoring Cleveland, wore white badges.

When the chairman tried to read his list of delegates, which would have excluded many pro-Weaver men, a near-riot broke out, and the old-line Democrats were worsted. A most remarkable political gathering, remarked historian R. G. Dill. It met as a Democratic convention and adjourned as a Populist auxiliary.

Patterson tried to get promises of patronage from the Populists for his machine. Waite refused to grant any concessions, but behind his back the Populist executive committee secretly promised Patterson that if the Populist ticket were elected, he could select certain appointees. Subsequently, Waite refused to abide by this "treacherous" arrangement.

While the Populist state convention was still in session, General Weaver and Mrs. Lease arrived to address it and to campaign in that state. Huge overflow meetings in Denver, Pueblo, Leadville, Aspen, and Grand Junction were held.

Waite stumped the state thoroughly, visiting all but seven counties. He spoke on free silver, the bettering of labor conditions, opposition to corporations (particularly railroads), and, as every good politicial should, on the reduction of governmental expenses. The campaign became a popular uprising. Crowds howled Democrat and Republican speakers from the platforms and seized possession of the halls. Businessmen were plainly told, said Dill, that if they supported the Republican ticket they would be compelled to go out of business. The *Rocky Mountain News* displayed a picture of a gallows for all who would strike a blow against silver's friends and assist silver's enemies. It advocated a boycott of all Republican businessmen.

The Republicans charged that the "calamity howlers" were ruining the state. No more eastern capital would be invested. Creditors were holding off paying their debts till after the election. The *Rocky Mountain News* replied that the state was suffering from a real lack of money due to bad currency laws, not to threatened Populist victory

Though the Weaver electoral delegates received a plurality of nearly 15,000 in Colorado, Waite was made Governor by a plurality of only 3,000. In the new legislature, the Populists barely outnumbered the Republicans, so a handful of Democrats held the balance of power. To hold them in line the Populists, to Waite's disgust, had to give them a share of patronage.

Waite's election aroused panic in conservative circles, but he proceeded with great caution. Before taking office, he consulted with his predecessor, visited the state penitentiary, which he had promised to reform, and inspected work on State Canal No. 1, an important irrigation project that he promised to complete.

On grounds of economy, he did not permit the usual inaugural ball. His inaugural address reiterated his fidelity to the Omaha program, but his proposals were mild. He was sternest towards the railroads. The existing railroad commission was ineffectual, and he asked for a new commission of three elected members whose decisions could not be taken to the courts. He demanded lower railroad tariffs, that all rate pooling be made illegal. The offer of free passes to any local or state official, or their acceptance, should be made a penal offence.

State lands should be leased only to bona fide settlers. Convicts were to be used only on public enterprises. He favored the eight-hour day and arbitration. Strikes and lockouts should be prohibited in all enterprises employing more than forty men. He recommended women's suffrage in municipal elections.

The Assembly was asked to memorialize Congress in behalf of direct election of United States senators and to forbid the government to issue bonds for the Nicaraguan canal, which, rather, it should finance, construct, and control. No bonds should be issued for the purchase of gold. Pensions should be paid in silver.

His administration was far from harmonious. Deadlock in the lower house led to endless discord. Much time was wasted trying unsuccessfully to impeach the Populist state auditor for using bribery to get his job. Nearly 1,000 bills were introduced, and nearly every one precipitated harsh interchanges. Necessary legislation was so delayed that the House had to sit 36 hours over the legal 90 days while different clerks read bills simultaneously. The only innovation was a bill submitting to the people a constitutional amendment in favor of equal suffrage.

In the ensuing Denver municipal elections, the Populist convention, on orders from Waite, spurned Patterson and all fusion. As Dill put it, the Populists kicked away the ladder by which they had ascended to power. As a result, the Republicans won in an election notorious for frauds. For Waite, many headaches were to follow.

Police scandals shook the city, and Waite replaced the chief of police. In April, a police agent was charged with collecting money from gamblers for protection, and Waite kicked two men off the police board.

These petty events were soon swallowed up by the growing

[261]

financial panic. On June 26, 1893, India closed her mints. In four days, silver dropped to sixty cents an ounce — about half what it had been. Colorado mines and smelters closed down. The Denver Real Estate Exchange and the Chamber of Commerce held panicky meetings to petition Waite for a special session so the legislature could declare a moratorium. Waite, remembering a year of headaches from the wrangling legislators, refused. A Leadville bank folded up. Others crashed in Golden, Pueblo, Jefferson, and elsewhere. Panic spread rapidly.

Early in July, a statewide silver convention was called in an attempt to get federal action to save the state from collapse. There Waite, the leading speaker, attacked monopolies and the "gold bugs." He closed eloquently: "It is better, infinitely better, that blood should flow to the horses' bridles rather than that our national liberties should be destroyed."

He had acquired a nickname — "Bloody Bridles." His speech went round the world, and though it had been roundly cheered by conservative silverites, businessmen, and mine owners, his words were broadcast over the nation as evidence of his fanaticism, of the folly and violence of the Populists.

A few days later, three savings banks folded up in Denver. The following day, three national banks and three private banks failed; the day after, three of the biggest banks in the state went under. Dry goods, lumber, and real estate firms, including the biggest department store in the city, gave up the ghost. Soon, 1,200 men and many women were being fed by charity. Murders increased. Men were lynched.

A State Relief Committee was organized, and a relief camp was set up on the Denver River Front. The National Guard supplied tents to 570 men, and fed breakfast to over 1,000. Five hundred men were shipped east in boxcars provided gratis by the railroad. Presently a big wing of Coxey's unemployed army came trudging in from the far West to add to the burden.

President Cleveland made matters worse by urging the extra

session of Congress to repeal the Sherman silver purchasing law. The debate "re-echoed on the plains and mountains . . . and in the streets" of Colorado. "Populist theories ruled the roost at every street corner," sputtered Dill, "and all the ills of life, real and imaginary, were attributed to the folly of the people in not heretofore recognizing the hidden beauties of the Omaha platform and of the People's Party."

When Congress actually outlawed silver coinage, Colorado's passion became a near gale. This body blow caused more economic collapse, and the Democrats and Populists rushed pell-mell into each other's arms and put up joint farmer-miner candidates. Patterson broke with the Democrats and joined with the Populists. The Republicans nominated the same old gang, so a citizens' ticket was drawn up in Denver, with leading businessmen as candidates.

Behind the scenes a cheap religious struggle was also brewing. All Republican candidates were said to be members of the A.P.A., a secret anti-Catholic, post-Know-Nothing, organization sweeping the country.

The citizens' fusion ticket was rushed into office. The Populists carried two-thirds of the state's counties. Women's suffrage was adopted by a 5,000 majority.

The federal repeal of the silver act had brought Waite roaring into action. This breach of contract by the federal government gave the state the right to coin its own money. He proposed that certificates of indebtedness on State Canal No. 1 be issued in small denominations as paper money, that the state send its bullion to Mexico for coinage, that Mexican dollars be made legal tender in Colorado. He was denounced over most of the nation as unpatriotic, a fool, and worse.

By December, Waite gave in to pleas for a special legislative session. But by then, the businessmen had turned against the call, fearing that in the stress of the moment Waite might attempt to put over pet projects of which they did not approve. Besides, business had begun to find its keel. The rugged individualists were again feeling rugged. Crops had been good, prices excellent; gold-mining had taken up some of the pinch. The business elements held a meeting in Denver to condemn a special session.

Waite declared opposition came from only a small business clique. How about the miners? He called a convention at Salida to hear their views. His opponents charged that only eighteen men showed up and only ten favored a special session. Waite painted the Salida meeting as a popular mandate and called on the legislature to convene, January 10, 1894, declaring that the mining interests of the state were in turmoil, that the panic had left living conditions so bad that prices needed regulating, that the debtor classes needed immediate assistance. The state should coin its own money. He demanded an eight-hour law, prohibition of child labor, an anti-usury bill, amendment of the chattel mortgage law, better employees' liability, prohibition of "sweating" by coal trusts and monopolies. He called for the Australian ballot and the initiative and referendum. Arrangements should be made for a constitutional convention. His proposals were mostly sound, urgent reforms, but an astounding hue and cry went up that the state was headed for revolution.

The precarious balance of power in the legislature promised little danger that anything would be done. No sooner was the Senate in session than the Republicans demanded that both houses adjourn *sine die* and blocked all action.

Public opinion had more influence on the House, but little was accomplished except that the legal rate of interest and penalties for delinquent taxes were reduced. Modified foreclosure regulations saved many merchants. Work on State Canal No. 1 was ordered resumed.

Soon Waite had to oust two corrupt members of the Denver Fire and Police Board. They refused to get out and had the backing of the local police. Waite had to send in the militia. When the guardsmen drew up before the city hall, the Fire and Police Board had assembled 400 armed men, policemen, and gamblers to resist ejection. The local bankers and businessmen, who had originally demanded that Waite purge the Board, now rushed to him to plead against violent action. Waite impulsively appealed to General McCook at Fort Logan to send in federal soldiers. This froze the status quo, for the federal soldiers would not oust local officials. Waite thereupon requested McCook to take his troops back to the fort. McCook refused.

All hands quieted down, pending a decision by the Supreme Court. It declared the Governor had a right to remove said officials, but not by force. Just how they were to be removed, the court did not elucidate. Once more Waite threatened martial law. Public opinion swung to his side, and the grafting recalcitrants folded up their tents and departed.

Coxey's Commonweal Army of unemployed, on their march to Washington, alarmed many people. Waite's enemies said the Commonwealers had come to Colorado because of his wild Populist ideas although "wings" of that army had invaded nearly every state in the Union. The Coxeyites arrived in Denver in May, 1894, and were put in the old relief camp on the river front and fed. Various schemes for moving them on were suggested. It was finally decided to construct boats and send them down river.

One hundred and ten boats were hastily built, each with a ten-man capacity, but departure on June 7 was not very successful, as most of the boats collapsed. About 500 Commonwealers collected at Julesberg and tried to board trains. Some succeeded, others were arrested and brought back to Denver.

The Governor was already troubled by bitter strike difficulties. On February 1, 1894, the mine-owners tried to impose a ten-hour shift. The miners promptly struck. Violence and arrests followed, and Sheriff Bowers of El Paso County called for state troopers. Waite, though up to his neck in the "city hall war" and the Coxeyite difficulties, started for the scene.

The mine-owners had hundreds of special deputies sworn in. On May 25, a mine shaft was blown up, and the union men captured the strikebreakers and fortified themselves on Bull Hill. Soon, 1,000 armed deputies were camped nearby, and open warfare was threatened. President Slocum of Colorado College tried to effect a truce but failed. Governor Waite called on miners and deputies to lay down their arms and disband. When he visited the miners' camp on Bull Hill, trying to arrange compromise, he was charged with siding with the strikers. He should blast them out, not treat with them.

However, the Governor, the union heads, and the mine-owners' representative met at Colorado Springs and reached an agreement, providing for an eight-hour day at $3.00 a day, that none but union miners be employed, and that no one be prosecuted for acts during the strike. The miners accepted. The owners balked, and the deputies advanced on Bull Hill. Waite planted the militia between the two groups, and General Brooks threatened to fire on the deputies.

Another compromise was worked out. The militia was to remain mobilized for thirty days, the deputies were to withdraw immediately, and the miners were to give up their arms and any property taken. Strikers for whom the sheriff had warrants were to be turned over to the authorities of an adjacent county.

No one was pleased. The moneyed element said Waite was illegally abetting the laboring men and making a play for the miners' votes. The workers bitterly charged that they had got nothing but the arrest of their leaders.

Three hundred strikers went to jail, but only five cases were called. The worst victim was the strikers' attorney, who was taken from his room, tarred and feathered, and left in a desolate spot.

Although condemned so hotly, Waite had secured a practical and peaceful solution by recognizing the rights of both parties and obliging them to reach a compromise.

Industrial war continued with the nationwide Pullman strike. Late in July, United States troops were sent into Colorado and made indiscriminate arrests without warrants. Waite, as did

Governor Altgeld of Illinois, Lewelling of Kansas, and most western executives, sent indignant telegrams of protest to Washington. Waite's communications were ignored. In the end, Cleveland's use of the federal army in peacetime to break the strike contributed to the ruin of his public career and his virtual elimination from the Democratic party.

The next Populist convention was held at Pueblo. Waite turned a flinty face against any fusion with the Democrats. Patterson's Arapahoe delegation vociferously demanded a hearing but was squelched. Dill describes it as a witches' Sabbath, or the unholy revels observed by Tam O'Shanter, in which the delegates, wrangling, hurling disgusting epithets, howled, shook their fists, and danced like dervishes. One enthusiastic admirer of Waite, drunk with excitement, penetrated the Arapahoe ranks, waving the Governor's portrait and yelling defiance. The portrait was seized and became the center of a seething mass fight.

The fusion minority report was greeted "with yells, shrieks of derision, laughter, and roars of anger." When Patterson made his way forward to speak, the chairman ordered him off, and Waite's followers fought to reach the platform to drag him out. "Denunciation, vituperation and abuse fell upon the boss who, two years before, had made the election of Waite possible." Gallery spectators took up the shouts. Patterson stuck it out, taking advantage of each lull to speak, only to be howled into silence. He left the hall. With him went Waite's chances of reelection.

Despite trouncings in two Denver elections, Waite was confident his party would sweep the state unaided by the Denver Democrats. The Populists took the field early and late. Audiences were immense. Waite's progress through the state was one big ovation. Men and women flocked to see and hear the man who had been more talked about, more mercilessly criticized, and more roundly abused than any man in the country. The alarmed Republicans poured huge sums into the campaign.

Waite carried the western half of the state almost solidly, but

[267]

his ship foundered upon Patterson's Arapahoe County rock, where the Republican plurality overwhelmed the heavy Populist vote in farmer and mining counties.

And so ended the Populist upsurge in Colorado, and so ended the career of one of American's most picturesque figures.

Waite was a dogmatic, impulsive, high-minded individual, with little tact. His passionate feelings and prejudices rarely permitted him to compromise in any common-sense fashion, and he made a number of very bad political blunders, though never of principle. His defects were as obvious as his courage and honesty, and he was, despite the uproar, one of the ablest governors in Colorado's history. But everything was done to undermine his reputation. Throughout the nation he came to be regarded as a hairy monster. The *Tulare Daily Evening Register* out in California declared (March 28, 1894), "The fool thinks he is no reformer if he does not kill somebody, tear something down and burn something up, and Governor Waite of Colorado is a fool."

V. M. Besser's manuscript-biography in the University of Colorado library declares: "With the passing of depression, the dimming by time of the intensity of the opposition, we see not a radical drastic man, but a far-seeing, just-minded one . . . sincere in his attempts; one who was unpopular in his own day because he was in many respects in advance of his time, who saw much that was to come despite opposition and who was ready to be an apostle to his creed and brave the dangers which as yet were strong enough to ruin him."

Confronted by corrupt and intrenched officeholders who refused to abide by the law, Waite, as Huey Long did later, resorted to strong-arm but legal measures, but not once did he step over the edge into violence. He killed nobody. He tore nothing improper down. He burned up nothing. His predecessors had shot down miners ruthlessly. Instead Waite prevented bloodshed. No man ever had a sobriquet less appropriate than his "Bloody Bridles."

[268]

Not until sixty years later was a civilized system of handling strikes worked out. Waite was one of the first men in the country to impose a more enlightened solution. The progressive currents he set in motion, the traditions of civil and human liberties he promoted, have never been entirely lost in Colorado.

XIII
COXEY'S ARMY

The disastrous 1893 panic continued in all corners of the nation. Bankruptcy and unemployment assumed vast proportions. There was little real improvement until the Spanish-American War.

"Those of us who lived in the West through the panic of 1893," wrote Othman Abbot, in his *Recollections of a Pioneer Lawyer*, "had lived through bitter experiences . . . men and women and children . . . that had once owned prosperous farms, lost everything, their early homestead, their young stock, the acres they had tilled."

But "a worse calamity — the terrible drouth of 1894 — that long summer day when the hot winds blew endlessly," hit them at daybreak. The prospects of a corn crop were promising, but by sundown the entire crop was destroyed. Farmers who had put in "the entire spring and summer at·hard labor in the fields were ruined . . . devastation and destruction were brought to all farming communities." Small businessmen and others also suffered cruelly in the ever wider circle of ruin that bank failures and crop failures brought in their train.

Marginal farms no longer supported the dwellers, even on the miserable standards of years past. Farmers and croppers were added to those drifting from place to place. Factories closed down; shutters went up on gutted stores; men lost their life savings in failing banks; they lost their jobs. People began starving in abandoned railroad and timber camps or took to the road. The country was overrun with tramps, beggars, thieves, and unemployed.

Greeley's advice, "Go West," was mocked at. Eyes turned east. Soon, marching feet moved east. The good free lands were gone — west or east. There were no more free lush pastures. The wall of the Rockies and the Pacific had stopped the great westward movement.

And so, on a chilly March 25, 1894, Coxey's army of the unemployed, "the Army of the Commonweal of Christ," began its march from near Chicago to Washington to demand of Congress the passage of measures to relieve starving workmen. Similar armies sprang up everywhere and set out on the same long trek.

Many men had proposed such marches in the past. It was not the first or the last, though perhaps the largest and most dramatic. Such marches, like the one in Russia in 1905 to ask the little Father for bread, are symbols of the eternal hope of troubled folk that those in power will soften their hearts or aid in rectifying intolerable conditions.

In the United States, Coxey's idea had been abroad for some years, as disaster piled on disaster at the foot of the closed frontier. As early as 1886, Joseph Buchanan, member of the executive committee of the Knights of Labor and of the secret revolutionary A.W.I., at a meeting in Platt's Hall, San Francisco, let his imagination run away:

"What shall starving men do *right now?*" a man in his audience cried.

"Go out and get a banner and paint on it, 'On to Washington' . . .

Go to the sand lots. We will open a recruiting office and when we have twenty marchers, we'll start down Market Street, gathering the hungry, the wretched as we go. We'll cross the bay and in Oakland will confiscate a train . . . or tramp along on foot, but with our faces ever turned toward the East. Then across to Sacramento Valley, over the Sierra Nevadas, through the Great American Desert, beyond the great continental divide, the great plain on the eastern slope, the fertile fields of the Mississippi and the Ohio Valleys, across the Alleghenies, nor cease our journeying until we camp on the Capitol grounds at Washington.

"We will gather the disinherited as we march and the millions of betrayed and plundered will cry with us 'ON TO WASHINGTON.' We will take the food we require for our actual needs, leaving vouchers to be cashed in Washington when the people once more regain their government.

"When we have massed our great host of Industrial Crusaders about the Capitol and packed Pennsylvania Avenue from the Capitol to the White House, we will demand of our servant Congress, that it give us at once the justice that has been so long delayed. If it heeds not our commands, if it still defies us, we will hurl the whole treacherous swarm into the Potomac."

Much in this way, but with not such violent intentions, Coxey's armies set out nearly ten years later, and several expeditions started from San Francisco.

In nearby Chicago, one freezing night the previous January, a thousand men without work had fought like wild beasts in the city hall for the food brought them. Now, men like these, not so very large a group, were setting forth toward the promised hope. Coxey, a well-to-do businessman, was their Moses, but he died on no Mount Nebo; he never reached it.

He was born on Easter Sunday, April 16, 1854, so the march to Washington was on his fortieth birthday. At fifteen he had quit school to work in the rolling mills, where he labored for ten years. He tried his hand as junk dealer and finally, in 1881, moved to Massillion, Ohio, where he purchased a sandstone quarry and prepared sand for steel and glassworks. He invested his profits in nearby farms and prospered greatly. At the time of the march, he owned a Kentucky stock farm, where he bred blooded horses and raced or sold them, and was probably worth close to a quarter of a million.

He had always had a reforming streak. In 1885, he had joined the Greenbackers and was a candidate for the state senate on a currency platform. He was now a strong supporter of the Populist party.

He looked like a well-to-do farmer, a prosy, medium-sized man, with a stubby moustache and rimless spectacles. He was voluble, but very calm, and very, very earnest.

One dark stormy night in December, 1891, when Coxey was driving home, floundering in the mud holes, he realized the need for good roads. Only the federal government, he believed, could put in an adequate system, and only Congress could vote the money. Public works and fiat money — would not that solve the whole unemployment problem?

He got busy at once and had a bill introduced in Congress the very next session, ordering the Treasury to issue $500,000,000 in greenbacks to be spent by the War Department at the rate of $20,000,000 per month on roads, wages to be $1.50 for an 8-hour day.

He promptly organized the J. S. Coxey Good Roads Association of the United States. His plan, he was told, offered nothing for cities. But a dream on New Year's Eve of 1893 gave him the solution for cities also. He told it to Carl Browne, then stopping at his home.

Browne was one of the curious wayward types Coxey was always picking up, philosophizing to, and helping. He was a picturesque westerner, a crackpot whom Coxey had met at the 1891 Silver convention in Chicago.

"I have it," said Coxey to Browne that New Year's morning, and he wrote out the Non-Interest-Bearing Bond Bill, which would provide for all sorts of public improvements. Any local or state government could issue non-interest-bearing bonds to be deposited with the National Treasury for notes, which money would then be used for streets, schools, courthouses, etc. The money would be retired in twenty-five years. This would provide "actual money in place of confidence money. Now that confidence has vanished, business has also vanished."

One day, when Coxey was driving with Browne to the quarry, the latter, who had been the private secretary of Kearney, an unemployed leader during the San Francisco sandlots agitation of the seventies, told of unemployment marches in the West.

"Browne," said Coxey, "we will send a petition to Washington with boots on."

They acted promptly. The time was set for early that March. The new march would be led by Generalissimo Coxey; Browne would be his chief aide. The raw material was at hand — plenty of jobless. The whole West was full of drifters. Already big gangs of men were traveling hither and yon, aimlessly seeking work and finding only hostile police and more unemployed wherever they went. Now, they would be given a mission and a goal.

Browne had the temperament of an actor, the showiness and magnetism that prosy Coxey lacked. A cartoonist, he had edited the radical San Francisco *Open Letter.* He was tall, heavy, with a deep booming voice, unkempt hair, and a disorderly beard streaked with gray. He always wore a fringed buckskin coat, decorated with Mexican silver *tostones,* high boots, an elegant sombrero, and, weather permitting, a fur cloak. In place of a collar and necktie he wore a string of amber beads, the gift of his dying wife. He was called "Old Greasy" because of his semi-Mexican attire and because he was not addicted to bathing. After the 1892 elections, he organized the Industrial Leagues, affiliates of the Populists, to provide disciplined support for propaganda, parades, honest counting, and poll-watching.

He was a well-known Lake Front speaker in Chicago — too well-known. Mayor Harrison, of Haymarket massacre fame, autocratically forbade his meetings, and when Browne called on him to make a protest, the mayor merely jibed at his odd dress. Browne got uppish, and the mayor banished him from the city.

He returned disguised as a patent-medicine vendor, helping A. P. Bozarro to sell a Kickapoo Indian blood rememdy. Whenever the police sniffed too closely on his trail, he dexterously shifted to his role of salesman.

Along with this bag of tricks, he propagated theosophy and reincarnation. All souls went into a common pot, and from that stew were fished out the souls of the newborn. Into that pot had also gone the soul of Christ. And Browne now discovered that he and Coxey had more than their share of Christ's soul. He called Coxey the "Cerebrum of Christ," he himself was the "Cerebellum of Christ." All others with more than average fragments of Christ's soul would automatically flock to their banners. By the time they descended on Congress, so much of the Savior's soul would be reassembled there that neither Hell nor the tools of Wall Street would be able to resist them. On the Commonweal banner of the great march was painted Christ's head (in Browne's own likeness), with the words, "Peace on Earth, Good Will to Men. He Hath Risen, but Death to Interest on Bonds."

For his "educational" lectures on the march, Browne prepared a "panorama" wagon and constituted himself a one-man literary bureau, signing all pronouncements, which were many: "Humble Carl." Three commissary wagons were to carry food for the marchers. A covered dray would house a small band.

Pending the start of the march, volunteers were housed in a circus tent. Curious characters presented themselves. Among the tramps, nondescripts, and legitimate unemployed was astrologer "Cyclone" Kirtland Douglas McCallum, the author of *Dogs and Fleas, by One of the Dogs.* He wore a plug hat and fur-lined overcoat. The famous cowboy, "Oklahoma" Sam Pfimmer, showed up "because his father had been a Greenbacker." Honore Jaxon, the Canadian half-breed of Riel's Rebellion, in full Indian costume and under contract with the *Chicago Times,* came with a letter of encouragement from Mrs. Mary Lease, "Weary" Bill Iler drove the panorama wagon; otherwise, he scarcely had energy enough to lift his food to his mouth. Browne's chief understudy was Louis Smith, a mysterious stranger, who refused to disclose his true identity and was rumored to be anything from a Pinkerton to a disguised banker. At one point he almost ousted Browne as acting leader. He turned out to be Bozarro, the vendor of Kickapoo medicine.

Twenty unemployed Cleveland iron-workers came into camp Local Populist leaders joined up. Each freight brought in its drible on the rods.

Snow flurries on the twenty-fourth dampened enthusiasm, and the start was made with only about a hundred marchers, and nearly half as many reporters, whom Browne called the Argus-eyed Demons of Hell, plus four telegraph operators and two linemen. At least one secret service agent, Matthew F. Griffin, was on hand.

Marshal Carl Browne, riding one of Coxey's best Kentucky stallions, led them down Main Street. Jasper Johnson, a Negro, carried the colors: the Christ banner of the Commonweal. Jesse Coxey, the General's sixteen-year-old son, wore a uniform with a blue coat and gray trousers to symbolize the reconciliation of North and South. Trumpeter "Windy" Oliver provided the bugle calls and brought up the rear. Coxey rode in a phaeton, followed by a carriage in which sat Mrs. Coxey No. 2 and their infant son, Legal Tender Coxey, and other relatives. The Scheduled Goddess of Peace, Coxey's daughter, was missing. Mrs. Coxey No. 1 wouldn't let her participate in such tarnation foolishness.

Most of the rugged foot-marchers looked like professional hoboes. Few had overcoats or blankets; few had decent shoes. They shivered, their lips blue. But they marched on and on for days and weeks, over the broad plains of America, across the great rivers of America, through the snow-filled gaps of America's mountains, along the hard pavements of great cities, and past the closed doors of smokeless depression factories — on and on trudged the ragged little band.

Not even McCarthy's stupidities, perhaps only major wars or Lindbergh's flight to Europe, have ever held the headlines so steadily with so much space day after day as did the march of Coxey's army.

As the march went on, professional hoboes dropped out on discovering it was no well-fed pleasure jaunt. Their places were taken by real unemployed, by farmers and by Populists. Coxey's currency and public works program dovetailed with their own ideas, and they sought to utilize the march for propaganda purposes. Populist leaders often paved the army's way with the local authorities to prevent police aggression and in gathering funds and provisions. At each point, they joined in the fervid speech-making, pointing out all the morals that could be drawn from the weary march of men unable to find work in a nation of such great wealth. The Knights of Labor also aided. Day and night, Browne kept up his harangues, "educating" his followers in his curious lore of religion, economics, and politics.

A welcome addition was A. H. Blum of Canton, Ohio, President of the Canton Iron Molders' Union, out of a job because he was boycotted for his union leadership. Another distinguished volunteer was Marshal John Shrim, tall and gaunt, with one glass eye, a union coal miner and editor of *The Mystic Messenger.* Another newcomer was Frank Ball, a Socialist. Very fervent in his belief that the march would bring real reforms was fellow-trudger Edward A. Moore, 1890 Populist candidate for Secretary of State in Colorado, now editing a Populist newspaper in Chicago. He was a former business partner of Mary E. Lease.

Discipline was good. Browne was an able leader, and made the marchers conform to rules. Those who got drunk or started fights were expelled. Freaks were driven out, especially those trying to capitalize on the march as a stunt.

In New Galilee, Ohio, it was generally admitted that the Coxeyites behaved better than the townspeople, who, very religious, disliked Browne's theosophy and insulted the marchers. But they did contribute food. Nothing, not even a chicken, was stolen.

[278]

The expedition was no bed of roses, for a fast pace was kept. In a forced march through snow a foot deep, over the Cumberland Mountains, the *Chicago Tribune* reporter said the army made eighteen miles in four hours. At night they were usually allowed to sleep in jail or in the city hall.

The army soon totaled about 300 men. At Alliance, Ohio, 10 men, bearing credentials from the People's party, came well-equipped with blankets and rubber boots. On occasion, college students went along for a ways, singing songs, giving yells, and entertaining the marchers.

In Allegheny and Pittsburgh, the Populists prepared a warm welcome, getting provisions and arranging meetings. In Pittsburgh, at the last minute the police thwarted publicity plans by shunting the marchers through back streets. Lone Coxeyites who strayed out of the assigned camp were arrested and sentenced. Vigorous protests were made by J. H. Stevenson, the Populist leader of Pittsburgh, and by James R. Sovereign, former head of the Knights of Labor, who showed up at various points along the line of march.

At Monongahela Wharf, 12,000 people crowded in to hear Coxey. The wheel of his phaeton was smashed by the crush.

By the time the works of the Carnegie Steel Company were reached, the army totaled 600 persons. On April 11, the Coxeyites marched out of Uniontown, a coal center, with four days' rations, to cross the difficult Alleghenies. They marched in a driving snowstorm, ankle deep in mud. The first night, drunk mountaineers galloped menacingly around the barn where they slept. A sheriff's posse good-humoredly, but sternly, escorted them straight across one county with only a single halt.

Weary and broken, the army reached Cumberland, where Coxey loaded them on barges at freight rates — two days' restful travel for $85.00 the lot. Browne compared it lyrically to the voyage of Cleopatra to meet Anthony.

Populist Henry Vincent wired the army that a thousand iron molders would join up at Rockville. News came that a second army, which had set out from San Francisco under Charles T. Kelly, had been fired upon by the Iowa militia with a toll of six dead.

At Rockville, Christopher Columbus Jones, a tiny man in a big silk hat, with long gray hair and a long pointed gray beard, who quoted poetry endlessly, led in fifty men, carrying flags, the vanguard of hundreds more. Jones believed faithfully in Coxey and his proposed bills and just as strongly in Browne's ideas of reincarnation. Among Jones's volunteers were a hundred students and two professors of Lehigh University. Jones's banner, it later turned out, was being carried by a detective in disguise.

The army reached the outskirts of the District of Columbia right on schedule — the last day of April. Formal entry was set for May 1, International Labor Day, the anniversary of the Haymarket martyrs of Chicago.

By that time, many other armies had been organized and were on their way, crisscrossing over the countryside for thousands of miles and meeting with all sorts of experiences and treatment.

Probably the largest was that organized in San Francisco by Colonel William Baker, soon taken over by General Charles T. Kelly, a former Salvation Army man and a born leader. A New Englander, he had drifted westward. Like Henry George, another drifter, he became a typesetter. His brief experience with the Salvation Army was due to love. He had to join in order to get the girl.

He was a small, frank, open-looking man, with a large nose and alert resolute blue eyes with a dreamy lingering gaze. His large moustache, scanty in the middle, failed to cover the cleft of his upper lip. He spoke with a soft persuasive voice and had much magnetism.

After parades and appeals for aid in San Francisco, the army moved over to Mills Tabernacle in Oakland, where citizens, rather than feed the marchers indefinitely, raised money to freight them on to Sacramento, the state capitol.

[280]

But the army refused to ride in boxcars like cattle, so the Oakland police arrested Kelly. The army refused to budge an inch unless he was returned, so the police brought him right back again. Kelly was then carried triumphantly on the shoulders of the army to the waiting freight train, on which they now agreed to embark.

At Sacramento, more than 1,000 were in the ranks. They were shipped quickly on to Ogden. Governor West of Utah angrily ordered the railroad not to bring them in and obtained court injunctions. But the train, with its strange human cargo, rolled steadily on toward the great Rocky Mountain commonwealth. West waited its arrival anxiously, with two companies of militia drawn up, two Gatling guns in place, a company of police — and *2,000 loaves of bread.*

The army was disgorged and resolutely refused to return west, even if the railroad would take it. Popular sentiment was with the marchers; labor unions paraded in their behalf, and the Governor discovered to his surprise that he was just "a bulldozer."

The marchers were herded into a swampy garbage dump where 3 men died and 30 fell sick. It was very cold.

Presently the men seized a 26-boxcar train and rolled on east. In Cheyenne, they were fed 13,000 loaves of bread and 5 beefs but weren't permitted to get off. The train was shoved right on.

At Topeka, the Populist party, which controlled the state, welcomed them fulsomely, and they were well fed. They moved on to Omaha. That city, after many sleepless nights of worry, discovered that the men were nonviolent and well disciplined.

Iowa officials had been frantic over the approach of the army. That the great commonwealth could be so dreadfully upset over 1,000 hungry shivering men now seems ludicrous. Officials blustered and threatened. They talked of shooting the marchers down. They spoke of rivers of blood. They talked of barricading the railroad bridge but feared to meddle with the federal receivership. They discussed other expedients. None seemed very intelligent.

[281]

No one had a stroke of humor. Governor Jackson, breathing fire and brimstone, rushed to Council Bluffs in person with his militia, telling the press all the things he would do and announcing: "They shall not pass." Newspapers sent "war correspondents."

Almost before Jackson knew it, the train had rolled smoothly across the bridge, and the army had scrambled off. By a pious trick, says Cole, in his *Iowa Through the Years,* "General Kelly turned General Jackson's war into a fiasco." On the approach of the militia, Kelly resorted to Salvation Army tactics and ordered his men to fall on their knees in prayer. "How would men in uniform attack men in rags who were praying and singing gospel hymns?" The report of six dead which had reached the Coxeyite army approaching Washington was apparently slightly exaggerated.

Onlookers were amazed not only at this holy ruse but also that thereafter the marchers held regular religious ceremonies even when there was no tactical need for them. "Prayers were offered up by the men so earnestly and full of touching pathos, that tears were brought to the eyes of hundreds of people," a local chronicler reported. The Wealers sang "Methodist hymns" as though really "trained for congregational singing."

The men were finally allowed to camp on the Chautauqua grounds. It had no shelter, and they had to sleep in rain and snow and mud. The dry amphitheater was occupied by ever-watchful militia.

Kelly now rode in and out of camp on a black horse, presented to him by a Council Bluffs admirer. He held meetings in Omaha, across the river, where Populist sentiment was strong.

Two hundred more recruits enlisted in Council Bluffs under the very nose of the discomfited governor. Kelly accepted 155, rejecting the others. Among those accepted was Jack London, who soon proved too anarchistic for the expedition.

All efforts to gain transportation now failed, so the army finally trudged off — afoot — toward Chicago. Omaha workmen, hearing of this great "injustice," marched across the railway bridge with drums and fifes and flags in angry protest and were joined by thousands of others demanding transportation for the army.

[282]

The angry sympathizers seized a train, but the railroad company tore up the tracks.

While the rails were being spiked back in place, Reverend J. G. Lemon of Christian House turned Paul Revere and galloped out through the spring mud to tell the army that the people of Council Bluffs had risen up in their behalf and were sending another train.

When it arrived, it had too few cars, so Kelly loaded his sick on it and sent it puffing back to Council Bluffs and led his forces on foot toward Des Moines, where the People's party had influential leaders.

When the army left Van Meter on April 28, rain was falling in torrents. In the mud and dark, many lost their way. Even General Kelly and the two women who accompanied him, Mrs. Ada Harper and Miss Anna Houston, went astray, and their closed carriage did not reach camp until the next day at 11:30.

The Des Moines sheriff and chief of police spent most of the night at nearby Valley Junction on the watch. About 9:00 A.M., the Kelly advance guard straggled into town wet and bedraggled. Their further advance was barred at Walnut Street bridge, and they were herded into D. B. Murrow's muddy cow pasture. Belated contingents continued to arrive.

Weaver came out to address them, and a citizens' committee provided them with a picnic-basket breakfast.

At four o'clock on a misty drizzling Sunday afternoon, wrote Cyrenus Cole in his *Iowa People*, the two generals (Kelly and Weaver) rode into the city at the head of a thousand men on foot (by actual count, 932). "General" Kelly sat on his horse, said one sarcastic observer, in imitation of the Savior entering Jerusalem and affected the postures of self-imposed martyrdom. He was a wiry man with a keen eye, but an eye of uncertain gaze. There was about him the vagueness and vacuity of the fanatic.

A platoon of police brought up the rear of the long wavering procession. The authorities had forbidden brass bands or any parading, and it was a sorry down-at-the-heels plodding. Nearly all were

[283]

in rags, many had no shoes. "Women wept and some men had to swallow their tears," said Cole. So this suffering little band was the invasion, which had frightened the fire-eating governor out of his wits!

The marchers were escorted to camp in an abandoned three-story stove factory. There, Professor Ott, of the local university, introduced Kelly to people gathered on the factory grounds in thousands, despite the rain falling in sluices.

Kelly thanked the people for their kindness. He spent the $378.50 collected for 222 pairs of shoes, but needed more supplies.

After the speech, the shivering, soaked army was given a hot meal. Spirits rose. Men stripped and wrung out their dripping rags to dry.

Two mass meetings were held, one at labor headquarters, the other in the opera. house. Weaver spoke at both places, declaring that the army wanted free silver and appropriations to irrigate arid western lands (neither idea had ever been mentioned in the various Kelly army communiques). Kelly spoke against the Chinese. A Mr. Nedrea told the crowd he'd rather be a dead Kelly than a live Cleveland; Weaver should be made President. The Industrial Quartet sang "Where is my Wandering Boy Tonight?" Sovereign, of the Knights of Labor, who had abandoned the main Coxey outfit to meet oncoming hordes, swore that the army would not go out of Des Moines on foot, even if the workers had to tie up all the railways in Iowa. Weaver, Sovereign, and other labor leaders then headed a big manifestation to call on the still-frightened Governor.

He agreed to get the army to the Mississippi, provided they would take a riverboat and not go into Illinois. But the railroads refused to move them at freight rates. It was finally decided to build flatboats to float them down the river.

On May 7, 500 Des Moines citizens marched to the boatyard, redubbed "Kelly's navyyard," and set to work under the direction of the local carpenters' union. They built 130 scows.

Although Kelly's yard hummed, nerves were getting frayed all around. The city's resources were already strained by its own numerous unemployed. Food was growing more scarce. Kelly accused Weaver and the citizens' committee of not taking proper care of the army as promised.

But at last, on May 9, a day hot as summer, the army, still about a thousand strong, embarked with shouts of joy.

As the army moved on, an article by Weaver justifying it appeared in the *Midland Monthly*. "They cannot till the earth on their own right for they have been fenced out by land monopoly . . . Employment cannot be found. . . . Their written petitions are spurned with derision and when they attempt to march in person to present their grievances, they are pursued by the wolf of hunger and beset with armed millitia and the policemen's club. . . . They want labor, independence, homes."

A few, like Jack London, merely wanted a lark. Many, being jobless, had nothing better to do. Many really were earnest for the cause.

The joy of the Kellyites in their scows did not last long. They passed gaily around the bend from the city, but the flatboats, hard to manage, were soon strung out for miles. Many got stuck at every turn on snags and sandbars. Water was scant; throats grew parched under the blazing sun, and smiles soon turned to scowls; no prayers or hymns now, remarked Cole, only considerable profanity.

But little by little they proceeded — the more skillful ones swiftly — past Newcomer's Point, past Hastie Point, around Rattlesnake Bend, past Tippie Point and Yellow Banks, past the old abandoned town of Dudley, past Adelphia, past all that was left of the LaFayette of 1851 — and so, on beyond the limits of Polk County. The sheriff escorting them went home and ate a good supper.

Jack London and his bunch discovered a trick of pivoting their boat that soon put them far in the lead. They gleefully presented themselves to farmers and town authorities as collectors of supplies for the army and lived off the fat of the land. The farmers grumbled at the Des Moines authorities for turning so many wandering men loose on them. The Iowa through which the Wealers passed that year, said Cole, was a desolate one, perhaps the most desolate in the history of the state. It was a year of great drouth. There were bare larders everywhere.

Many of those stranded, or whose scows collapsed, swarmed along the back roads. However scant the food supply, it was better than that obtainable on an empty river. The crews who stuck it out were lucky to get even one full meal a day, and they suffered innumerable accidents. Hunger, cold nights, sickness took their toll. One by one the rafts were tied up, abandoned, or sold. Only a few navigators reached the mouth of the Des Moines; fewer still reached St. Louis.

In some places they fared well. Those who reached Ottumwa were bountifully fed and visited by 10,000 curious, cordial people. At Quincey, Alderman Thad Rogers put them up at his hotel and fed them 1,000 pounds of meat and 1,000 loaves of bread, at his own expense. As the flotilla drifted downstream, the banks were often lined with spectators and, according to Jack London, sometimes the industrialists had to go many miles before finding a secluded spot to make their toilets.

Below Ottumwa, "Kelly's marines" fought Rock Island Railway deputies. The next day 25 Pinkertons were routed, 2 captured and disarmed. Eleven days out from Des Moines, what was left of the army, after chilling winds and driving rains, reached the Mississippi. While the men were encamped on the levee near St. Louis, a mob attacked them, fracturing one man's skull.

St. Louis did itself proud. An excursion steamer, gaily decorated, with brass band and labor leaders aboard, towed the scows into the city with much fanfare.

The Kellyites drifted on to the mouth of the Ohio, where the boats were destroyed. The army was barred from Cairo, but Kelly finally secured barges to be towed up the Ohio.

At Evansville, Indiana, Kelly's army had again grown in size and numbered 1,100 men. At Louisville, Kelly and Baker were arrested. From there on, the police everywhere tried to scatter their followers.

Kelly finally reached Washington on July 12, announcing that 600 men were coming up. But one large detachment was jailed for 15 days in Wheeling, West Virginia. Only a small number finally struggled into the capitol.

Numerous other armies started in the West, Northwest, the Rockies, New England, and elsewhere. General Lewis C. Fry's army, organized in Los Angeles, was finally dumped off a train in the handful of shacks of Sierra Blanca on the Texas desert. The state rangers wouldn't let them leave there on foot, and the railroad company wouldn't put any trains through. They went hungry for days while Governor Hogg squabbled with the railroad for leaving them stranded in a barren desert to murder them by torture and starvation. The people of El Paso, previously thrown into hysterical panic on news of the army's approach, having found the marchers harmless, sent a large supply of provisions and hired a special train to carry them on their way. And so the Fryites finally emerged from the Texas wilds. Six hundred reached St. Louis on April 3, a month before Kelly's outfit. In Terre Haute, they paraded and sold copies of Populist Henry Vincent's *Story of the Commonweal* — already they had a history. Local Populists raised money for transportation, but the railroads refused to accept less than the regular fare. After numerous adventures with federal troops and police, Fry's group reached Washington on June 16.

Mrs. Anna F. Smith of California, after conducting many drills, led 1,100 "industrialists," many of them women, to Sacramento. There disputes arose over leadership. Finally, jointly with "Colonel" Barker, she led a group of about 300 south through the San Joaquin Valley. In Fresno, where they arrived May 30 with blistered feet, Reverend Collins (who a few days previously had tried unsuccessfully to kick all the Armenians out of his congregation because they ate garlic and didn't wash their feet) made his own personal three-hour investigation of the camp and reported a large percentage of professional tramps with jail records who frightened women into giving them food. He saw the men sinfully playing cards, and others full of booze "every day." "A dangerous class of men!" he concluded.

"We have people enough in our town who require assistance," said the *Tulare Daily Evening Register* as the Barker-Smith army drew nigh, "and this band of hoboes is not worthy. Don't give a single dime."

But the Populists were strong in Tulare and had their own newspaper there, so when Mrs. Smith arrived ahead of the army on an afternoon freight to give one of her harangues on the street and pass the hat, she got many dimes.

The army was herded into camp just beyond the town, and local officials collected $30.00 and a wagonload of provisions for them. "They are not a nice looking lot of men at all" said the *Register,* but "a good bath and clean raiment might make them look better."

At the town of Pixley, the army stopped a freight train with sacks stuffed with weeds, which they called dummies, and swooped down on the cars.

Sheriff Kay ordered the engine disabled, then hurried back to Tulare, where he enrolled 35 deputies.

When he got back about midnight, the Wealers had retired for the night among the crevices on the lumber car, on top of boxcars, or were strewn alongside oil tanks, "seemingly engaged in sweet repose as though slumbering on the downiest couch in the White House, that mecca for which they claimed to be bound," said the *Register.* At early dawn, the army commissary department struggled to set up a cooks' headquarters.

Sheriff Kay parleyed with Colonel Barker for over an hour. The Wealers flatly refused to leave on foot and spread their blankets on top of the cars, arranged their bundles, hoisted their flags, lit their pipes, and stretched themselves out comfortably.

Kay's deputies kicked them off. The Wealers "vented uncomplimentary remarks," and when the train started off without them they took after it, "yelling, hooting, cursing, their pockets and hands filled with rocks." Besides stones, said the *Register*, the Wealers also had clubs, lath hatchets, knives, and a few guns. They cut the air hose and disconnected several cars.

The sheriff had to shove them off these again, and the train finally pulled away with all its cars minus marchers. After an hour's parley, it was agreed the army would be given rations for a good meal and that their effects would be moved on for them if they would walk as far as Delano by that evening. Kay purchased flour, crackers, potatoes, onions, salt, coffee, and other provisions. Fresh meat was secured in Delano.

The Wealers arrived there at 6:30 P.M. and marched through the town to the sound of fife and drum, flags flying, and camped in the railroad cattle corral.

In Bakersfield, after much fuss and feathers, the Kern County supervisors chartered a freight train, "loaded the whole caboodle into it," and sent them off for Mojave on the desert.

"The hobo special" reached there about 4:00 P.M., June 6. At the first order of the sheriff, the army clambered off into the teeth of a cutting sandstorm. It was so bad, the men were given permission to return to the cars, and by 11:00 P.M. apparently all were asleep.

A mile south of Mojave, the 12:15 eastbound Santa Fe freight was flagged. Almost before the engineer and fireman knew it, a dozen Wealers leapt out of the dust-filled air and took possession of the engine while the whole army climbed aboard the cars. Once more they were rolling eastward in grand style.

It was a clever coup, but a brakeman, who had gotten away, hotfooted it back into Mojave to spread the news. Los Angeles was telegraphed for fifty deputy sheriffs to stop the stolen freight at Barstow.

All the Wealers were hauled back to Mojave, where they were sentenced to four months in jail. But the names of Smith and Barker did not figure in the proceedings.

Doctor J. H. Randall's army, perhaps the only out-and-out Populist outfit, left Chicago on May 1 with 450 men. Many World's Fair detectives joined up, and several became head marshals.

Fifty-four-year-old Dr. Randall was a Union veteran, ex-dentist, ex-labor organizer, ex-Greenback editor, one of "the best stump orators in the business." Visitors to Randall encampments had to pay admission. At La Porte, the doctor was arrested, but the mayor soon discovered it was cheaper to release Randall and speed the army on its way than to feed it and pay special deputies $5.00 a day. In Valparaiso, the Wealers were forcibly vaccinated.

At Mansfield, the Populists staged a mass meeting of 7,000 in the park. Randall, they claimed, was making a straight People's party appeal. By then he had seven fine horses, two new Studebaker wagons donated by Populist farmers, and a buggy and saddle horse given him by a Populist doctor. The army had five flags and two big red umbrellas.

Through Pennsylvania, Randall's route was laid out by the People's party Central Committee so as to arouse the most interest among voters. Populist candidates harangued all meetings en route. In Pittsburgh, June 18, a grand rally of Commonweal leaders and Populists was held. Coxey put in an unexpected appearance on the platform.

Later middle western and far western armies, as time went on, received less sympathy. The federal authorities were even more determined to break them up.

Sanders' Railroad Army set out from Cripple Creek, Colorado, with a captured local switch engine and flatcars. Engines were turned over on the track ahead of them to stop them, but they built the tracks around such obstructions, and finally, getting hold of a good engine at Scott, Kansas, whirled toward Topeka so fast they could not hold their flags up against the wind.

Populist Governor Lewelling had promised to take good care of them on the courthouse grounds, but the federal marshal kept them on the cars and took them off to the Fort Leavenworth Military Reservation, where rifle-armed deputies were stationed on the surrounding hills.

Thirty escaped and caught a train to Kansas City, where they joined "General" Bennett's army, which marched through the streets singing a song to the tune of "John Brown's Body." Two hundred were sent to jail.

A Silver Legion also set out from Colorado under "General" Hamilton. He soon landed in jail. General Grayson's army, another Colorado outfit, eventually also joined up with the Bennet expedition. A large New England contingent successfully joined the Coxey outfit in the capital.

But other groups were now being clubbed, half-starved, or jailed by federal marshals. Hogan's band of miners in the Northwest soon clashed with federal deputies. Eventually Hogan was sentenced to six months for contempt of court, forty others were given thirty-day sentences, but the army moved on, drifting down to Bismark on flatboats. Four hundred strong, they finally reached St. Joseph, Missouri, in July.

About the only army that ever got out of the Northwest successfully, though many started, was that led by "Jumbo" Cantwell and his "modish, diamond-adorned" little wife. He and his 300 men reached Minneapolis and eventually showed up in Washington.

The first Coxey army, as related, had reached the capital on schedule, camping on the outskirts on April 30. Before its arrival, officials had grown so alarmed, their knees quaked. Higher-ups expressed grave fears for the life of the President and solemnly anticipated a bloody attack on the double-barred Treasury, "with its vast store of gold and silver and paper."

That any such ideas had ever entered the head of a single Coxey it could not be proved, but awaiting the pitiful little band of unarmed, half-starved, ragged marchers were 1,500 crack troops. A thousand more stood ready to be rushed in from nearby cities. The National Guard was also ready, shoes shined, guns polished. Two hundred special policemen were sworn in and armed. Special sharpshooters were added to the regular Treasury guards and waited breathlessly, perched on roofs, scrolls, and behind pillars.

Populist congressmen had not been idle. Senator Peffer of Kansas had introduced Coxey's good-road bill, but it had been reported out unfavorably. On April 14, Peffer introduced a bill condemning the use of force to keep the Coxeyites out of the District. It provided for a special reception committee of nine senators. Senator William Allen of Nebraska, supporting the proposal, asked why paid lobbyists were received in Washington with open arms, and unemployed citizens were met with military force? The lobbyists were doing the country more damage than all the Coxey armies. Senator Joseph R. Hawley of Connecticut retorted that Allen's speech contained "the bacteria and bacilli of anarchy." By a small majority, Peffer's resolution was shelved.

Populist Congressman Haldor E. Boen of Minnesota introduced a resolution instructing the Secretary of War to provide grounds and tents for all organized bodies of laborers. Populist John R. Davis introduced a bill directing the Secretary of War to enlist half a million men in a volunteer industrial army to be given army clothing, food and pay, and to be employed on public works, the cost to be defrayed by a treasury issue. Both measures were smothered.

April 25, the Populist congressional caucus adopted a resolution favoring fair treatment for the Coxeyites, and Allen introduced it in the Senate. More bitter speeches pro and con resulted. The great march had certainly stirred up a hornet's nest.

Coxey dutifully obtained the required police permit for his parade. The chief of police reminded him that it was illegal to carry banners through the Capitol grounds or to hold meetings there. Speaker Crisp said Coxey was trying to intimidate Congress.

At the Coxey George Washington Camp on the outskirts, Brother Browne drilled his weary men for the coming parade.

The procession (led by a platoon of nine policemen) started down an empty tree-lined road. As they came to the streets of the capital, the Commonweal six-piece band pounded out a discordant "Marching through Georgia." Coxey was in one carriage with Mrs. Coxey No. 2 and infant Legal Tender Coxey; Mrs. Annie La Porte Diggs of Kansas was in another. Mounted on a thoroughbred horse was Coxey's seventeen-year-old daughter by his earlier marriage, who had finally succeeded in running away from home and was now in all her glory in a snow-white riding habit as the Goddess of Peace. Her flowing golden hair glinted under a tiny white parasol. Her horse pranced; she was pretty. Spectators cheered. Her face flushed, and she smiled winningly.

A special Philadelphia "army" brought up the rear with a shriek of bagpipes and another Goddess of Peace — a bovine girl, "good-looking, plump, a red-cheeked maiden of eighteen," riding an old docile farm plug. She was draped in the Stars and Stripes, a gilt star glinted from her blue turban; her dark hair streamed loose down her back. Her escort was little wizened Christopher Columbus Jones, who rode a spirited black charger he could hardly manage. He was plain scared. In his tall silk beaver and long gray beard he looked like a wizard or necromancer.

The little band of 500 ragged men, spruced up as well as they could for the occasion, with their pathetic attempts at American middle-class folklore, symbolized by Coxey's daughter on a Kentucky thoroughbred, the Pennsylvania Dutch girl on her farm plug, the squeaking little band, and smudged placards, trudged down noble Pennsylvania Avenue. Some carried staves with cards bearing the Wealer motto: "Peace on Earth, Good Will Toward men, but Death to Interest on Bonds." It was not exactly the motto of desperate men planning to storm the Treasury against sharpshooters; it was scarcely the slogan of lawless men ready to do battle with the United States Army or planning to dash in to assassinate President Cleveland.

But against this little handful of unarmed folk, half-starved, broken by adversity, bewildered by the city, all the majesty of the armed forces of a mighty nation had been arrayed by the jittery bureaucrafts. Federal soldiers stood tense, Winchesters in hand, alert in their barracks for the call. The brave National Guards of adjacent states were drawn up ready to fly to the safety of the city. There were many more policemen than Coxeyites.

[293]

The avenue was black with people — more than had ever turned out for any Presidential inauguration in past history — to look at this feeble Sunday-best attempt. There were a few jeers, but for the most part the onlookers generously cheered the little band on its way.

At the head of the avenue before the Capitol, the police majestically blocked the street from curb to curb. The Commonweal army did not debate the issue. Quietly it turned aside and halted on B Street.

Coxey, Browne, and Jones walked alone toward the Capitol. The pillars of that great edifice did not cave in at the approach of this queer trio of faintly cracked American citizens, but the mounted police galloped frantically after them.

Browne almost reached the Capitol steps. He was easily identified by his buckskin coat, his big sombrero and his glistening Mexican silver *tostones,* not the most practical garb for a dangerous conspirator. At the foot of the steps the police grappled with him and beat him badly, although he made no resistance and merely shouted, "I am an American citizen . . . my constitutional rights."

But Carl Browne had no constitutional rights that fair day of May 1, 1894 He was an American citizen, but he could not walk up the Capitol steps to his Congress. He was a dangerous idea. He believed in Christ; he believed that men had souls; he believed that unemployed men should have jobs; he believed in a lot of queer things. Undoubtedly he was wrong in all of these beliefs; undoubtedly they menaced the very pillars of the government. He must have been wrong, for the newspapers said so. One minute they had reviled him, another they had ridiculed him, still another they had quivered with the danger to society if such as he were allowed in the Capitol. He was roughly hustled away.

Coxey, looking like the prosperous little businessman he was, also reached the steps and also was surrounded. He drew a written protest from his pocket and, as the police dragged him off with more than necessary violence, tossed it to the reporters.

Little Christopher Jones, with his big silk hat and his long beard, was certainly not a very well-disguised conspirator. Certainly he did not look like one of the lobbyists Allen had talked about. It was strange what a commotion such a funny little man could cause among the high and mighty, what nightmares he had brought to the spreading asses in swivel chairs, what a mighty array of military force this queer little fellow had caused to be brought to the Capitol of the great free Republic!

The crowd booed the police and cheered the conspirators. Otherwise it was wholly orderly. But the police were nettled and let loose with their clubs among the peaceful onlookers. Simultaneously, mounted patrols charged, with a clank of spurs. Fifty spectators were beaten up or trampled under foot.

In the meantime, two children, young Jesse Coxey and Mamie Coxey — in conformity with the good biblical aphorism — led the now leaderless, quite unarmed, law-abiding, but tired and half-starved army back to camp. It was cheered all the way.

That night Browne issued Special Order No. 1. He spoke of Rothschild, of the Belshazzar of old, of good roads, and of the damp dark dungeon in which he had been confined for nearly five hours.

He and his two dangerous associates had been charged with — trampling on the grass. The charge did not seem quite in keeping with the general fear or all the pomp and circumstance of war, the vast forces that had been raised up against them. It did not quite jibe with the brutal police-clubbing of bystanders.

"Liberty," perorated Browne, "lies weltering in her own blood in the capitol city tonight, stabbed in the homes of friends and supposed guardians."

Coxey's protest was also published. "We stand here today to test these guarantees of our Constitution — 'the right to assemble and petition, and of free speech.'" It did not sound quite like the language of men coming to assault the Treasury vaults.

Upon the Capitol steps he had been forbidden to tread had been spread recently, he said, "a carpet for the royal feet of a foreign princess" at the cost of the public Treasury. "Up those steps, the lobbyists of trusts and corporations have passed unchallenged on their way to committee rooms, access to which we, the representatives of the toiling wealth-producers, have been denied." He might have added — what history has later revealed — that in those very hours, the sacred Treasury was being looted. It was being looted by the men who held the guns. It was being cynically looted by deals behind closed doors by "Wall Street" financial leaders. Against them no sharpshooters could be stationed.

On May 2, Congressman Tom L. Johnson called for an investigation into the violence on the Capitol steps. His resolution was buried in committee. Allen introduced a similar resolution in the Senate. It suffered a similar fate.

The case of the three leaders came to trial with a large battery of defense lawyers, including Populist Senator Allen and half a dozen Populist congressmen.

May 8, the three were found guilty of carrying banners, and Coxey and Browne, of walking on the grass. They were given twenty days imprisonment for the former offense and fined $5.00 for the latter offense.

The banners were merely 3 inch by 2 inch badges pinned on their coats, the sort that the members of every back-slapping lodge wear when they come to goggle at Washington. But the Treasury had been saved.

Coxey and Browne now tried to get a hearing for their bills before the House Committee on Labor but were not permitted to appear. Mrs. Coxey No. 1 now threatened to sue her erstwhile spouse for abduction of Mamie, the Goddess of Peace.

Coxey was released from jail, Sunday, June 10, and drove off in a four-horse phaeton, stopped at a hotel to clean up, then went out to George Washington Camp.

Various contingents of Commonwealers continued to arrive. On July 4, there was another parade, which included Coxey's contingent, representatives of the western armies led by "Jumbo" Cantwell, Indiana Commonwealers, and a rear guard of Negro marchers.

That day special patriotic shows, with an admission charge, were staged at both Fry's camp and at Coxey's camp. In the latter, the Wealers enacted the "Death of Liberty." A large impressive Goddess of Liberty, after various antics, was borne swooning off to the panorama wagon, recently repainted and redecorated. Presently, from this improvised dressing room emerged a man — now clean-shaven, since he could not otherwise have portrayed the Goddess of Liberty — in a buckskin coat with Mexican *tostones* and a big sombrero.

A few days later, Browne led sixty men to New York "to see the bosses themselves."

The various camps were improved, tin-can or thatched shacks were put up, the grounds were kept spic-and-span, paths and roadways, "some quite artistic," were built, steps were cut in steep embankments. But admission fees fell off, and stomachs soon growled for food. It was tougher sledding every day. By the first of August, there were still over 1,000 hungry men in the capital.

Coxey, however, was not there, neither was Browne. Those bright stars had faded from the sky. Coxey was now running for Congress on the Populist ticket and could not be 2 places at once. To his honor, he returned periodically to advise them and try to help them, and he made speaking tours around the country, collecting provisions and funds for them. He still advised more men to march on Washington. If only 2½ percent of the unemployed made the pilgrimage, 100,000 men would be encamped in the shadow of the Capitol; then Congress would have to do something.

But every day the Washington Wealers were having a harder row to hoe. Several of Coxey's men worked all day for a bushel of potatoes. Ten men worked a day and a half for a beef cow. When it was dragged to camp, rain put out the cooking fires, and the campers had to eat it raw.

The men continued to appeal to Congress. Fry's group at Rosslyn camp had Peffer present a petition to the Senate with a well-studied plan of how the situation could be met. Their total wealth, they said, wouldn't purchase a decent coffin. They asked for work.

August 20, the police barged into Coxey's camp and wrecked it.

Little by little the men drifted away or were sent off. Some were even shipped clear to Los Angeles. One contingent sent back warm thanks for kind treatment — at home they would continue to fight for liberty and equality at the ballot box.

A camp over the border in Maryland was raided and all the men sent to the workhouse. The Virginia authorities called out three companies of militia and helpfully drove the men from another camp back into the District of Columbia.

Greatly angered by such occurrences, Coxey hurried back to Washington but was unable to get his men released from the workhouse by writs of habeus corpus. He did salvage his seven blooded horses, which he shipped back to his farm. Once more he left, this time to attend the Ohio Populist convention. Presently the governor of Maryland shipped the workhouse prisoners out of the state.

And so, my children, in the year 1894 was saved the Treasury of the United States:

> 'Twas in the year of ninety four
> That Coxey's army marched,
> The golden Goddess of Liberty before;
> They came all ragged and parched.
>
> But Cleveland held the fort, fat and true,
> The army stood bravely by,
> And all the office-holders, too,
> Ready all, to do or die.
>
> They saved the nation; they saved the gold;
> "Nay, thou shalt not pass,"
> They all cried out right brave and bold,
> And on bad man Coxey they laid hold
> For walking on the grass.

XIV
SILVER KNIGHT
ON A CROSS
OF GOLD

William Jennings Bryan was emotionalizing himself through the higher walks of American politics. In 1894, he refused to run for reelection to Congress for a third time and angled for a senatorship, but the Republican legislature of Nebraska was not convinced that the home-boy's brilliance was more important than rewarding the party faithful. If not the senatorship, why not the Presidency?

Though only thirty-four, Bryan set out ardently to promote this still loftier ambition. With more than the confidence of his years, he lost no time in sounding out the party powerful. Already he had strong financial backing from the wealthy western silver interests, who were paying him well for his speech-making and were heavily subsidizing the activities of the bimetallic leagues, under whose auspices he lectured up and down the country. If the silverites, of whom Bryan was now the outstanding leader, could wrench control of the Democratic machine from Cleveland, no other man — except possibly Silver Dick Bland — was in a better position to lead the hosts than the young Nebraskan with the most winning silver voice in the country.

He approached Governor Altgeld of Illinois. "You are too young," was the gist of Altgeld's reply. "Later on. Be patient."

He sought out Boss Hill, of New York, who mortally hated Cleveland. Hill was too much a gold bug to sympathize.

But Bryan knelt in prayer, as he did before and after all speeches, and God told him he was ready to be anointed.

He had been born in Salem, Marion County, on March 19, 1860. His father was a Baptist, his mother a Methodist, so his Sunday school opportunites, as he said in his *Memoirs,* were doubled. For a time he wanted to be a Baptist preacher, but the requirement of overall baptism deterred him. When still quite young, he joined the Presbyterians, thus making the day of rest a busy day indeed.

He was inculcated from childhood with a crusading zeal against liquor, gambling, and similar evils. As soon as his fingers could hold a pen, he signed the prohibition pledge and joined a temperance society after hearing a little girl recite: "The lips that touch liquor shall never touch mine." The last year of his long life he spent writing letters to congressmen, attempting to persuade them to exclude from the mails newspapers with betting and lottery ads, not perhaps realizing that his own Florida land-booming was not much different.

At one time he wanted to be a farmer and raise big pumpkins, but before he was ten his mother was making him stand on a chair and declaim, so he became a lawyer and politician. He wanted to take piano lessons, but his father put his foot down on that, saying the best music for a boy was the handsaw. All his life, though he never acquired the slightest musical appreciation, he had great fondness for popular sentimental tunes and rhetorical poetry. His appreciation of art was limited to Bodenhausen's "Madonna" and a Y.M.C.A. picture entitled "The Breaking of Human Ties." His great talents lay in other directions. Politics and aesthetics are usually oil and water.

Bryan went off to Whipple Academy at Jacksonville, then to Illinois College. He rejoiced that while at those institutions he did not fall under the spell of the teachers of physical sciences or the "mind-worshippers" but retained his early religious faith. He spent much time culling apt phrases from the Bible, declaiming, making speeches, engaging in political debate. Then and ever afterwards, Bryan was full of proverbs, verses, and quotations from Scriptures. He took special elocution lessions and won a prize for a recitation.

His future wife, Mary Elizabeth Baird, described her first impression of him at that time: "He entered the room with several other students, was taller than the rest, and attracted my attention at once. His face was pale and thin, dark eyes looked out from beneath heavy brows; his nose prominent — too large to look well, I thought; a broad, thin-lipped mouth and square chin completed the contour of his face." Her classmates warned her that Bryan was "too good." But she liked his smile, which in those days, before his face filled out, extended "from jowl to jowl." One observer remarked that Bryan could "whisper in his own ear."

He went on to the Union College of Law for two years, where he was connected with the office of ex-Senator Lyman Trumbull, Lincoln's friend, then took up practice in Jacksonville. October 1, 1877, he moved to Lincoln, Nebraska.

A year and a half later he was nominated for Congress, largely because no one else wanted the nomination in an overwhelmingly Republican district. He was "a sacrifice upon the party altar." But in the debates his smooth cadences put his Republican rival to rout, and he marched off to Congress at the age of thirty — at a campaign cost of $33.85.

He waited nearly two years before giving his maiden speech — probably his longest interval of silence since his mother stuck him up on a chair. His theme was the lowering of the tariff.

The upholders of a high tariff, he declaimed, were "fit companions for the people who are supposed by Bastiat to have petitioned the French legislature to find some way of preventing the sun from shining because it interfered with the business of the candlemakers [laughter]."

Mr. McKenna: "Do you really believe that the protective policy is similar to the pickpocket policy of putting a man's hand into another man's pocket and extracting money from it?"

Mr. Bryan: "Yes, that is my belief."

Mr. McKenna: "How do you justify your position, not in economics but in morality, for reporting out a bill which leaves thirty-nine percent taxes on woolen clothing?"

Bryan had a prompt explanation. "Mr. Chairman, if I found a robber in my house, who had taken all I had, and I was going to lose it all or else get back one half, I would take the half [laughter and applause on the Democratic side]. . . . There is a difference between a bounty and a protective tariff that the Bible describes when it speaks of 'the destruction that wasteth at noonday, and the pestilence that walketh in darkness' . . .

"And yet this party that boasts of striking the manacles from 6,000,000 slaves is engaged in driving the fetters deeper into the flesh of 65,000,000 free men. . . .

"Out in Nebraska there was a time when we had almost one sheep for each man, woman and child. We look back to it as the mutton age of Nebraska [laughter]. But alas! That happy day has passed. . . . Now, if every woman in the state named Mary insisted on having a pet lamb at the same time, we would have to go out of the state to get lambs enough to go around [laughter and applause].

"Homer tells how Ulysses escaped from the cave of the Cyclops by means of a sheep. We read in the Bible that when Isaac was about to be offered up, a ram was found caught by the horns in a thicket, and offered in his stead, and in the Fourth Chapter of Genesis, I think in the second verse — my Republican friends, of course will remember [laughter] — it is recorded of the second son of the first earthly pair, 'Abel was a keeper of sheep.' And from that day to this the sheep has been the constant companion of man in all his travels, and it has differed from the modern owner perhaps the most in that it is recognized as the symbol of meekness [laughter]."

This ability to play on easy emotions rather than to present adult argument was to carry him far. He was usually on the side of the angels, always adamant in his youthful hinterland moral prejudices, always for "the people" rather than "the interests." Though he accepted handouts from the western silver interests, he always berated the intrenched powerful. He had his fingers on the pulse of the strong Middle West and was at war with the powerful financial East, which had made so much hay out of the bloody Civil War harvest. If his thinking was fuzzy, his pungent words glittered. He was always the prima donna and the actor; his hunger for success and notoriety was strong. He might not know music or art but he was always a great poetaster and a magnificent phrasemaker.

Though often a side-stepper and compromiser, he issued many a clarion call, many a fearless challenge. He called Congress sharply to task for the Homestead riots and the Pinkertons. Law and order should be maintained only by the proper authorities, not by individual companies. The "safety and even life of the citizen" should not be "imperilled by a private and irresponsible soldiery."

In a speech delivered August 16, 1893, he told Congress, "The poor man is called a Socialist if he believes that the wealth of the rich should be divided among the poor, but the rich man is called a financier if he devises a plan by which the pittance of the poor can be converted to his use [laughter and applause]."

He asked Joe Bailey of Texas to recommend him some good books on the money problem. He had a tremendous capacity for quick assimilation, and barely a month later launched forth where angels fear to tread. He soon discovered that few folk knew the ins and outs. Because it was such an intricate subject, even the best authorities disagreed violently. It was one of the safest of themes. The tangled monetary question of the day baffled the wisest, but nearly all men believed that mismanagement of the currency lay at the root of many of their difficulties, as it did. In such a confused arena, it was not so difficult to become a true prophet. There was plenty of truth in his accusations, if not in his remedies.

"The poor man who takes property by force is called a thief," he told Congress, emphasizing a favorite theme, "but the creditor who can, by legislation, make a debtor pay a dollar twice as large as he borrowed is lauded as the friend of sound currency [laughter and applause]. The man who wants the people to destroy the government is an anarchist, but the man who wants the government to destroy the people is a patriot [applause]." He clinched it with a Biblical citation. "Has some new dispensation reversed the parable and left Lazarus in torment while Dives is born aloft in Abraham's bosom [laughter]?

"You may think that you have buried the cause of bimetallism, you may have congratulated yourselves that you have laid the free coinage of silver away in a sepulchre, newly made since the election, and before the door rolled the veto stone. But sirs, if our cause is just, as I believe it is, your labor has been in vain; no tomb was ever made so strong that it could imprison a righteous cause. Silver will yet lay aside its grave clothes and its shroud. It will yet rise and . . . and its reign will bless mankind [applause]."

He spoke in behalf of the income tax, and ridiculed the threats of wealthy men to leave the country. Where would they go? They would meet up with an income tax everywhere else in the world. Of all the mean men I have known, he said, "I have never known one so mean that I would be willing to say of him that his patriotism was less than two percent deep [laughter and applause]."

A colleague suggested Monte Carlo.

Bryan: "And give up to the wheel of fortune all the wealth of which he would not give a part to support the government which enabled him to accumulate it [laughter and applause]."

Shortly before leaving Congress, he spoke on the Pacific Railroad Bill with biting sarcasm, in the true mood of the Middle Border. It affected two classes of people, he said, "those who have been guilty of defrauding the government in the management of the roads and those who for the next fifty years will pay the rates charged by these roads for transportation." The title of this bill

should be changed to: "A bill to so amend the eighth command-
ment that it will read: 'Thou shalt not steal on a small scale;' it
aims to visit the iniquities of the fathers upon the children of
somebody else unto the third and fourth generations [laughter]."
In ringing tones he voiced the popular demand of the day: "I appeal to you to foreclose these lines, squeeze the water out of the
stock, reduce the roads to a business basis, and allow the Western
states to secure reasonable rates for their citizens [applause]."

Numerous bold speeches of this type were delivered over the
two terms Bryan was in Congress, and they marked him as one
of the strongest voices of the Middle Border, the cleverest speaker
in Congress, and a man to be reckoned with. But by the end of his
first term, he mostly concentrated on the silver question. In 1892,
he introduced a silver resolution in the state Democratic convention
that threw that body into an uproar. Back in Congress, he entered
the lists strongly for bimetallism.

"Historians tell us that the victory of Charles Martel at Tours
determined the history of all Europe for centuries. It was a contest
between the Crescent and the Cross. . . . A greater than Tours is
here! In my humble judgment the vote of this House on the subject
under consideration [repeal of the Sherman Silver Act] may bring
to the people of the West and South, to the people of the United
States, and to all mankind, weal or woe beyond the power of
language to describe or imagination to conceive."

David F. Houston, who heard Bryan speak on the silver question,
said years later, "I discovered that one could drive a prairie schooner
through any part of his argument and never scrape against a fact
of sound statement." However, most hearers, said N. R. Werner,
did not want a fact or a sound statement; they were impressed with
the power of his eloquence and the strength of his heart. Such a
masterful Bible-quoter could not be wrong.

If his silver tongue, the tinsel of his public utterance, often had
a hollow sound, and his reasoning never went deep, his eloquent
emotional fervor, his wit and cleverness, his power of phrase-making,

[305]

his ability to voice the fears and hopes, the grief and dreams of the common man — these were beyond almost anyone else's of his day. Had he been less opportunistic, less shaken by the winds of chance, had he been a trifle less ambitious, he might have become one of the greatest men in the history of the country and have carried through to accomplishment some of the things he advocated. Already, those early days in Washington, he was known for his stand against the financial boodle gangs and his stand on the money question. Mostly he was right, and certainly the repeal of the Sherman Silver Act was a terrible blow at the country's prosperity and helped bring popular unrest to the boiling point. We have already observed what it did to Colorado.

Young Bryan pitted himself against Cleveland and the whole party machine and gained nationwide notoriety. More and more he became the people's apostle in those years of panic and depression, of Coxey's armies and of the great railroad strike.

Refusing to run for a third term in Congress, Bryan accepted the editorship of the *Omaha World-Herald*. This was both an advantage and a handicap. Bryan could not smile on paper, but he sent marked copies of his editorials on the silver question to every influential Democratic politician in the country. He got the lists of delegates to all Democratic conventions, national and local, and bombarded them personally with articles and correspondence. And during the next two years, he spoke in all the states South and West on silver, usually under the auspices of Bimetallic and Silver Leagues. He was laying his plans, stone by stone, to storm the national convention.

Thanks to well-subsidized propaganda and hard times, the silver question was now agitating everybody. It was splitting the Republican party; it was raising up a storm of revolt against the eastern bosses of the Democratic party; it was a frequent plank in Prohibitionist platforms. It was shunting the new Populist party onto an empty siding, leaving more than half the members stalled on the main line of legitimate farmer demands, while the other half, like Bryan, hoped to win office and influence by seizing hold of one shining but superficial panacea.

Silver was really a fake issue, a demagogic bauble. It threw dust in the eyes. It took men's mind off important issues and created a babble of voices and unreasonable emotions. It ignored broader currency questions; it ignored all the basic economic and political demands of the day. It was merely a bright Christmas star for simple minds. It meant little, except to frighten eastern believers in a tight gold standard out of their wits and to excite the farmers with false hope.

Perhaps the silver question gained ascendency precisely because it was a fake issue. In time of crisis, most men are afraid to face real issues or deep problems. Their troubles and fears drive them to seek an easy escape. Men find it hard to agree at such times on necessary reforms and changes. Silver provided a shining symbol. It allowed no intricacies. You could be for it or against it. You had an issue. It was a banner and flag, an emblem, just as gold was, something simpler men would rally around and fight under. One flag was that of the common man. The other was the flag of the oppressors.

And so the fake issue grew into a full-fledged popular cyclone that threatened the existing parties and the privileged powerful. Soon the question became: Who will ride this silver hurricane? A man like Weaver of the Populists, a far deeper thinker than Bryan? He, too, was basically a currency reformer, and he saw this might be his one great opportunity. Populists, who had tasted office and found more honey there than out on the prairies, saw it as a chance to hold on to their gains and their jobs. Such men were willing to toss aside the farm program, laboriously built up by trial and error through the Grange and the Alliance, and carried time and again to the polls with increasing success. But like the Democratic bosses, the Populist currency bosses failed to see in young Bryan the New David who would walk away with their glory and knock out — almost — "the Goliath of Gold privilege."

Bryan himself had few doubts about his own role or what was to happen. More than anyone else, except perhaps Coin Harvey, who was not a politician, Bryan had helped puff this false issue into a tempest, and it was easy to picture himself as the silver knight of the silver crusade. He did not leave it to eloquence and personality. He worked hard and methodically. By the time he entrained for the Democratic convention in Chicago in July, 1896, he had his fishhooks in every little pool of the Democratic party and many other pools. He was already confident he would draw out the prize and be nominated for President.

The myth persists that Bryan, a relatively unknown man, moved by eloquence and inspiration, seized the coveted honor wholly by his famous "extemporaneous" Cross of Gold speech. Nothing could be farther from the truth. No one ever prepared his nomination or his speech with more care. Behind him, by 1896, were the rank and file of the Democratic West and South; behind him was the unrest of a difficult period of panic; behind him were powerful silver-mining interests.

In 1896, the *Chicago Chronicle* editorialized: "Of late years they [the silver-mine owners] have found it profitable to keep a large number of orators, lecturers, and other spokesmen on the road, preaching to people already limping as a result of bites of the free silver cur, the sovereign remedy of applying the hair of the dog to the wound. Among them men who have been thus employed and carried on the payroll of the big bonanzas for a number of years is William Jennings Bryan of Nebraska. A paid agent and spokesman for the silver combine . . . The richest men of the world, the proprietors of the big bonanzas, hire orators like Bryan exactly as other wealthy men use fiddlers. . . . Silver orators, like fiddlers, come in at the back door of the big business and eat at the servants' table. . . . Bryan's nomination . . . [is] an insult to the American people of no small proportions."

That is only a small part of the whole story, of course, and far from being an insult to the American people, his nomination represented one of the few times in the life of the major parties that a man of the people and for the people, whatever his shortcomings, has ever won the coveted nomination. Bryan worked hard to get it, and even some of the silver people must have had a few nervous qualms, for, whatever their fight to improve the silver situation, these interests were deeply involved with the financial East and not the Middle Border revolt. They, too, had used armed guards and state and federal troops to kill workers.

Bryan's great address was not extemporaneous at all. Most of it had already been published in his paper. He had tried parts of it out on audiences in the sticks time after time. He had prepared every syllable, every comma, every accent, every gesture, every facial expression, beforehand, and he had practiced it time and again before the mirror.

As the Democratic convention approached, the two men most often mentioned for the nomination were Silver Dick Bland and Horace Boies of Idaho. Bryan cleverly refrained from endorsing either of them. To Champ Clark, on the eve of the Chicago convention, he said he wished he could disguise Champ as a delegate from Nebraska.

"Why?" . . .

"To put me in nomination."

Surprised, Champ asked, "Are you a candidate?"

"Yes and I will get the nomination."

"How? . . ."

"Bland will not be nominated because it is too early to nominate a candidate from one of the old slave states." Other proposed candidates were not well enough known. "Vice-President Stevenson will not get it because he has sat on the fence too long."

Not all was settled yet. There was still a possiblity that Bryan's silver delegation to the convention might not even be seated. A "gold" delegation was claiming to be the rightful representatives of Nebraska democracy. But the "baby Demosthenes," as John Hay called him, was full of confidence. He might be, as the testy preju-

[309]

diced Marse Henry Watterson declared, not only "a boy orator" but also a "dishonest dodger . . . daring adventurer . . . political fakir," but he knew where he was bound.

First he attended the Republican convention at St. Louis as a correspondent for the *World Herald* and watched the proceedings closely. What his opponents did would help him chart his own course. It also gave him an unobtrusive chance to contact silver Republicans, such as Teller of Colorado, who planned to bolt if "gold" became a Republican plank and silver was made a Democratic plank. Numbers of such Republicans, good machine men, were willing to walk right into the Democratic parlor.

The bitterness among Republican gold and silver factions was strong. Mark Hanna had worked for years to make certain that William McKinley would be nominated. The time came. But would it be on free silver or a gold plank? Or would Hanna's advice be followed that the issue be dodged and the fight made solely on the tariff?

When the currency issue was raised, the convention exploded. Men stood on their desks and roared. Hanna sat stolidly chewing his cigar. As he expected, his machine worked smoothly, and the thorny currency question was sent to committee, put into the hands of the safe "gold bugs" of the party for strangling. The "inviolable" gold standard plank went through — probably written by Melville E. Stone of the Associated Press, "because," as someone said, "he was the only one present able to spell the word inviolable." When the Silver Republicans rose and left the hall — an out-and-out bolt — Hanna still stolidly chewing on his cigar with a "good-riddance" attitude.

In the midst of the turbulent scene, reporter Wallace Dunn found unusually large feet planted on his scribbled news bulletins. They belonged to Bryan, standing on the desk, watching fascinated, busily planning his own coup at Chicago. When Gold Republicans shouted at the departing silverites, "Go to Chicago . . . Take the Democratic train," Bryan's face gleamed with satisfaction.

In the windy city for the great Democratic day, he registered quietly at a cheap hotel. He always affected unkempt locks and seedy attire, and the clerk demanded pay in advance.

The Democrats were also badly split over the ticklish silver-gold issue. The initial fight came over the temporary chairman. The party bosses had decided on powerful Senator David B. Hill as a sop to strong anti-Cleveland elements, but as a check also — since he was a New York "gold bug" — to the pro-silver forces. The true temper of the convention showed itself at once; the careful plans of the old-liners were shattered after the first moment; the enthusiastic silver delegates swept Hill aside and put in Senator Daniel from Virginia. Already they controlled the strategic credentials committee, and they did not hesitate to use their weapons. Gold delegates, according to Rufus Hardy, Texas Democratic Chairman, were "ejected . . . without a shadow of justification. . . . The convention, assembled under such methods, by party manipulators, had disenfranchised every honest-money Democrat in Texas."

"To one suddenly arrived from a foreign country, and unacquainted with the actual conditions," said one gold delegate, "to have heard all the talk, in which there was so little toleration for the despised gold-bug, the conclusion would have been inevitable that the American Republic sat crouching under the blighting shadow of England's financial dominance, and that this frantic, gesticulating, steaming crowd of excited free coinage apostles had gathered in quest of a leader of the revolution that should wipe Great Britain off the map and fling Wall Street into the middle of the East River. . . . Grover B. Cleveland and Wall Street — that indefinable conglomeration of corporate avarice, rapine and plunder — had entered into a conscienceless . . . conspiracy to 'crucify mankind on a cross of gold' by pilfering the laborer of every dollar wrought in the sweat of his brow, and by planting the gaunt wolf of hunger on the threshold of every farm house in the land."

General hatred of Cleveland helped the silverites. Under the leadership of Bryan, Altgeld, and Tillman, "they proposed to ride down, with the cruelty of cossacks, precedent, tradition, and everything else without respect to whether it was decent or necessary."

These harsh contemporary comments, one-sided and perhaps shortsighted, revealed the deep feeling and passion of the hour, the deep division in men's minds and souls that racked the entire country, all the bitterness that had accumulated with the crass plundering of the gilded age. Whatever the outcome in the convention or in the country, the handwriting seemed clear: the course of the nation would be changed.

While credentials were being examined, Senator Daniel, in a typical Southern speech, full of sunrises, sunbursts, and horizons, advocated silver coinage at sixteen to one. Governor David Overmeyer of Kansas told the convention solemnly that the seat of the empire had now been transferred from the Atlantic states to the Mississippi Valley. Governor Altgeld of Illinois, who, more than anyone else, had broken Cleveland's power in the convention, spoke of farm mortgages "held by English moneylenders."

The Nebraska silver delegates, including Bryan, were duly seated. Friends beat time with their feet, and the delegates roared approval. Two Kentucky delegates did a wild dance. A Montana delegate rushed up to present the chairman with a silver gavel.

Today that old issue of gold *versus* silver is unimportant. There was not much sense in it even in 1896. Silver was only a crude symbol that drew the lines between the sections and the classes, and today the heated passions seem childish and ridiculous, except that men always grow most emotional and bitter over what they understand least. But in '96, the hosts drawn up for battle on that false issue were determined to give no quarter.

The next day, Bryan maneuvered himself into the position to be the one to close the debate. Hill would speak for gold. For the silverites, Ben Tillman, "the South Carolina flamethrower." fired the first gun. He was a striking, rugged figure.

"The whole 'tout ensemble' of the man," said one delegate, "suggested a block of granite . . . fighting jaws . . . figure compact

[312]

and square . . . features . . . regular and clearcut as if chiseled in stone. One eye is gone, and his seamed and ugly face . . . appears to scowl under a sardonic shadow. His voice sounds like a buzz-saw ripping through a gnarled log, but it fills the air like a gong when delivering that rubbing stroke which brings out the full sound of the metal."

Never a tactful man, Tillman made the mistake of harping on sectional antagonisms. He pictured silver as the battle of the West and South against the northeastern states. Truthful as this was, the fiction of party and national unity had to be maintained, and he was roundly hissed.

The speaker turned his solitary orb, from which leaped the flames of defiance, toward the gallery from whence came the insult. "There are but three things that hiss: a goose, a serpent and — a man," he said. It had been said before, but no man had ever said it like the mad South Carolinian. But he was hissed again and floundered.

Venerable Sam Jones of Arkansas rose and repudiated Tillman and his "rabid utterance." Next came David Bennet Hill, the patriarch of the party. He was a "gold bug," but he hated and had fought Cleveland, and the delegates hated Cleveland, and though they had refused to make Hill chairman, now, as he mounted the rostrum, "salvo after salvo of applause united in an ovation that was tempestuous."

Emotions, aroused by preliminary controversies, were mounting toward the crest — the orgiastic revivalism so typical of American religious and political life. The shouts of 20,000 people rose "like old Ocean's surge, breaking upon resounding cliffs," rose and fell, rose and fell. Everybody stood in his chair, up three sides of the coliseum, "in tier after tier, from the parallelogram-shaped section, occupied by the delegates, to the far away descending roofs." For 19 full minutes, the pandemonium kept up.

"I am here to unite, not to divide, to upbuild, not to destroy, to plan for victory, not to plot for defeat," Hill pleaded.

[313]

Finally Bryan rose eagerly to speak — tall but stocky, pale, with long black hair and a beaked nose. His nervous thin lips, tipped with worry, wore an uncertain wide-slit smile. But worried though he might be, from the very first moment his voice struck its full resonance. It was "like the chiming of cathedral bells," reported one rapt listener.

He said modestly that he was presumptuous in presenting himself against such distinguished gentlemen, but this was no measuring of abilities, no contest of persons. Then his phrasemaking rhetoric hit its full stride: "The humblest citizen in the land, when clad in the armor of a righteous cause, is stronger than the hosts of error. I come to speak to you in defense of a cause as holy as the cause of liberty . . . the cause of humanity."

He traced the rise of the silver cause, and, as his eloquence expanded, the silverites began to beam. There on the platform, big ex-Governor Hogg of Texas, 6 ft. 2 in. in his socks, could not conceal his delight.

Bryan flouted the idea that the silver men were disturbing business. Was not the employee as much as the employer a businessman? Was not the farmer also a businessman? The merchant at the crossroads store? The miners "who go down a thousand feet into the earth or climb two thousand feet upon the cliffs, and bring from their hiding places the precious metals to be poured into the channels of trade?" Were they not as much businessmen "as the few financial magnates who, in a back room, corner the money of the world? We come to speak for this broader class of businessmen?"

In 1896, this specious sort of talk was radical doctrine indeed. It aroused the Middle Border folk to wild glory, and it filled the eastern financiers, the big metropolitan newspapers, and the men of commerce, with terror. Today it sounds more like familiar chamber of commerce argument — so does the flow of time polish the stones.

The silverites had nothing against those who live on the Atlantic coast, said Bryan, but the hardy pioneers — he pointed west — were "as deserving of consideration . . . as any people in the country."

It is for those that we speak. "We do not come as aggressors. Our war is not a war of conquest; we are fighting in the defense of our homes, our families and prosperity. We have petitioned, and our entreaties have been disregarded; we have begged, and they have mocked when calamity came. We beg no longer; we entreat no longer; we petition no more. We defy them!" he shouted in dramatic pose, and again the thunder of applause shook the auditorium.

Why was silver more important than the tariff question? he continued, and balanced his phrases to a literary answer. "Protection has slain its thousands, the gold standard has slain its tens of thousands."

He referred to McKinley: "Why, the man who was once pleased to think that he looked like Napoleon — that man shudders today when he remembers that he was nominated on the anniversary of Waterloo. Not only that, but as he listens he can hear with ever-increasing distinctness the sound of waves as they beat upon the lonely shore of St. Helena."

Amazingly enough, the new commoner had copied this blast directly from a fellow opposition congressman who had earlier accused Bryan himself of resembling and imitating Napoleon, and now he used it to single out his future opponent and announce his inevitable defeat.

An "indignant people," declared the young Nebraskan, pointing up the western anti-foreign, anti-British prejudices, would visit their "avenging wrath" on a man who would place "the legislative control of our affairs in the hands of foreign potentates and powers."

He spoke of two opposing concepts of government that were to be heard as late as Hoover's day and beyond. "There are those who believe that if you will only legislate to make the well-to-do prosperous, their prosperity will leak through on those below. The Democratic idea, however, has been that if you legislate to make the masses prosperous, their prosperity will find its way through every class which rests upon them."

He played upon another familiar western prejudice. The cities were for the gold standard. Yet if the cities were burned down, but the farms were saved, the cities would spring up again "as if by magic." But destroy the farms, and "grass would grow in the streets of every city in the country."

He returned to the nationalistic, anti-British isolationist note and cleverly pivoted it on a note of patriotism. The United States was fully able to legislate for itself alone. It did not have to follow the lead of a foreign power. Here, he claimed, was the issue of 1776 all over again. "Our ancestors, when but three million in number, had the courage to declare their political independence of every other nation; shall we, their descendants when we have grown to seventy millions, declare that we are less independent than our forefathers? . . .

"Instead of having a gold standard because England has, we will restore bimetallism, and then let England have bimetallism because the United States has it . . ."

For his final words he borrowed a complicated metaphor from a cartoon that had been published four years earlier in a Populist newspaper in Iowa. "Having behind us the producing masses of this nation and the world, supported by the commerical interests, the laboring interests, and the toilers everywhere, we will answer their demand for a gold standard by saying to them: You shall not press down upon the brow of labor this crown of thorns, you shall not crucify mankind upon a cross of gold."

This was the grand climax of one of the world's most historic speeches, and Bryan stood there in the awed silence of those thousands upon thousands "like some god of the storm."

The silence cracked, and the thunder rolled in from the sea. The convention literally went insane. Men yelled, shrieked, wept, clawed, marched. A burly long-whiskered Georgian ruthlessly trampled his way forward with the standard of his state raised aloft. A Cherokee delegate from the Indian Territory plunged headfirst through the New York delegation. The blue guidons that marked the position of the various delegations were snatched from their

[316]

fastenings and, while the Coliseum rocked in the tempest of emotion, were grouped about the Nebraska standard in wild jubilee. A grand march of glory started.

Bryan, white with exhaustion, was lifted to the shoulders of more than a dozen men. He was feeling sick and begged to be put down. But he was slapped on the back, his hand was shaken, he was shouted at, his feet were danced upon.

"Those who listened to Bryan's speech," declares biographer Werner, "received an emotional experience that remained with them for years; it was like hearing Jenny Lind or Patti sing, and innumerable grandchildren were assured that never had there been the like of it in the memory of man." The speech swept the nation, and William Allen White believed that if the elections had been held within a week or so, Bryan would have been easily elected.

Yet it was mostly sound and fury, signifying nothing. In itself it was not a great speech at all, nor was it even a great issue. It was merely a great emotional occasion. His words were perfectly chosen for the feelings of the moment, properly pitched to meet the current prejudices of the hour, and planed down to the general ignorance of the day. It was a sublime example of what mediocrity could achieve; a mighty victory of emotion over reason, the culminating proof that Bryan had indeed escaped the clutches of the men of science and the "mind-worshippers."

Bryan later made many blunders, he did many noble and ignoble things, he lived a long life and filled high posts; but at that moment when he stood like a god of the storm above the hushed multitude, that was the supreme moment of his career. There was crystallized the whole gusty essence of the man on the highest peak possible for him ever to reach.

The following day on the fifth ballot Bryan was nominated amid marching banners and shouts. He was at a barber shop getting shaved. His enemies insisted this, too, was a studied stunt.

The nomination for the Vice-President was put off for two days. To offset the impetuous Bryan and his supposed radicalism, to placate the East, Arthur Sewall of Maine, a wealthy banker and ship builder, was nominated. Teller of Colorado, close to the wealthy silver-mining interests, sent Bryan a most curious public message: "All the power of money and organized wealth, corporations and monopolies of all kinds will be against us . . . It is a contest for industrial independence and for freedom from the domination of foreign powers and foreign capitalists." And so, according to disgruntled Democrat Hardy, with the assistance of Mr. Teller, a lifelong and distinguished Republican, and the advice and suggestion of leading Populists, there was adopted "what they have falsely labelled a Democratic platform."

The campaign of 1896 became that of a brilliant western demagogue, a man of the people, against sedate, proper, and mediocre McKinley, backed by the millions of the financial East and the millionaires of the new West. The symbols were gold and silver — and mystic symbols they were. People were being stampeded after false gods, and the less reason they had for their emotions, the more violent they became.

"The free Silver movement," said Henry Demarest Lloyd, former editor of the *Chicago Tribune*, a monetary expert and one of the more brilliant minds of the Populist party, "is a fake. Free Silver is the cow-bird of the Reform movement. It waited until the nest had been built by sacrifices and labor of others and then it laid its eggs in it, pushing out the others which lie smashed on the ground It is now flying around while we are expected to do the incubating. I for one decline to sit on the nest to help any such game.

"I may vote for Bryan as the Knight of the Disinherited, like Ivanhoe, but he will not be the next President, and I am content . . ."

It was the eternal dilemma of voters in the curious American two-party system. It was all romantic nonsense, but Silver was a gallant knight who would somehow tumble down the power of the bankers and bring prosperity to all, though few of those so excited about it had any inkling of just what the free coinage of silver would or would not do. But gold was the symbol of unjust power;

it was the habiliment of the dragon guarding the sleeping beauty of liberty and the treasure that belonged to worthier but poorer men. Bryan, in short, was the people's man. McKinley was Big Business, or as the Democrats put it, forgetting their own Sewall, "the office boy of corporate wealth." "The plutocrats" were certainly alarmed, but as Congressman Tom Johnson of Ohio remarked, "what they feared was not free silver — but free men."

The East — so ignorant of the West — was indeed terribly frightened, and Mark Hanna and his associates played upon that fear to pry out a campaign fund of $16,000,000 to Bryan's $1,000,000 in the effort to save the Republic. As the national candidate who can call upon the largest campaign fund has always been elected (except in the case of Lincoln), the outcome of the battle was to be expected. Even so, it was a close race.

Industrial leaders issued dire warnings of dread consequences if Bryan were elected. They told their employees they would have to shut down the day after election. M. E. Ingalls, President of the Chesapeake and Ohio Railroad, announced his company would have to stop all improvements everywhere, discharge many employees, and reduce the pay of the rest. Bryan was pictured as an anarchist, an infidel, and an anti-Christ with one foot on the Bible, desecrating it, though no one cherished that book more than he.

The Bryanites did the best they could with limited funds, much of which came from the silver barons. According to Mark Sullivan, the Big Bonanza proprietors put up $228,000, more than one-fourth of the entire campaign fund, and distributed 125,000 copies of Coin's *Financial School*.

Men were troubled in spirit those days, and party lines were jumbled. Silver Republicans bolted. Gold Democrats bolted. The latter put forward the "true" Democratic candidates, General John Palmer of Illinois and the Confederate hero, General Simon Bolivar Buckner of Kentucky. The facetious called them "anarchists," an ironical designation, for Cleveland endorsed them.

[319]

Above all, the Populists were in a bad way. For some years, their leaders, among them Weaver, had increasingly laid aside broader reforms to put all their energies into the one basket of silver, and they were now driven to champion not their own cause, but the candidate of the Democratic party who half-disdained their support. At the 1896 Populist party convention in St Louis, the vast majority of the delegates were Mid-Roaders who realized that fusion and the nomination of Bryan meant destruction of their broader program and an end to the party.

For southern Populists, who had been on the verge of taking over the Democratic party but had reluctantly pulled out to form the new party, leaving control in the hands of the Bourbons, fusion meant political suicide. They would not be taken back into the Democratic fold.

The Mid-Roaders at St. Louis were tricked by the new bosses of the party, particularly by officeholders and especially by Weaver, Senator William V. Allen of Nebraska, and National Chairman H. E. Traubneck, Jerry Simpson, General Field, Lewelling, and Coxey. At crucial moments, to disconcert or check the Mid-Roaders, the lights were turned off, and delegates blundered around in the dark, yelling, tearing their clothes, getting pokes in the eye. Mid-Road committee meetings were sabotaged and thrown into bedlam.

Senator James K. Jones, Democratic National Chairman, was practically a member of the convention. Busily he promoted the cause of silver and of Bryan and Sewall, promising delegates every-thing — cabinet positions, jobs, moonshine, starshine, and pie in the sky.

Four hundred bimetallist delegates convened in Music Hall and worked on individual Populists to bring about a solid front against the imperial hosts of gold. There was an angry ruckus when the Populist assemblage sent a delegation to their convention.

The most effective of all perhaps was Governor Silas A. Holcomb of Nebraska, who descended on the sessions with 150 energetic pro-silver agents to buttonhole, lobby, and win over delegates.

Weaver nominated Bryan. "There is a tide in the affairs of men . . . [which made it necessary for the Populists to nominate] that matchless champion of the people, that intrepid foe of corporate greed, that splendid young statesman . . ."

As the cheering mounted, four men came in a side door with a big yellow cross topped by a crown of thorns. Bryan was chosen by a landslide vote. But 300 rock-ribbed Mid-Roaders made a forlorn counter-demonstration and left the hall. The vote was no victory; it was the beginning of the end for Populism.

The silver Populists almost feared to peep in Bryan's direction lest he toss their nomination back at them. Unwilling to endorse banker Sewall, they had put up a different Vice-Presidential candidate, fiery Tom Watson of Georgia. Bryan never accepted either nomination. Except for using Weaver here and there, he scorned the Populists as poor relatives of whom he was ashamed. He had nothing to do with Watson, and the Georgian was treated like a poor unwelcome relative by his own party. The Populist bosses feared to support their own Vice-Presidential candidate. Their one chance, they believed, to get reelected or to obtain patronage was to cater to Bryan.

Bryan knew the Populists would have to vote for him, that his election now depended not on them, but in allaying earlier fears of his radicalism. He had to cut into the more conservative vote on the Atlantic seaboard.

Bryan easily drew nearly all the many schools of reform into his silver net. There was no other place to flounder. At the same time, his smooth cadences drew off the heat of farmer militancy, refilling the vacuum with the passion of emotional revivalism. Perhaps it was the inevitable fate of a frontier mind that had listened to too many windy preachers.

But even before the campaign was over, Bryan had ceased to be the true leader of the western hosts. By one act of crude opportunism, he tossed it all away. At Cooper Union in New York, where he was expected to put Tammany in its place, whatever the cost,

[321]

he said, "Great is Tammany and Crocker is its prophet," and Tammany had never been a grosser filthier institution than it was under Tweed and Crocker. America gasped, and Bryan's "broken scepter was crunched in the Tiger's grinning jaws." After that, wrote William Allen White, he was "a shorn Samson."

For Bryan it was a meteoric rise and fall. He had shot into the sky for only a day, and gone out, though the long tail of his glimmering fall was to shower sparks over the American scene until the time of World War I — his post as Cabinet Minister, his silly part in the Dayton evolution trial, and his stint as a Florida land salesman.

Logically, Bryan, the orator, should have been rushed pellmell into the White House, and nearly was. But by the close of 1896, it was becoming evident he was already a belated prophet. The age of oratory was over well before the end of his campaign.

Between the age of eloquent revivalism and the age of the radio crooner, the age of gold and steel was to intervene. William McKinley, riding to victory on torrents of gold, aided by the steel propellers of the industrialists and new munition-makers, and by the guile, ability, and wealth of impresario Mark Hanna, moved into the White House to inaugurate the new era of militant internationalism, of war and expansion. The long farmers' revolt was over at last.

But the land was still there! More acres were dying. In spite of expansion and industrial prosperity, men were becoming tenants and sharecroppers faster than ever. With new war and new industrialism widening the margins of prosperity for so many, a quarter of a century and more would drift by in the grip of the bigger and better optimism, before the nation would again really take some stock of its land resources and its human resources on that land.

XV
JOAD ON THE ROAD

In the 1930's, the Joads, the dispossessed farmers of the Middle Border, began pressing out *The Grapes of Wrath* along the western highways. They joined the "farm-tramps," the migratory seasonal crop workers, who jitter from camp shack to camp shack, with little security or regular employment, with few sanitary conveniences, and scanty educational and health opportunities for their children.

Many of the new "Migs" were from drouth-stricken Oklahoma, where drifting dust and foreclosures and the tractors of ever-expanding big plantations overwhelmed the old homesteads. And so the new westward-bound migrants were usually called "Okies," though actually they came from nearly every state east of the Rockies, from the gullied cottonfields and dying acres of Georgia and Alabama; from the foreclosed lands of Texas, where the mechanical plow and cottonpicker had romped across the boundaries of small holdings and homes, obliterating them; from the tired acres of Connecticut and Massachusetts; from the stripped timberlands of Louisiana and Minnesota; from the parched inlands of Kansas and Nebraska; from the gritty skies of the Dakotas.

A new system of quickie machine-farming had seized great areas in Indiana and Illinois. Hurriedly, long-conserved lands were raped with bumper crops for a few years, then turned back to large-scale tenants, bound to go bankrupt or barely survive on the leached out acres. Small farmers were driven out and joined the new westward march. The old muskrat trapping lands of Louisiana, greatest fur-producing state in the Union, were all seized by hook or by crook, and many trappers, not willing to submit to the new debt-feudalism, joined the westward trek. It was estimated that new machinery in Iowa had reduced the need for farmhands by 100,000. And so, nature and science, greed and lack of science, depression and neglect, ruined soil and drouth, machinery and land-concentration, all combined to send a mighty river of folk flowing toward the setting sun.

World War I had enormously expanded agriculture. It made the cultivation of marginal or sub-fertile lands temporarily profitable again, and thereby hurried them on to the grave of land made forever useless, already a desert empire vaster than any Alexander ever dreamed of conquering, as large as all the cultivated lands of Europe outside Russia. It led to the plowing up of new acres of sod-land never meant to be plowed, thus exposing fine topsoil to wind erosion. It caused the more rapid exhaustion of good lands, the quicker ruin of lands already half-lost. This reckless process continued during the post-war boom until disaster, man-made and nature-made, hit, and the caravans of leaky radiators, piled bedding, cook stoves, busted rockers, and irritable unwashed children started out on Highway 66 for the Golden Gate.

By 1934, in the South alone some 4,500,000 rural inhabitants, mostly white, were being kept from starvation by local state and federal handouts. The Negroes really starved. In some communities of the north-central states, up to 80 percent of the population was on relief.

[324]

The agricultural decline in much of the deep South, of which the Great Depression was merely the climax, was visible in places as early as the Civil War. In the Piedmont area, it had set in as early as 1880, and in most regions by 1920. The best lands, in the so-called Black Belt, remained monopolized by survivors of the old plantation system or by large corporations. Human conditions in that belt of the richest southern lands were almost as bad as any place on earth, and the system was largely maintained by a totalitarian system of mob terrorism and race hatred. On the richest soil there, one found the poorest people.

Georgia, which in earlier periods had been the most productive agricultural state in the Union, had so declined that by the third decade of this century, the majority of the rural population was without decent housing, proper food, education, or medical care. Whole counties lacked so much as a public health officer. Even by the lowest conceivable standards, Georgia was sub-standard. It had become a great rural slum. In some places over 40 percent of the land had been destroyed and abandoned. Georgia, by the time of the Great Depression, had become a distinct liability to itself and to the nation. By then four-fifths of its land was planted to corn or cotton, and the production per acre was far below that of the nation as a whole, while the cost of producing that smaller yield had become greater than almost anywhere else, this despite low living standards. To harvest the rolling eroded soil on poor hills meant that human beings had to be hired at a few cents an hour in order that the products could compete with the mechanized output on the more fertile level lands of Texas and California and the Mississippi bottom lands. By 1928, a prosperity year, the gross farm operator's income for all crops sold, traded, or used by his family, totaled less than $600 annually for 35.9 percent of all rural producers in the state. Cash income was even less.

In Iowa, one of every seven farms was foreclosed, many even before the depression. They had been taken over by the sheriff and the families ousted; 60 percent of the remaining farms were mortgaged by 1931. During Hoover's two-cars-in-every-garage campaign, part of the proof of prosperity of his four-year rule was the picture of a vine-covered cottage in Cedar County, an idyll of the rustic happiness farmers enjoyed.

But by March, 1931, 1,000 hungry farmers in a Cedar County town drove off law-officers and the veterinarian who came to test their herds. So the Cow War began.

The leader, Milo Reno, who had attended the 1892 Populist convention and now headed up farm insurance cooperatives and the Farmers' Union, was telling them the tests were not accurate, nor were the farmers adequately compensated for their animals the government killed. They believed it was a plot of the big packers to get meat cheap. Why was the meat of murdered tubercular animals eatable and milk not salable?

Five hundred Cedar County farmers hired a special train to the Des Moines capitol. Milo Reno's men were specially organized into the Farmers' Protective Association, which had no money, to avoid possible injunctions and lawsuits. It was headed by big-jawed Jake Lenker, a dour relentless man, and Paul Moore, a slim Irish Republican who liked to recite Edwin Markham's "The Man with a Hoe."

The legislators were wise enough to turn the house chamber over to the farm speakers, who snarled into the microphone; one recited poetry:

> Knights went forth with lances,
> Clad in coats of mail,
> Now they go forth with squirt guns
> And shoot cows in the tail.

But no attention was paid to the legislation demanded, and presently the law attempted to kill the herd of well-to-do Curt Mitchell. The farmers, unawed by the sheriff's guns and threats of tear gas, kicked them and the veterinarian off the premises. Gover-

[326]

nor Dan Turner ordered the state militia to stand by, but in the end Mitchell's cows and his fine blooded-bull were not destroyed, and for a time the authorities avoided Cedar County. But soon, state officials, backed by the Governor's agents, were driven off a farm by shotgun and the egg-throwing of wife and daughter. The veterinarian was literally kicked in the pants and told "to git." But three farmers were arrested, and the Governor appointed an ex-Des Moines chief of police to get together armed deputies. They singled out the farm of Jake Lenker to force him to permit his herd to be tested. Five hundred farmers hemmed in the deputies, who used tear gas. The farmers came in fighting with clubs, bricks, and bare hands, and ducked the Governor's assistant attorney into the horse pond. The deputies' car tires were punctured and the windows broken. They had to flee on foot.

Governor Turner called out the National Guard to put down the "insurrection." Jake Lenker was seized and locked in a horse-stall. He jeered to reporters that the Governor did not know what he was gassing about. Hoover took prosperity away from us and hid it around a corner. Turner wasn't going to get away with it.

But his herds were tested, and he and Paul Moore were sent to jail for three years, though paroled in four months. The real issue, of course, was not cow-testing but fifty years of farm depression in the West, now topped by a whopping national depression.

Milo Reno deplored violence but led the farm hosts in ever wider and wilder protests. In 1932, he called the farmers to the Des Moines fairgrounds to decide on a farm-strike, i.e., to hold all their products off the market until the price went up. Three thousand showed up, and the strike was set to begin August 8. Tens of thousands of pledged signatures were obtained. Why not? Milk was selling for two cents a quart. Other states rallied behind the idea, particularly North Dakota, and Minnesota, where the Farmer-Labor party was born and took over the state. Other farmer holdouts occurred in Kansas, Oklahoma, Montana, South Dakota, and Nebraska.

The chief fight in Iowa was around Sioux City, where the embattled farmers turned back the milk trucks of nonstrikers after dumping their milk. Road barricades were established. The sheriff rounded up 100 armed deputies.

The farmers crowded around them, and, after a few threats and the throwing of a deputy's shotgun into the weeds, the minions of the law folded up their tents. Freight trains carrying milk and/or livestock were stopped. The strike was successful. But the prices did not go up.

The conflict spread to Omaha. There, fifty deputies attacked a strikers' camp with tear gas and bullets. The strikers smashed the windows of the deputies' cars and drove them off. But by morning, fifty Holiday men were in jail in Council Bluffs.

Farmers from all over the state began converging on the city. Machine guns were set up to defend the jail, soon surrounded by 3,000 protestors, for the time quietly, but the sheriff knew that when the moment came, they would attack, whatever the cost. The sheriff accepted a piece of property as bail-bond for the whole arrested caboodle and hurriedly released them all.

But on the night of August 31, a fusillade of bullets from a county sheriff's posse ripped into a strikers' camp, Cherokee, killing 1 person, wounding 14. Reno was so shocked that he called off the strike, which was not producing better prices, to return to a middle-western governors' conference to consider ameliorative measures for the farmers. But many farmers refused to give up, and pitched battles, 100 or so men on either side, took place. On September 9, 5,000 farmers surged through the Omaha streets in mass protest.

The governors did nothing, ignored all farmer demands, and Reno called another strike, this time in all the West and in the South. It was not particularly effective, but Hoover and Curtis were smothered at the polls. The depression by then had reached its lowest point, with some of the biggest banks in the country closing their doors. Wheat was twenty-five cents a bushel, hogs netted less than $1.00 apiece.

As prices sank still lower, farms and goods, horses and mules and cows, were seized for debts. Properties everywhere were going under the auction hammer. A remedy was found—the famous penny sales. Thousands of farmers gathered at each auction, kept everybody else away, and purchased the property for a few cents or a few dollars. It was then deeded back to the owner. These auctions became gala fiestas. The women served chicken, pie, and coffee. The crowds roared with laughter when a two-cent bid for a horse would be solemnly raised to three cents. It was customary at such affairs to hang a noose from the hayloft track, as a warning of what awaited those who attempted to break up the proceedings.

The idea spread like wildfire all over the country, even to Pennsylvania and New York. Legislatures and governors began declaring debt moratoriums. The farmers considered this reasonable. If the United States could give moratoriums for foreigners and foreign governments owing money, surely the farmers had an even more legitimate right to such protection.

But plenty of farms were waiting to be auctioned off; the lawyers easily found loopholes, and by the April after Franklin D. Roosevelt had taken office, great bands of angry landless or jobless farmers roamed the highways and byways in much of the West, taking over forced sales and surrounding county courthouses to threaten judges and the authorities not to carry on any more sales. Roosevelt asked for time to work out a proper program, but mostly his efforts seemed to give preference to talk and more talk.

Impatient farmers gathered around the sheriff of Dennison County, who was selling seized corn. They swept up in cars, caught about thirty deputies, badly mauled them, and let them go.

At Primghar, deputies fought off farmers where the sheriff foreclosed a farm. The only satisfaction the farmers got on this occasion was to force the mortgage-holders' lawyer to kiss the American flag. They invaded the courthouse but were driven down the stairs by deputies' clubs. Nursing their bruises, they went to Le Mars and slipped into the courtroom of Judge C. C. Bradley, who was hearing a suit to set aside the moratorium. Some did not remove their

[329]

hats, which held their bandages on their battered heads. Others smoked cigarettes. Judge Bradley's gavel rapped in wrath.

The anger of the farmers boiled over. They swarmed right over the bench and slapped the old judge's face. They demanded that he promise not to sign any more foreclosure papers. He refused. They slapped him again and again. He still held out.

Using handkerchiefs for masks, they took hold of him, blindfolding him, led him out, and threw him into a car. A mile and a half outside of town, they put a noose around his neck and threw the rope over a high-power line. They told him to kneel down and pray for better times for the farmers. He did so. But he still refused not to foreclose their farms. Grease was smeared on his head. The rope was hauled up, just enough to render him unconscious, then the mobsters fled. His neck was badly burned.

He came to, got the noose off, and stumbled back toward town.

The governor rushed in troops; fifty farmers were arrested and held in bullpens. Among them were some of the most respectable men in the community.

Reno again deplored the violence but reminded his listeners that the incident was not unique in human history, for wherever courts had failed to maintain equality and justice they had been overthrown, ignored, and abolished.

He called another strike for May, 1933. Roosevelt appealed for more time. Reno acceded, and thereby manacled his own revolt. All summer Roosevelt and Wallace talked mightily about helping the farmer. Farm loans were arranged for, but only one farmer in fifty, Reno pointed out, could qualify to meet the government requirements.

The old greenback cries were heard again — the Frazer-Lemke Bill was introduced. It was ignored. Instead, the government cut veterans' pensions as a deflationary move. By August, when another strike was called, Roosevelt was less alarmed. He had hit on his big spending panacea and expected to be able to smother any real trouble. Reno went right ahead, declaring the strike was to support the Frazer-Lemke Bill and the cost-of-production plan by which the farmer would be guaranteed as much return as it cost him to produce his crop. He forced another western governors' conference. Only Bill Langer, Governor of North Dakota, went along with Reno's ideas. He established a farm embargo and backed it up with the state militia.

The strike was not a success. October was corn-husking time, and farmers were too worn out to man the barricades on the roads. But ties were stacked on railroad tracks, blocking trains. They were dragged into the roads before approaching trucks. In Minneapolis, packinghouses were obliged to shut down. Wisconsin farmers cut off all milk to Chicago.

Wallace, red in the face, shouting double cross, denounced the Holiday leaders as leeches on the farmers' backs. Reno snapped back that he was "a disgrace to the office he is supposed to hold." He challenged anybody on earth to prove that he had improperly taken one thin dime from the Farmers' Union or the Cooperatives.

Government action was speeded up. By November, Washington was giving farmers loans on sealed corncribs up to one-third above existing farm prices. Even on hogs. A wheat subsidy program was almost ready. The money was sufficient to pump off the high crest of revolt.

Even so, the whole Farm Holiday movement had been one of the more dramatic occurrences in the long history of farmer revolt. It had "scared the eastern bankers and politicians into acquiescing in farm subsidies," said one paper. But Reno was now harassed by government auditors and snoopers. The news organs staged a smear campaign against him, calling him anarchist, socialist, communist, fascist. He struck back by calling Roosevelt and Wallace tools of Wall Street, which must have startled most financiers on that narrow thoroughfare. There appeared to be some evidence for the "fascist" charge about Reno. He had briefly ganged up with Father Coughlin and Huey Long before realizing that they were charlatans. By the spring of 1936, he was a lonely, broken old man who wanted to die. And he died.

By 1936, when Reno died, there were already more than 600,000 families in the United States on land incapable, even in ordinary prosperity times, of producing a decent livelihood, and the aggregate of such lands was by then 100,000,000 acres. Though World War II again made the utilization of improper lands possible, the acreage of submarginal lands being used and further destroyed was even greater.

During the depression, the government had spent hundreds of millions of dollars attempting to do away with submarginal farming and to save soil, but in World War II much of that effort and expense went for nought. Even before the war, less than half the 55,000,000 farm acres in Georgia. South Carolina, Alabama, and Florida were suitable for farming purposes, and 500,000 people there were stranded in poverty and near starvation. With the war, many of those improper lands went back into use.

The result of such trends in the nation at large has meant the relatively steady decline of free individual farm ownership. Between 1890 and 1930, the farm population (exclusive of farm labor) *increased* 35 percent, but the number of owners with unmortgaged farms *decreased* 30 percent; by 1935, 40 percent, and the percentage of rural dwellers in America declined and continues to decline. Mortgage-free farm operators came to represent less than one-third of the total of farmers. Today there are fewer than 2,000,000 fully independent farmers in the whole nation. Thus, while our soldiers won territory abroad, the American farmer lost much of his own territory at home. In 1820, the percentage of farm-working population was 71.8. By 1950, it was only 11.6 and is still declining. Since the 1935 peak, the number of farms declined from nearly 7,000,000 to less than 4,000,000 in 1959, whereas total acreage increased slightly, and value of farms rose from $33,600,000,000 to $130,000,000,000.

By 1933, the farmers' net capital (including that of millionaires and corporation farm owners) had shrunk from $34,000,000,000 in 1924 to $19,000,000,000. The average farmer was suffering a capital loss of about $255 a year. As in the nineties and before, the American farmer was still living off his fat, off social increment, as much as off his crop. But many had eaten themselves to the bone and had given up; the remainder were growing thinner.

By 1937, an average of four-fifths of the value of mortgaged farms was held by landlords and mortgage companies, and the average income of mortgaged farmers was actually less than that of tenant farmers. From 1926 to 1934, nearly 2,000,000 farms were foreclosed.

Tenantry increased from 25 percent of all farmers to 42 percent in 1935. By the early thirties, share croppers operated over 10 percent of all farms; in the South, 39 percent. In addition, in 1930 there were more than 4,000,000 paid or unpaid (food-and-keep) workers — over one-fourth of all persons gainfully employed in agriculture had joined the proletariat. In other words, by 1930 about 80 percent of the rural population of the United States belonged in the class of wage workers, sharecroppers, tenants, part owners, and mortgaged farmers. Many of the last-named were worse off in terms of annual income than the tenants. This, history tells us, is near the revolutionary explosive point. National depression was part of the answer.

On top of that, America had wasted its lands through ignorance and greed. Some farmers who, after the Civil War, wept over the lost fertility of their acres, had brought this to pass by their own wastefulness and ignorance and were far more to blame than the so-called "railroad barons" and the so-called "Shylock bankers." They themselves had destroyed the wealth of America. This was an inevitable part of the price of small-farm independence, without corresponding individual scientific knowledge, a price the United States has paid, and a price it is still paying to the tune of billions each year in the form of involved bureaucratic opportunism.

And so, by the thirties, the land collapse in America had set in motion a gigantic army of people. The Okies and Migs, the Joads, joined the big army of "farm tramps" already shuttling from crop to crop, living in tumbledown shacks, tents, or barracks, enjoying

[333]

only a few months of poor wages, suffering acute hardships most of the year; the children getting only scraps of education, plus rickets and disease, and putting down no roots. In addition to these restless driven hordes, by 1935 some 900,000 tenants had become migrants in the sense that they remained on the same path of land only one year. The submarginal farmers, some 3,000,000, if not shifting from bad lands to bad lands, were increasingly isolated from commercial exchange yet unable to be properly self-supporting. Millions, of course, were absorbed into the army and into war industries, which temporarily changed the picture.

The new westward movement did not head toward a new frontier or free lands. The free lands were gone. The uprooted folk headed toward the greatest center of industrialized agriculture in the world. By 1930, 36.7 percent of all large-scale farms ($30,000 or more a year output) in the United States were located in California, as compared to less than 1 percent in Mississippi, where large holdings are the rule. California had nearly 5 times as many large-scale cotton plantations as Mississippi. It had 40 percent of all the nation's large-scale dairy farms; 44 percent of large-scale general farms; 52 percent of all large-scale poultry farms; 60 percent of the large-scale truck or fruit farms. Besides being the world's most concentrated area of large-scale agriculture, California agriculture is probably as technically efficient as any in the world, this in part due to the early crusading of Henry George.

But from the standpoint of human welfare and social values, it is one of the world's worst agricultural systems, less humane than the feudal sharecropping system of the South. In the South, many workers have access to soil for their own use. In California, most are hired for a few weeks or months, then cast adrift. California therefore, was the migrants' poverty paradise; and there the migrants headed; there, to survive, they worked more cheaply than had the previous migrants, the Japanese, Filipinos, and Mexicans, whom they displaced, amid occasional scenes of race violence and mob hysteria.

[334]

The New Deal faced a desperate depression situation. It faced the accumulated mistakes of the wasteful methods of frontier settlement. That system had broken down. It faced the problem of submarginal production, of ruined land, of land going to ruin. It faced the decadent plantation system of the South and its wasteful sharecropper system. It faced the problem of agriculture being industrialized, of land monopolies and concentration; it faced a growing rural proletariat.

The dilemma was great. How could the farmers be helped? Raise prices? Then the misery of the hordes of urban unemployed would be made greater. Raise wages also? When factories were going bankrupt? Then the farmer would still fail to receive any larger proportion of the national income.

A multiplicity of methods·were used, contradictory, opportunistic, bureaucratic. It was not a solution by free farmers, as might have been possible in the nineties, a movement that was beaten down, betrayed, and wiped out. It was a solution imposed from above, in the name of economic liberation.

Despite the threatened hardship on the unemployed, efforts were made to raise prices. This was accomplished by arbitrary edict and by artificially creating scarcity. Scarcity was created by crop restriction, crop destruction, government buying, enforced hoarding, overseas dumping (the government taking the loss). The bitter pill was coated by such phrases as "parity price," "rationalization," "regional planning," "ever normal granary," etc.

Artificial price-raising produced a number of evils. It increased the hardship of the unemployed and the industrial proletariat. It progressively lost the world market for the United States and promoted greater production in other countries, viz., cotton-growing in Mexico, Brazil, Peru, Salvador, Colombia, Argentina, Africa, Egypt, India, etc. It promoted large-scale inefficiency. It kept up the process of soil exhaustion.

Crop restriction had a number of evil consequences. It closed up processing plants, increasing unemployment and income. It made the economic condition of the railroads worse. It destroyed many business enterprises devoted to distribution. Many cotton distributors fled abroad and set up offices in Brazil, Mexico, and Africa.

In the second place, it froze agriculture into a pattern. This favored established better-heeled farmers, blocked new enterprise, kept alive inefficient agriculture, including outmoded plantation agriculture in the South. It hit the small producer; crop curtailment meant that often he could not survive. It created, more than ever, a class system in agriculture.

It made the plight of the Okies, the migrants, and the itinerant farm workers much worse and limited possibilities for employment of the rural proletariat.

Hoarding also had many bad consequences. It temporarily halted price-drops; but over longer periods it seriously depressed the market here and abroad, costing huge government subsidies.

And all these measures increased the bureaucracy, multiplied red tape, caused the government to take losses on purchased products, hence in nearly every direction represented loss to the nation at large and the taxpayer, including the farmer.

But prices could not be raised sufficiently, because of the danger of greatly increasing the general cost of living and completely losing the world market.

Subsidies were a further premium to the backward plantation agriculture of the South. Subsidies further increased the cost of the bureaucracy — more governmental machinery. They further froze the agricultural pattern. At the same time, they made all farmers dependent upon the government, made them fillers-out of endless forms. The farmers were becoming sharecroppers for the State.

The farmer was subsidized to grow less food, and with greater efficiency, in order to keep the price up. Then, in order not to lose the foreign market, exports of some commodities also had to be subsidized or bought up by the government to distribute free to foreign countries, thus injuring agriculture in friendly free enterprise lands and ruining our own textile industry. Excess farm products, finally, under Kennedy and Johnson, were dumped by Food for Peace, ruining vast farming areas abroad, creating great resentments and difficulties for U.S. foreign policy makers.

In the thirties, the preliminary "reforms" created further dilemmas. To make it possible for the unemployed and underprivileged to meet food costs, they had to be subsidized with blue tickets to get food cheaper than their neighbors — more bureaucracy. The farmer was subsidized to grow less; the foreign consumer was subsidized to buy more; the underprivileged at home were subsidized. The treasury paid out money to grow less, paid out money to store that little less, paid out money to sell that less. It was a losing game all the way from the slaughtered pig to the human stomach. Visible subsidies, unabashed, unblushing subsidies, crept up toward the billion dollar mark, and in recent years, costs have hit as high as eight billion. Eisenhower campaigned on a platform to cut them down and restore free enterprise. He quadrupled the expenditures.

There were also many invisible subsidies to the farmer, some of them improper, some highly commendable. He was paid to build cribs and warehouses to store products subsidized and kept off the market. He was subsidized to plant different crops such as soy beans and peanuts. He was subsidized by the TVA and rural electrification, which provided him with lower power rates — a more legitimate subsidy. He was provided with cheaper money through federal lending agencies. But all of it increased government bureaucracy and government costs, and the outright money subsidies chiefly fostered more large-scale farming, often at the expense of small farmers. This promoted industrialized farming, for, among other things, the government subsidy could be kept wholly by the big entrepreneur. And so, more sharecroppers and tenants were driven into semi-vagrancy.

For the rural proletariat, very little was done. A few soup kitchens, public relief with much red tape, food handouts, a few model

migrant camps; and even these far below American standard —
little circus showplaces here and there in California, Oregon,
Washington, and Utah. And even these camps, though they aroused
kulak hostility, were in fact a further subsidy to the large-scale
farmer, since thereby he could pay lower wages.

The farmers' share of the national income, a few New Dealers
thought, could be raised by farm efficiency. But this provided a
new contradiction. Greater efficiency meant more production,
which made the price-pegging more difficult and required more
subsidies to be dished out, ever more governmental bureaucracy,
more invisible costs. But in any event, such efficiency was more
enduring and constructive, for it was adding new wealth and capital
— the main highway to permanently self-sustaining agriculture.

Among such efforts at greater efficiency were the creation of
better lands through reclamation, irrigation, and scientific treatment, the rehabilitation of bankrupt farmers with food, land, equipment, fertilizer, and implements to farm their land better and
more profitably, the resettlement of farmers from land unable to
produce properly to fertile acres. Soil conservation, terracing, the
use of alternative crops, tree-planting (in Donnelly's day this was
branded as "crackpot"), proper conservation of organic materials
in the topsoil to promote fertility and increase yield, absorb moisture
and prevent soil and water erosion, made strides. Billions have
been spent upon federal and state agencies for technology and
education. If all this required more bureaucracy and higher governmental costs, new wealth was created and better instrumentalities
for producing more wealth resulted. Many benefits have been sound
and permanent — technical progress but social decline.

Unfortunately, a large share of the rich new lands, created by
great irrigation projects and made available with the best of modern
science and engineering, were settled and farmed by the most
anti-social, primitive, and unscientific methods. This was true of
one great enterprise in the state of Oregon, where pauperized
folk were sent in, without proper tools, capital, or housing, in the

old hit-or-miss frontier fashion, and were unable to utilize the magnificent opportunity properly, with no true benefit for themselves or the community. Without having been given sufficient machinery, tools, or education to meet modern requirements and competition, they merely provided a pathetic contrast to the enlightenment and modern technology which had made the new land available, a sad contrast between their equipment and capacities and the tremendous engineering skill and science that had put them there. It was another example of how far our social thinking lags behind our technical abilities.

Resettlement, if costly, was fine, and might, if properly carried out, have paid for itself. However, to gain more bureaucratic leverage, Henry Wallace, who at first did not control resettlement, knifed both it and rehabilitation, two of the best features of the agrarian New Deal, and for the most part turned a deaf ear to the problems of the migrant workers.

In general, the New Deal increased bureaucratic power over the farmer and intruded, often cumbersomely, into every minutia of his producing life. It made every farmer over into a red tape form-filler, exposed him to constant inspections and fines, increased the costs to the taxpayer, introduced charity handouts (subsidies) on a vast scale, and, except for technical advances and soil conservation efforts, further crippled agriculture in many directions as an independent going concern in these United States.

It did not prevent extreme individual suffering in many areas. But it caused a great deal of suffering in other directions, and it has made agriculture into a costly national liability. Benefits within the industry itself were not fairly distributed and are not today. The farm worker received little direct help from the program, and he comprises one-fourth of the rural population. The sharecroppers and tenants were also deprived of many benefits. In general, the program was heading for colossal failure, a price-juggling and quantity control system that was running increasingly into insoluble contradictions.

This failure, which Wallace's reputation would not have survived, was hidden by World War II, in the same manner that agricultural collapse had been hidden by World War I, later by the Korean and Viet Nam Wars. These wars bailed out agriculture. In the Second World War and then the Cold War, government mismanagement and mistaken policies have also been bailed out, but sooner or later more basic problems of the industry will have to be faced. The problems then will be more acute and grievous.

World War II, followed by the Cold War, injected much prosperity into agriculture, but mostly aided large-scale commercial farming. The war accelerated the increasing use of farm products by industry, for alcohol, synthetic rubber, explosives, plastics, textiles, etc. This prosperity has served as a false narcotic, for the war, plus price support and subsidy, have caused ruin of American land faster than ever — as Secretary Clinton Anderson put it, to a "murderous" extent. Much of fifteen years of sound conservation effort were wiped out.

Still greater concentration of land-holding and large-scale machinery methods was promoted. True, many independent farmers went back to submarginal lands momentarily profitable, but these may again be hopelessly stranded when normal production and exchange are restored. If they are protected by false price supports for too great a time, even more land will be ruined.

Yet even with this great war stimulation, agriculture had to be helped by price supports and subsidies, still does. Not only are these benefits not equitably distributed among the rural population as a whole, but this imposes a quadruple burden on the consumer. He pays a tax subsidy. He pays for a second-tax outlay for the complicated bureaucratic machinery to administer the subsidy. He pays higher prices for food. The high cost of farm products means a corresponding percentage increase in processing and distribution — all down the line, through factory, wholesaler, truck and railroad handlers, and retailers. Thus, even though the consumer pays the double subsidy and double taxes, he must pay again through higher prices at silo and crib, and these prices swell proportionately all down the line of processing and distribution.

The Brannan agricultural plan of 1949 — voted down in Congress through the pressure of interested groups profiting from the extravagant system—represented one of the finest pieces of economic legislation yet proposed to cut through some of the tangle of farm bureaucracy and the costly artificial method of guaranteeing larger, if inadequate, farmers' profits, in good part at the expense of the general taxpayer and the consumer. Through the plan, even smaller subsidies than those being paid out would have sufficed to have guaranteed survival and profit to farmers, while permitting the consumer to get farm products at reduced prices. The plan if generally adopted might have wiped out at least 50 percent or more of the artificial cost of the industry to the country at large.

What are the future prospects of American agriculture, and the people who keep it going?

Whether more normal supply and demand reasserts itself or whether complicated bureaucratic methods of dealing with the problems persist, the rapid industrialization of agriculture is certain to continue. Farming in the United States has become increasingly a large-scale capitalistic enterprise. Even before the war, middle-class farmers were finding it difficult to compete on the one hand with inefficient plantation agriculture, which cut costs through large acreage and human exploitation, and on the other with large-scale modern agriculture, which cut costs, but not prices, through migrant labor, mass production, and smaller profits per commodity unit.

Technology will continue to impose new revolutionary changes and bring about methods and possibilities unknown to Daniel Shays or Jerry Simpson. Most modern agriculture, in a sense, began only when Justus von Liebig showed the way to increased yield through commercial or chemical fertilizers. Following Mitscherlich's discovery, forty years ago, of the basic laws of plant growth, a whole new science was inaugurated. Nitrogen studies

[341]

have provided us with knowledge of the absolute maximum possible for the growth and yield of any given plant. Practical applications have proved that, almost regardless of the original nature of the soil, if it has any potentiality whatever, it can be made over without prohibitive cost into a balanced soil superior to that ever provided by nature, and that any irrigated land can be put in shape to produce close to the maximum. In California, some time ago, Dr. Geriche, by chemical cultures, grew 2,000 bushels of potatoes and more than 200 tons of tomatoes per acre.

In recent years, also, the excessive use of fertilizers and neglect of the basic properties of the soil and its necessary organic materials, on which depend the nutritional value of the products, have been steadily rectified after the first flush of bonanza fertilized supercrops often resulted in a decline of food and vitamin values. Plant breeding, of which hybrid corn is one example, has created disease-resistant strains with greater yield or more uniform growth, which in turn makes more possible large-scale mechanization. The scientific revolution extends into the study of nutrition, chemistry, physics, electronics, invisible rays of all sorts, medicine, health — every field of human investigation. One wit has declared, "We now know more about plant needs than we do human needs."

Thus science is rapidly offsetting many ignorant and wasteful methods. The vast fertile empire that extravagant eager America so willfully destroyed, may again become of some utility as we acquire the ability to manufacture new low-cost chemicals and learn new agricultural techniques. Many acres considered lost may be reclaimed and made profitable again. Science opens the possibility that American agriculture may again someday take its place in the sum total of American enterprise as a profitable undertaking rather than being as it has so long in so many places merely a handmaiden of increasing population real-estate speculation, and later of government paternalism.

Science also opens up the possibility of growing products not merely quantitatively but with such increased nutritional and vitamin values as will modify and improve human physical vigor and even character. Today, even if we do not use our new knowledge except sporadically, science tells man not only how he can produce food in far greater quantities and more cheaply but also how to create soils superior to any provided by Nature, how to turn out products with the highest measure of food value for health and energy. Organic farming may also have its day in court, indeed may be the basic solution for less commercialized farming, if such a way of life is not to perish entirely.

But even with large-scale production, the use of more capital, machinery, and true scientific methods, something better than the California system is required if modern standards of living are to be extended to the entire rural population and particularly to the farm workers. No industry is valid that cannot support such a standard. Substandard wages and living conditions, even in the face of colossal subsidies paid out by the federal government to industry, represent a loss to the nation as a whole, whatever benefits lowered costs or greater profits may bring to certain sectors. The problem, therefore, is not merely one for technology, but for social readjustment.

The problems of land ownership, marginal production, education in proper farm methods, of fair relationships between farm workers and farm owners, between farming, and processing and manufacturing, between city and land dwellers, are still with us regardless of scientific improvements. If the equitable distribution of land is not to be an issue, then the proper distribution of the products of capital and labor becomes an issue.

If another bad drouth or another bad depression hits us, the Joads may take to the road again, no longer a combination of small capitalists and workers, no longer farm owners trying to save their land and their homes, but a marching army of disinherited proletariat. Their problem becomes that of the industrial worker, but without similar means of defense or cohesion. Their lot can scarcely improve greatly unless the relations of factory and land are properly balanced in the overall economy of the country. Undoubtedly this has been the aim of much farm legislation during the past two decades, but within agriculture itself protection has not been spread fairly to all groups. Today the old frontier is gone. The men who stood at the crossroads in the Midwest, the men of the westward movement who faced the era of modern industrialization and who fought for a system of free small landholdings, lost their fight, and today such a fight would make no sense at all. Probably there will be, can be, no more Shayses or Kellys, Weavers, Simpsons, or Donnellys. A stand cannot be made at the same old crossroads, for they are gone forever.

Seen in retrospect, the failure of the farm leaders of the last century was inevitable, just as the earlier enclosures were inevitable in England. The real revolutionists of the era were not the Peffers and Simpsons, but the so-called "Robber Barons," the industrialists, and presently the scientists and technologists, who were carrying on to completion the earlier "industrial revolution" of England.

Essentially, the Populists, though so harshly denounced, were conservatives, and, however radical their talk, not radicals at all. From the standpoint of industry, of agriculture itself, and of technology, they were foredoomed to eventual failure along economic lines. But in the transition of America from a farming nation into an industrial colossus, their conservatism, though branded as dangerously radical, played a great part in promoting and strengthening many democratic liberties that might have been wholly lost in the transition. Even though they failed in their main intent and in so many directions, in others they did not fail, for they strengthened American democracy considerably. They revalidated, at least for a time, the principles of free expression, free assemblage, and free elections, which processes they helped democratize.

Whether these rights will survive in the hands of uprooted urbanites, remains for the years ahead to reveal. Whether the death of a whole way of life, the alienation of most of the population from the land, the substitution of a more mechanized type of citizen with little health-giving relation to the soil of America, will bring greater happiness or strength, is still to be told. As more people are stripped from the land, millions of acres are lost by paving more roads and by the constant expansion of the urban sprawl, with its increased smog and pollution, its ghettos and its crime, and the bureaucratic monstrosities of a falsely labeled welfare state. Millions more acres have been appropriated by the U.S. Army, the greatest landowner on earth, as we proceed toward the permanent warfare state. We may yet have to revaluate our whole concept of a so-called progress, prosperity, and power. What seems inevitable is not always good. As Kipling pointed out, the iron shard is scarcely a dependable or desirable instrument, even for world power.

Nearly all the political demands of the Populists have been enacted into law, and though the midwesterners failed as farm prophets, they wrote into our codes many sound regulations for industry and agriculture that prevented abuses and made the whole process of our great industrial revolution more orderly and respectful of human rights. Without the rights which the Populists won for us, which they helped conserve for us, we would scarcely claim to be a free people in a free land, as we do claim to be.

But liberty must be written in new terms by each succeeding generation, and the frontier of scientific and industrialized agriculture now opening up will require new types of leaders to conserve and expand human rights and opportunities. For however much the Populists erred in measuring the course of future history and developments, their goals were great humanitarian goals, and though the struggle may change in character, the effort to broaden and vitalize American democracy must be a continuous process.

In that continuing effort and aspiration, the Populists provided us with some of our greatest traditions — and some of our present hypocrisies. They were appalled in their day by the alienation of

[345]

government from popular controls; they would be more appalled today, both by that and by the organized control of the mass mind, the sort of propagandistic control that produced mass support for Hitler and Mussolini and constantly exalts the State over individual human beings, makes them compliant with the wishes of the State — be it in Russia or be it in the United States. They were trapped by the closing of the frontier; they were overwhelmed by the onrush of industrialization and the creation of a new power-structure, economic and political.

The newer technical revolution of automation and electronics is now sweeping the land toward a new world which will demand its own political and economic structure, which is already shaking down the institutions and traditions of our land. New tools have been provided, which if they don't destroy mankind, can free him to savor incredible new opportunities. Or they can cast him into a new type of slavery, the well-fed slavery of an ant society. It will largely depend upon who controls the new instruments of power and the purposes for which they are used.

One belief the Populists had: that mankind was or could be master of his own destiny. It is a good belief to have. Whether it is entirely valid may be debated. Mostly, history teaches, man en masse has merely rushed from one disaster into another. His leaders have rarely been men of vision or courage, but men seeking power, preying on ancient prejudices and bigotry, and riding herd with ideas that knowledgeable men long ago abandoned. In short, for the most part, man's science and instrumentalities for altering the face of the globe have surpassed his capacity to use them intelligently or worthily. Ignatius Donnelly observed that man's inertia and his inability to accept new ideas were like a great, almost impassable, snow-clad ridge that blocked his way to the promised land.

One of the basic tenets of Populism was that men first had to be informed before they could accomplish anything important. They started a hundred newspapers; they distributed millions of pamphlets and books; they engraved their messages on the brains of millions. Today even that has become more difficult for honest men. The matter has been made more complicated. Knowledge itself has become more institutionalized, more controlled, though words and paper have become cheaper and more widely disseminated. Who controls the knowledge has become a more pertinent question than knowledge itself so far as national and international survival are concerned, so far as political and social progress are concerned. All we can say is, the Populists made a good fight while it lasted; they are an integral part of the history of our land; they changed the thought and the pattern of American life. We can still learn much from their methods and their ideas.

SELECTED READING LIST

The selected reading list does not constitute a bibliography, which would contain thousands of references consulted in the preparation of this volume. The following categories, with a few exceptions, have not been included in this list: local, state, and federal documents; manuscript material and collections of clippings from university libraries; contemporary magazine and newspaper articles; handbooks, campaign books, and song collections; local and state histories; accounts of frontier life; books on the silver controversy; biographies and autobiographies of contemporary figures; novels.

Adams, James Truslow. *The Epic of America*. Boston: Little, Brown, and Co., 1931.

Aiken, D. W. "The Grange: Its Origin, Progress and Educational Purposes." Department of Agriculture, Report II, no. 55-64. Washington, D.C.: Government Printing Office, 1883.

Allen, Emory Adams. *Labor and Capital*. Cincinnati: Central Publishing House, 1891.

——————. *The Life and Public Services of James Baird Weaver*. Cincinnati: People's Party Publishing Co., 1892.

Allen, William V. "The Populist Program," *Independent* (New York), LII (February 22, 1900), pp. 475-76.

_____. "Western Feeling Toward the East," *North American Review* (New York), 162 (May, 1896), pp. 588-93.

Ashby, N. B. *The Riddle of the Sphinx.* Des Moines: Industrial Publishing Co., 1890.

Beard, Charles A. *Contemporary American History, 1877-1913.* New York: Macmillian Co., 1914.

Beard, Charles A., and Mary R. *The Rise of American Civilization.* 2 vols. New York: Macmillian Co., 1927.

Beer, Thomas. *Hanna.* New York: A. A. Knopf, 1926.

_____. *The Mauve Decade.* New York: A. A. Knopf, 1923.

Bellamy, Edward. *Duke of Stockbridge.* New York and Boston: Silver, Burdett and Co., 1900.

_____. *Looking Backward, 2000-1887.* Boston: Ticknor and Co., 1888.

Bemis, E. W. "Discontent of the Farmer," *Journal of Political Economy* (Chicago), I (March, 1893), pp. 192-213.

Bentley, Arthur F. *The Condition of the Western Farmer as Illustrated by the Economic History of a Nebraska Township.* Baltimore: Johns Hopkins Press, 1892.

Blood, F. G. *Hand Book and History of the National Farmers' Alliance and Industrial Union.* Washington, D.C.: Mutual Benefit Association, 1893.

Brewton, William W. *The Life of Thomas E. Watson.* Atlanta: the author, 1926.

Buck, Solon Justus. *The Agrarian Crusade.* New Haven: Yale University Press, 1920.

Carr, Ezra S. *The Patrons of Husbandry on the Pacific Coast.* San Francisco: A. L. Bancroft, 1875.

Chamberlain, Henry R. *The Farmers' Alliance, What It Aims to Accomplish.* New York: Minerva Publishing Co., 1891.

Clark, John Bunyan. *Populism in Alabama.* Auburn, Alabama: Auburn Printing Co., 1927.

Commager, Henry Steele (ed.). *Documents of American History.* 3rd ed., New York: F. S. Crofts & Co., 1943.

Coxey, Jacob A. *The Coxey Plan.* Massillon, Ohio: J. S. Coxey, 1914.

Darrow, James W. *Origin and Early History of the Patrons of Husbandry in the United States.* Chatham, New York: Courier Printing House, 1904.

Davis, James Harvey (Cyclone). *A Political Revelation*. Dallas: Advance Publishing Co., 1894.

deFord, Miriam Allen. "The Amazing Ignatius Donnelly," *American Parade* (Girard, Kansas), II (January-March, 1929), pp. 44-48.

Delap, Simeon. "The Populist Party in North Carolina," *Trinity College Historical Society Papers* (Durham), ser. xiv (1922), pp. 40-74.

Diggs, Annie Le Porte. "The Farmers' Alliance and Some of Its Leaders," *Arena* (New York), V (April, 1892), pp. 590-604.

_____ *The Story of Jerry Simpson*. Wichita: Jane Simpson, 1908.

_____ "The Women in the Alliance Movement," *Arena* (New York), VI (July, 1892), pp. 161-79.

Donnelly, Eleanor Cecilia. *Domus Deii*. Philadelphia: P. F. Cunningham & Son, 1875.

Donnelly, Ignatius Loyola. *The American People's Money*. Chicago: Laird & Lee, 1895.

_____ *Atlantis*. New York: Harper & Bros., 1881.

_____ *Caesar's Column*, by Edmund Boisgilbert, M.D. (pseud.) Chicago: F. J. Schulte & Co., 1890.

_____ *The Cipher in the Plays, and on the Tombstone*. Minneapolis: Verulam Publishing Co., 1899.

_____ *Doctor Huguet*, by Edmund Boisgilbert, M.D. (pseud.). Chicago: F. J. Schulte & Co., 1891.

_____ *The Golden Bottle*. New York and St. Paul: D. D. Merrill Co., 1892.

_____ *The Great Cryptogram*. Chicago, New York, and London: R. S. Peale & Co., 1888.

_____ *Ragnarok*. Chicago: D. Appleton and Co., 1882.

Dorfman, Joseph. *Thorstein Veblen and His America*. New York: Viking Press, 1934.

Dunning, Nelson A. (ed.). *The Farmers' Alliance History and Agricultural Digest*. Written by a board of editors. Washington: Alliance Publishing Co., 1891.

Farmer, Hallie. "Economic Background of Frontier Populism," *Mississippi Valley Historical Review* (Cedar Rapids, Iowa), XIII (December, 1926), pp. 387-97.

_____ "The Economic Background of Southern Populism," *The South Atlantic Quarterly* (Durham), XXIX, no. 1 (January, 1930), pp. 77-91.

Fossum, Paul R. "The Agrarian Movement in North Dakota," *Johns Hopkins University Studies in Historical and Political Science* (Baltimore), XLIII, no. 1 (1925), pp. 1-183.

Fuller, Lear W. "A Populist Newspaper of the 'Nineties: *Aspen Union Era*," *Colorado Magazine* (Denver), IX (1932), pp. 81-87.

Garland, Hamlin. "The Alliance Wedge in Congress," *Arena* (New York), V (March, 1892), pp. 447-57.

——————. *Main-Travelled Roads.* New York: Macmillan Co., 1899.

——————. *A Son of the Middle Border.* New York: Macmillan Co., 1926.

Garvin, William L., and Daws, S.O. *History of the National Farmers' Alliance and Co-operative Union of America.* Jonesboro, Texas: J. N. Rogers & Co., 1887.

George, Henry. *Progress and Poverty.* 50th anniversary ed., New York: Robert Schalkenbach Foundation, 1929.

George, Henry, Jr. *The Life of Henry George.* 2 vols. New York: Doubleday & McClure Co., 1900.

Harmon, Ralph. "Ignatius Donnelly," *Minnesota History* (St. Paul), XVII, no. 3 (September, 1936), pp. 262-75.

Harrington, Wynne Powers. "The Populist Party in Kansas," *State Historical Society Collections* (Topeka), XVI (1925), pp. 403-50.

Harvey, William H. *Coin's Financial School Up To Date.* Chicago: Coin Publishing Co., 1895.

Haynes, Frederick Emory. *James Baird Weaver.* Iowa City: State Historical Society of Iowa, 1919.

——————. *Third Party Movements Since the Civil War, With Special Reference to Iowa:* Iowa City: State Historical Society of Iowa, 1916.

Hicks, John D. "The Farmers' Alliance in North Carolina," *North Carolina Historical Review* (Raleigh), II (1925), pp. 62-87.

——————. "The Origin and Early History of the Farmers' Alliance in Minnesota," *Mississippi Valley Historical Review* (Cedar Rapids, Iowa), IX, no. 19, 22, (December, 1922), pp. 203-26.

——————. "The People's Party In Minnesota," *Minnesota Historical Society Bulletin* (St. Paul), XII (1931), pp. 3-20.

——————. "The Political Career of Ignatius Donnelly," *Mississippi Valley Historical Review* (Cedar Rapids, Iowa), VIII, no. 1, 2, (1921), pp. 8-132.

——————. *The Populist Revolt.* Minneapolis: University of Minnesota Press, 1931.

Holmes, George K. "A Decade of Mortgages," *Annals of the American Academy of Political and Social Science* (Philadelphia), IV (May, 1894), pp. 904-18.
————. "The Peons of the South," *ibid.*, III (September, 1893), pp. 265-74.
Hudson, Joseph Kennedy. *Letters to Governor Lewelling.* Topeka: Topeka Capital Co., 1893.
Josephson, Matthew. *The Politicos, 1865-1896.* New York: Harcourt, Brace and Co., 1938.
————. *The Robber Barons.* New York: Harcourt, Brace and Co., 1934.
Kelley, Oliver Hudson. *Origin and Progress of the Order of the Patrons of Husbandry in the United States . . . 1866 to 1873.* Philadelphia: J. A. Wagenseller, 1875.
Kent, W. H. *A Historical Review of the Causes and Issues That Led to the Overthrow of the Republican Party in Kansas in 1892.* Topeka: Topeka Daily Press, 1893.
Kramer, Dale. *The Wild Jackasses.* New York: Hastings House, 1956.
La Follette, Robert Marion. *La Follette's Autobiography.* Madison, Wisconsin: Robert M. La Follette Co., 1913.
Larson, Henrietta M. *The Wheat Market and the Farmer in Minnesota, 1858-1900.* New York: Columbia University, 1926.
Lauck, William Jett. *The Causes of the Panic of 1893.* Boston and New York: Houghton, Mifflin and Co., 1907.
Lloyd, Caroline Augusta. *Henry Demarest Lloyd, 1874-1903.* 2 vols. New York and London: G. P. Putnam's Sons, 1912.
Lloyd, Henry Demarest. *Lords of Industry.* New York and London: G. P. Putnam's Sons, 1910.
London, Jack. "A Jack London Diary: Tramping with Kelley Through Iowa," *Palimpsest* (Iowa City), VII (May, 1926), pp. 129-58.
McCabe, James Dabney. *History of the Grange Movement,* by Edward Winslow Martin (pseud.). Philadelphia and Chicago: National Publishing Co., 1873.
McCormick, Fannie. *A Kansas Farm.* New York: J. B. Alden, 1892.
McMurray, Donald Le Crone. *Coxey's Army.* Boston: Little, Brown, and Co., 1929.
McVey, Frank L. *The Populist Movement.* New York: Macmillan Co., 1896.

Malin, James Claude. "Notes on the Literature of Populism," *Kansas Historical Quarterly*, (Topeka), I, no. 2, (February, 1932), pp. 160-64.

Manning, Joseph Columbus. *Fadeout of Populism, Presenting in Connection, the Political Combat Between the Pot and the Kettle.* New York: T. A. Hebbons, 1928.

Miller, Raymond C. "The Economic Background of Populism in Kansas," *Mississippi Valley Historical Review* (Cedar Rapids, Iowa), XL, no. 4 (March, 1925), pp. 469-89.

Moore, Frederick. "The Condition of the Southern Farmer," *Yale Review* (New Haven), III (May, 1894), pp. 56-7.

Morgan, J. T. "The Danger of the Farmers' Alliance," *Forum* (New York), XII (November, 1891), pp. 399-409.

Morgan, W. Scott. *History of the Wheel and Alliance and the Impending Revolution.* Fort Scott, Kansas: J. H. Rice & Sons, 1889.

Morris, Richard B. (ed.). *Encyclopedia of American History.* Rev. and enl. ed., New York: Harper, 1961.

Nevins, Allan. *The Emergence of Modern America, 1865-1878* New York: Macmillan Co., 1928.

Nixon, H. C. "The Cleavage Within the Farmers' Alliance Movement," *Mississippi Valley Historical Review* (Cedar Rapids, Iowa), XV (June, 1928), pp. 22-33.

——————. "The Populist Movement in Iowa," *Iowa Journal of History and Politics* (Iowa City), XXIV (1926), pp. 3-107.

Nugent, Catherine (ed.). *Life Work of Thomas L. Nugent.* Stephenville, Texas: C. Nugent, 1896.

Oberholtzer, Ellis Paxson. *A History of the United States Since the Civil War.* 5 vols. New York: Macmillan Co., 1917-1937.

Paine, A. E. *The Granger Movement in Illinois.* Urbana, Illinois: University Press, 1904.

Parrington, Vernon L. *Main Currents in American Thought.* 3 vols. New York: Harcourt, Brace and Co., 1927-1930.

Paxson, Frederic L. *Recent History of the United States, 1865-1927.* Rev. and enl. ed., Boston and New York: Houghton Mifflin Co., 1928.

Peck, Harry Thurston. *Twenty Years of the Republic, 1885-1905.* New York: Dodd, Mead & Co., 1907.

Peffer, William A. *The Farmer's Side.* New York: D. Appleton and Co., 1891.

Pierson, Charles W. "The Rise of the Granger Movement," *Popular Science Monthly* (New York), XXXII (1888), p. 199.

Polk, Leonidas L. "The Farmer's Discontent," *North American Review* (New York), CIII (April, 1891), pp. 423-30.

Powderly, Terrance V. *Thirty Years of Labor.* Columbus, Ohio: Excelsior Publishing House, 1889.

Rightmore, W. F. "The Alliance Movement in Kansas — Origin of the People's Party," *Kansas State Historical Society Transactions* (Topeka), IX (1906), pp. 1-8.

Robinson, Daniel M. *Bob Taylor and the Agrarian Revolt in Tennessee.* Chapel Hill: University of North Carolina Press, 1915.

Rochester, Anna. *The Populist Movement in the United States.* New York: International Publishers, 1943.

Schlesinger, Arthur Meier. *The Rise of the City, 1878-1898.* New York: Macmillan Co., 1933.

Sharp, J. A. "The Entrance of the Farmers' Alliance into Tennessee Politics," *East Tennessee History Society's Publications* (Knoxville), 9 (1937), pp. 77-92.

Shaw, Albert. "William V. Allen: Populist," *Review of Reviews* (New York), X (July, 1894), pp. 30-42.

Sheldon, William Dubose. *Populism in the Old Dominion.* Princeton: Princeton University Press, 1935.

Snyder, Carl. "Marion Butler," *Review of Reviews* (New York), XIV (October, 1896), pp. 429-33.

Steward, Ernest D. "The Populist Party in Indiana," *Indiana Magazine of History*, XIV (December, 1918), pp. 332-67.

Thompson, J. M. "The Farmers' Alliance in Nebraska," *Proceedings and Collections of the Nebraska State Historical Society* (Lincoln), X (1902), pp. 199-206.

Turner, Frederick J. *The Frontier in American History.* New York: H. Holt and Co., 1920.

Usher, Ellis B. *The Greenback Movement of 1875-1884 and Wisconsin's Part in It.* Milwaukee: E. B. Usher, 1911.

Vaile, Joel F. "Colorado's Experiment with Populism," *Forum* (New York), XVIII (February, 1895), pp. 714-23.

Veblen, Thorstein. *The Theory of the Leisure Class.* New York: Macmillan Co. London: Macmillan & Co., Ltd., 1899.

Vincent, Henry. *The Story of the Commonweal.* Chicago: W. B. Conkey Co., 1894.

Watson, Thomas E. *The Life and Speeches of Thos. E. Watson.* Nashville: 1908.

Weaver, James B. *A Call to Action.* Des Moines: Iowa Printing Co., 1892.

Werner, Morris Robert. *Bryan.* New York: Harcourt, Brace and Co., 1929.

White, Melvin J. "Populism in Louisiana during the Nineties," *Mississippi Valley Historical Review* (Cedar Rapids, Iowa), V (June, 1918), pp. 1-19.

White, Roland A. *Milo Reno.* Iowa City: Athens Press, 1941.

Woodward, C. Vann. *Tom Watson, Agrarian Rebel.* New York: Macmillan Co., 1938.

Woody, Carroll H. "Populism in Washington," *Washington Historical Quarterly* (Seattle), XXI, no. 2 (April, 1930), pp. 103-19.

INDEX

Smith, Anna F., 287, 288
Smith, Louis, 277
Socialist Labor party, 198, 206
South, the, 66-67
Sovereign, J. R., 85, 189, 206, 279, 284
Spencer, Herbert, 154
spiritualism, 137, 158
Stanford, Gov. Leland (Cal.), 21
Stanley, Henry M., 141
Stevens, Thaddeus, 186
Stevenson, J. H., 279
Stevenson, Vice-Pres. Adlai E., 309
Stone, Melville E., 310
Storer, Bellamy, 193
Streeter, A. J., 88, 207, 229
strikes, 29, 200, 327-328
subsidies, farm, 336-337, 338, 339, 340, 341, 343
subsidies, government, 24-25
Sub-Treasury Plan, 90, 93-94, 100, 216
suffrage, 13-14, 222
suffragettes 11, 61, 86, 171, 206,
Sullivan, Mark, 319

tariff, 201, 302, 315
taxes, 25, 227, 230, 304
Teller, Henry, 258, 310, 318
tenant farmers, 89, 97, 189, 333
Thompson, John, 54
Tilden, Samuel J., 183
Tillman, "Pitch-fork" Ben, 67, 72, 87, 311, 312, 313
Tocqueville, Alexis de, 33-34, 149
Todd, Chaplain, 239-240, 246

Tracy, Harry, 100, 221, 229
Traubneck, H. E., 320
Tresillian, Judge, 251
Trideck, Harold, 6
Trimble, Reverend Doctor John, Jr., 42, 53
Trumble, Lyman, 301
trusts, 99
  See also monopoly
Turner, Frederick Jackson, 3, 25
Turner, Gov. Dan (Iowa), 327
Twain, Mark, 23, 140
Tweed, Boss, 322

unearned increment, 31, 32, 34
Union Labor party, 86, 128, 170, 206

Valesh, Eva, 207
Vanderbilt, Cornelius, 183
Van Wyck, Charles H., 72, 207
Veblen, Thorstein, 32
Vickery, Fanny, 207, 208
Videttes, 171, 180, 206, 233
Villard, Henry, 84
Vincent, Henry, 279, 287
Vinson, Clara (Mrs. James Weaver), 193

wages, 27, 28, 31, 81
Waite, Davis H. "Bloody Bridles," 72, 88, 210, 255-269
Wallace, Henry A., 36, 90, 136, 330, 331, 339, 340
Watson, Tom, 6, 14, 67, 72, 87, 95, 100, 136, 155, 169, 179, 209, 211, 321